A LIGHT
SHALL BREAK
Forth

Other volumes in the BYU–Relief Society Women's Conference series

A LIGHT
SHALL BREAK
Forth

TALKS FROM THE
2005 BYU WOMEN'S CONFERENCE

DESERET
BOOK
SALT LAKE CITY, UTAH

Photographs on pages 106, 107, 108, and 110 are by Miguel Sayago and are used courtesy of the Inter-American Foundation.

Library of Congress Cataloging-in-Publication Data

Women's Conference (2005 : Brigham Young University)
  A light shall break forth : talks from the 2005 BYU Women's Conference.
     p. cm.
  Includes bibliographical references and index.
  ISBN 1-59038-546-2 (hardbound : alk. paper)
  1. Mormon women—Religious life—Congresses. 2. Church of Jesus Christ of Latter-day Saints—Congresses. I. Title.
  BX8641.W73 2005
  289.3'32082—dc22   2005033597

Printed in the United States of America
R. R. Donnelley and Sons, Crawfordsville, IN

10   9   8   7   6   5   4   3   2   1

Contents

THE POWER OF THE LIGHT OF CHRIST

"A Light Shall Break Forth"

Sandra Rogers

In the early morning of a spring day in 1820, a young man resolutely walked toward a grove of trees near his home. No living mortal, especially not the young man himself, comprehended the eternal significance and consequence of what he was about to do, though prophets of old had looked forward to and foretold the event. The boy went to the quiet grove seeking the answer to a question that had perplexed him for some time. It was a question that his mother had often pondered herself. Once, when she had been extremely ill, she had thought, "'I am not prepared to die, for I do not know the ways of Christ,' and it seemed to me as though there was a dark and lonely chasm between myself and Christ that I dared not attempt to cross. . . . I covenanted with God that if he would let me live, I would endeavor to get that religion that would enable me to serve him right."[1]

The question had to do with, as the young man later wrote in one account, his "all important concerns for the wellfare of my immortal Soul which led me to searching the scriptures believing as I was taught, that they contained the word of God thus applying myself to them. . . . I pondered many things in my heart concerning the sittuation of the world of mankind [and] my mind became exceedingly distressed for I became convicted of my sins and by searching the scriptures I found that mankind did

---

Sandra Rogers is international vice president of Brigham Young University and teaches Gospel Doctrine in her ward.

not come unto the Lord but that they had apostatised from the true and liveing faith and there was no society or denomination that built upon the gospel of Jesus Christ as recorded in the new testament and I felt to mourn for my owns sins and for the sins of the world; . . . therefore I cried unto the Lord for mercy for there was none else to whom I could go to obtain mercy."[2]

With those questions about the salvation of his soul burning in his heart and mind, Joseph Smith knelt among the trees to pray. His inquiry about which church he should join was founded on his deep desire to be reconciled to God. As he attempted to pray, he was seized by a hideous power, and thick darkness enveloped him. Just when he imagined that he was doomed, he saw a pillar of light exactly over his head, above the brightness of the sun. When the light fell upon him, he saw God the Eternal Father in brightness and glory, who called him by name and, pointing to the other glorified Being, said, "This is My Beloved Son. Hear Him!" (Joseph Smith—History 1:15–17).

On the occasion of the unveiling ceremony of the statue of Joseph at the First Vision which is in the atrium of the Joseph Smith Building on the Brigham Young University campus, Elder Henry B. Eyring said:

"There are other figures not sculpted here which I would like you to imagine with an eye of faith. . . . God the Eternal Father and His Beloved Son, Jesus Christ, appeared to open this dispensation.

"From studying the various accounts of the First Vision, we learn that young Joseph went into the grove not only to learn which church he should join but also to obtain forgiveness for his sins—something he seems not to have understood how to do. And in more than one account, the Lord addressed the young truth seeker and said, 'Joseph, my son, thy sins are forgiven thee.'"

"This piece of art," Elder Eyring continued, "represents that moment when Joseph learned there was a way for the power of the Atonement of Jesus Christ to be unlocked fully. Because of what Joseph saw and what began at this moment, the Savior was able, through this great and valiant servant and through others that He sent, to restore power and privilege. That power and privilege allow us, and all who will live, to have the benefit of Christ's Atonement work in our lives."

Elder Eyring then said: "I testify to you that Jesus is the Christ. I know

He lives. I know Joseph saw Him. And I know that because He lives and because Joseph looked up and saw Him and because He sent other messengers, you and I may have the thing that the Prophet Joseph wanted as he went to the grove: To know, not just to hope, that our sins can be washed away."[3]

Do you remember the moment when you learned there was a way for the power of the Atonement of Jesus Christ to be unlocked fully for you? When you truly believed there was a way for you to be reconciled to God?

The light of the fulness of the gospel, heralded by a visit of the Eternal Father and His Beloved Son in answer to Joseph Smith's prayer 185 years ago in a grove of trees in New York State, ushered in the long-awaited restoration of all things, the dispensation of the fulness of times. On that spring morning, a light, no, I would say, *the light* of God the Father and His Son, Jesus Christ, broke the chains of darkness. The world had been struggling in darkness for centuries. Brave religious reformers and statesmen and -women had begun to push back the shadows of superstition and falsehood, but it was not until Joseph Smith decided to ask a question about the fate of his own soul that the light returned to earth for all of us. Through Joseph Smith, Christ restored the true doctrine of the gospel and the authority and keys to administer the ordinances of the gospel and the kingdom. From that day, that light—the restored fulness of Christ's gospel—began its penetration to every corner of the world, to every heart, chasing away every doubt and shadow.

The Lord reminded Joseph Smith of the things He had taught His disciples when He was here on earth. After reviewing with them the Apostasy, the scattering of the Jews, and the perilous last days when the love of many would wax cold, Jesus gave the ancient Twelve reassurance that "when the times of the Gentiles is come in, a light shall break forth among them that sit in darkness, and it shall be the fulness of my gospel" (D&C 45:28).

Jesus Himself explained what the fulness of the gospel was when He visited the American continent:

"And this is the gospel which I have given unto you—that I came into the world to do the will of my Father, because my Father sent me.

"And my Father sent me that I might be lifted up upon the cross; . . . that I might draw all men unto me, that as I have been lifted up by men even so should men be lifted up by the Father, to stand before me, to be judged of their works, whether they be good or whether they be evil. . . .

"And it shall come to pass, that whoso repenteth and is baptized in my name shall be filled; and if he endureth to the end, behold, him will I hold guiltless before my Father at that day when I shall stand to judge the world. . . .

"Now this is the commandment: Repent, all ye ends of the earth, and come unto me and be baptized in my name, that ye may be sanctified by the reception of the Holy Ghost, that ye may stand spotless before me at the last day.

"Verily, verily, I say unto you, this is my gospel; and ye know the things that ye must do in my church; for the works which ye have seen me do that shall ye also do" (3 Nephi 27:13–14, 16, 20–21).

Through the truths revealed to Joseph Smith and his successors, we know that mortality is informed by eternity. We understand that there was indeed a divine plan in the beginning. That plan included a Savior, who took upon Himself our sins, our pain, our sorrow, our sufferings so that we could, through His sweet grace and our repentance and obedience, be reconciled once again to God. We can trust that Christ has been sent "to bind up the brokenhearted, to proclaim liberty to the captives, and the opening of the prison to them that are bound; . . . to comfort all that mourn; to appoint unto them that mourn in Zion, to give unto them beauty for ashes, the oil of joy for mourning, the garment of praise for the spirit of heaviness; that they might be called trees of righteousness" (Isaiah 61:1–3).

Can you feel the power of Joseph Smith's testimony when he said, "I had seen a vision; I knew it, and I knew that God knew it, and I could not deny it, neither dared I do it"? (Joseph Smith—History 1:25). Not only could he not deny it, but he embarked on a life of persecution, criticism, and hardship because of it.

Just three years after the calamity of Far West, the tragedy of Haun's Mill, and the injustice of Liberty Jail, Joseph Smith wrote the 1842 Wentworth letter that included what would eventually be known as the Articles of Faith. That letter also courageously included this prophecy: "The Standard of Truth has been erected; no unhallowed hand can stop the work from progressing; persecutions may rage, mobs may combine, armies may assemble, calumny may defame, but the truth of God will go forth boldly, nobly, and independent, till it has penetrated every continent, visited every clime, swept every country, and sounded in every ear, till the purposes of God shall be accomplished, and the Great Jehovah shall say the work is done."[4]

On one occasion, the angel Moroni told Joseph Smith, "Your name shall be known among the nations, for the work which the Lord will perform by your hands shall cause the righteous to rejoice and the wicked to rage: with the one it shall be had in honor, and with the other in reproach; yet, with these it shall be a terror because of the great and marvelous work which shall follow the coming forth of the fulness of the gospel."[5]

Nothing exemplifies this promise of Moroni more than two statements from two different men. In 1854, Illinois Governor Thomas Ford wrote, "Thus fell Joe Smith, the most successful imposter in modern times; a man who, though ignorant and coarse, had some great natural parts, which fitted him for temporary success, but which were so obscured and counteracted by the inherent corruption and vices of his nature that he never could succeed in establishing a system of policy which looked to permanent success in the future."[6]

This truly is a case of a light shining in the darkness and the darkness comprehending it not. Joseph Smith wasn't establishing policy; he was doing God's work by restoring the truth that would "bring to pass the immortality and eternal life of man" (Moses 1:39).

Contrast Thomas Ford's assessment of Joseph Smith with that of John Taylor following the martyrdom: "Joseph Smith, the Prophet and Seer of the Lord, has done more, save Jesus only, for the salvation of men in this world, than any other man that ever lived in it. . . . He lived great, and he died great in the eyes of God and his people; and like most of the Lord's anointed in ancient times, has sealed his mission and his works with his own blood" (D&C 135:3).

Joseph Smith stood by Christ, and now the faithful stand by Joseph.

Isn't it grand and joyous to be alive in this last dispensation, when the light of the fulness of the gospel is sweeping over the earth? How many of you remember joking about missionaries in Russia? How many of you remember when dedicating a temple once a decade was the normal pace?

What a blessing it is to be able to witness in our own lives the fulfillment of prophecy and to be part of this great work.

From the original six members of the Church who gathered in the Whitmer farmhouse in Fayette, New York, in 1830, the Church has grown to over 12 million members. Slightly over half the members now live outside the United States; 53 percent are female. The Book of Mormon is available in over 100 languages. Basic Church curriculum materials are available in 175 languages. While English is still spoken by half of the members of the Church, one-third, or over 3.5 million members, speak Spanish. The other eight top languages in the Church are Portuguese, Tagalog, Cebuano, Japanese, Samoan, Ilokano, Korean, and Tongan.[7]

Now, sisters, the organization of the Relief Society was a key part of the Restoration. We know the history—as sisters in early Nauvoo began to organize themselves to do acts of service and charity. We know Eliza R. Snow drafted a constitution, which Joseph Smith called the best he had seen, and we know that he offered the sisters something better. Joseph Smith organized the Relief Society to complete the organization of the Church. He taught the early Relief Society sisters that the purpose of the Relief Society was not simply to relieve the poor; it was to help save souls—to bring them to Christ and the fulness of the gospel. Joseph encouraged the sisters to expand their hearts and to be charitable to one another. In many ways, Joseph and the early leaders of the Relief Society envisioned the work of the organization as helping women "[put] off the natural man" (or woman, in this case) and become "saint[s] through the atonement of Christ" (Mosiah 3:19).

Our dear sisters in Relief Society have always been an important part of this glorious wave of light and truth that has been sweeping the earth since 1830. The entire Church is blessed by the commitment and consecration of pioneers in every land who have received the fulness of the gospel; who have understood that "sacrifice brings forth the blessings of heaven"[8]; and who, despite all trials and challenges, still sing with thankful hearts, "All is well! All is well!"[9]

Sister Jane Manning James was born a free black woman in 1822 in Fairfield County, Connecticut. She was baptized in 1841 and led a group of family members to Nauvoo, where she was welcomed by Joseph Smith, who told her, "You are among friends." The journey wasn't without difficulty. Jane wrote: "Our feet cracked open and bled until you could see the whole print of our feet with blood on the ground. . . . But we went on our way rejoicing, singing hymns, and thanking God for his infinite goodness and mercy to us in protecting us from all harm and healing our feet." Jane arrived in the Salt Lake Valley on September 22, 1847. She shared her own meager supply of flour with Eliza Lyman, who had nothing and was starving, saying, "I try in my feeble way to set a good example for all."[10]

There are countless stories just like this one among our early pioneers. My humble prayer is that when I meet Jane Manning James or the others, I can put on the altar of sacrifice for the kingdom something equal to her bleeding feet and her last pound of flour.

During my mission in the Philippines, I had the opportunity to share an apartment with one of the Filipino missionaries. When the first patriarch was called for the Philippines while she was serving her mission, Perla had the opportunity to receive her patriarchal blessing. I remember when she returned to the apartment after her blessing, her eyes glowing with light. I asked her what was the most special part of receiving a patriarchal blessing. She said, "Now I finally know who I am." She explained that during many years of Spanish rule, Filipinos were made to feel that they were not as good as Spaniards and that even though the Americans who followed were more benevolent than the Spanish, Filipinos still felt inferior. "Now," she said, "I know I belong to the Lord's family and am not inferior to anyone."

After being released from her mission, Perla obtained a master's degree and married. She was often recruited to go abroad to teach, as are many Filipinos. Perla always felt that even though their financial circumstances were desperate, she needed to stay in the Philippines and build the kingdom there. When her husband was called to be the stake president, she wrote me a short note. She said, "Now that my husband is the stake president, the presiding authority asked that my callings be reduced so that I can support him in his work. I hardly know what to do. All I do now is teach early morning seminary, gospel doctrine, spiritual living and lead the choir."

When I had the opportunity to do my dissertation research in Nigeria, I was excited to go to a country where the gospel was so new. The official work of the Church began in Nigeria not long after the 1978 revelation on the priesthood. I spent much of my time in Nigeria in Lagos. Sister Faustina Haizel, a Ghanaian living in Nigeria, was the Relief Society president. At that time one of the important elements of being Relief Society president was being able to read the English lesson manual and teach the Relief Society curriculum. Faustina taught almost every Relief Society lesson.

I remember one humorous occasion. When it was time for Relief Society, there were only four sisters in attendance—one of the American missionaries, the wife of the Australian mission president, me, and Faustina. The lesson was on the blessings of the temple. Faustina was prepared and started giving the lesson. About halfway through the lesson, she stopped and said, as Africans do: "Ah! What am I doing giving this lesson? I am an African sister who has never seen a temple much less gone inside one, and I am giving this lesson to three white women who have all been to the temple." We all laughed at the irony of the situation, but I knew how much the temple meant to Faustina. Before I left Nigeria, she gave me a copy of her birth certificate with instructions that should she die before having the opportunity to go to the temple, I should take the birth certificate and do her temple work.

I am not going to need to do Faustina's temple work by proxy. Instead, we were able to go together to the Mount Timpanogos Utah Temple just three years ago. And now, from her window in the Church area office in Accra, Ghana, she looks out over the beautiful Accra Ghana Temple. Imagine the miracle it is for the Saints in Ghana to see this temple finally come to pass. What a marvelous work and a wonder, for just about 18 years ago the Church operation in Ghana was completely closed. The Ghanaian government had heard propaganda about the LDS Church and decided to seize the Church's assets and to close chapels and all other Church buildings. The radio and television media bombarded people with horrible stories about the Church. They said Joseph Smith was a criminal who died in prison. They said the Church persecuted blacks. They said the temples were places where evil things happened. During this difficult period, the Saints met quietly in one another's homes and kept the faith. During this time, Faustina wrote to me, saying, "The gospel is a pill I have swallowed, and it is already working its good in me. Do not worry about me. I will always be faithful."

Jane, Perla, Faustina—incredible examples of what occurs when the light of the fulness of the gospel breaks forth in a person's life.

We can feel the blessings of the Restoration in every aspect of our lives as the truths of the gospel of Jesus Christ provide an anchor and guide for us and our families. We are blessed to know that all things here on earth are more clearly and fully seen in the light of the restored gospel. The light that is spreading across the world is a light that lifts burdens and overwhelms the powers of darkness. This light of the gospel will lift our spirits, improve the way we feel about ourselves, illuminate our countenances, and inform our thoughts and actions. It provides answers, comfort, and peace. It can change everything about us if we will let it, as Faustina said, "work its good" in us.

I remember a particularly dear family I taught in the Philippines. First the oldest son was baptized, then the parents, then the youngest brother, then the youngest sister. Their home was a small structure in the shadows of a large church and other tall buildings. But I can testify that as the light of the gospel penetrated that small, humble home, even the shadows cast by the buildings around it seemed to be removed in the radiance of the joy of those who lived the gospel within its tiny frame.

Now, sisters, with the many blessings we receive because of the Restoration, we also have the obligation to share the light of the fulness of the gospel with others. Let me offer this analogy. With few exceptions, I am a very careful driver. I try to be cautious and courteous. But some months ago I crossed lanes in front of someone and came a little too close. I just hadn't been paying attention. In the past, the few times I've done that I have been embarrassed but soon got over it. But this time I was profoundly mortified and the feeling stayed for days. Why? Well, when I purchased a new vehicle two years ago, I decided to be a loyal employee and get BYU license plates. Now when I cut someone off, my BYU plate is right in the face of the other driver. Now when I don't seem to know where I'm going, my BYU plate is right out there. The worst situation was several months ago when a friend and I decided to go to a play at Pioneer Memorial Theater at the University of Utah, BYU's friendly rival. We wanted to have dinner at a nearby restaurant, and I was having trouble finding the right streets and parking spots. The stress was almost more than I could stand. I hoped that if any University of Utah fans saw my strange driving, they would be like Elaine Anderson, a member of the Women's Conference committee, and be less inclined to blame my erratic driving on BYU. I felt I was being held to a higher-than-ever driving standard because I was now labeled "BYU." I felt loyal and did not want my university—which was now clear to everyone on the road—to be dishonored by my behavior. In fact, I practically wanted to give the plates up, it was so stressful.

But those experiences made me think about another label I have taken upon myself that is far more significant and eternal than a BYU license plate. Every Sunday when we take the sacrament we "witness unto . . . God, the Eternal Father, that [we] are willing to take upon [us] the name of [his] Son, and always remember him, and keep his commandments" (Moroni 4:3). Not one of us is "received unto baptism save [we take] upon [us] the name of Christ, having a determination to serve him to the end . . . , [and] relying alone upon the merits of Christ, who [is] the author and the finisher of [our] faith" (Moroni 6:3–4).

I have been asking myself more often, because of a simple decision to buy a BYU license plate, what am I doing with His name? President Hinckley was once asked, "Since you do not use the cross, what is the symbol of your religion?"

President Hinckley replied that "the lives of our people must become the most meaningful expression of our faith and, in fact, therefore, the symbol of our worship."

President Hinckley went on to say: "No sign, no work of art, no representation of form is adequate to express the glory and the wonder of the Living Christ. He told us what the symbol should be when He said, 'If ye love me, keep my commandments' (John 14:15).

"As His followers," President Hinckley said, "we cannot do a mean or shoddy or ungracious thing without tarnishing His image. Nor can we do a good and gracious and generous act without burnishing more brightly the symbol of Him whose name we have taken upon ourselves. And so our lives must become a meaningful expression, the symbol of our declaration of our testimony of the Living Christ, the Eternal Son of the Living God."[11]

Isaiah said it this way:

"Arise, shine; for thy light is come, and the glory of the Lord is risen upon thee.

"For, behold, the darkness shall cover the earth, and gross darkness the people: but the Lord shall arise upon thee, and his glory shall be seen upon thee.

"And the Gentiles shall come to thy light, and kings to the brightness of thy rising" (Isaiah 60:1–3).

The Restoration, the light breaking forth to those in darkness, began with Joseph Smith's prayer in 1820. In a tribute to Joseph Smith in 1845, Parley P. Pratt exhorted the Saints:

"He has organized the kingdom of God.—We will extend its dominion.

"He has restored the fulness of the gospel.—We will spread it abroad.

"He has kindled up the dawn of a day of glory.—We will bring it to [meridian] splendor.

"He was a 'little one,' and became a thousand.—We are a small one, and will become a strong nation.

"In short, he quarried the stone. . . . We will cause it to become a great mountain and fill the whole earth."[12]

I bear to you my testimony of the reality of the Atonement, of a living Christ, of the Prophet Joseph Smith, who ushered in this dispensation of the fulness of times. I bear testimony of the reality and power of the Restoration and the blessings it brings to our individual lives. Now, for the sake of our own souls and for the sake of our families and for the sake of all the honest in heart who are looking for truth and light and watching us, I pray that we might feel the desire to "break forth" the light of the fulness of the gospel in all that we do. I pray, sisters, just as Joseph Smith encouraged his friends, that we can "go on in so great a cause" (D&C 128:22).

NOTES

1. Lucy Mack Smith, *History of Joseph Smith, Revised and Enhanced,* ed. Scot Facer Proctor and Maurine Jensen Proctor (Salt Lake City: Bookcraft, 1996), 47.
2. Joseph Smith, *The Papers of Joseph Smith,* 2 vols., ed. Dean C. Jessee (Salt Lake City: Deseret Book, 1989), 1:5–7.

3. Henry B. Eyring, remarks given at the unveiling ceremony of the First Vision statue by Avard T. Fairbanks at the Joseph Smith Building, Brigham Young University, October 17, 1997.

4. Joseph Smith, *History of The Church of Jesus Christ of Latter-day Saints*, ed. B. H. Roberts, 2d ed. rev., 7 vols. (Salt Lake City: The Church of Jesus Christ of Latter-day Saints, 1932–51), 4:540.

5. *Messenger and Advocate* 2, no. 13 (October 1835): 199.

6. Thomas Ford, in Smith, *History of the Church*, 7:35.

7. See "Key Facts and Figures," http://www.lds.org/newsroom/page/0,15606,4034-1---10-168,00.html

8. W. W. Phelps, "Praise to the Man," *Hymns of The Church of Jesus Christ of Latter-day Saints* (Salt Lake City: The Church of Jesus Christ of Latter-day Saints, 1985), no. 27.

9. *Hymns*, no. 30

10. Quoted in "Life of Continual Faith," *Church News*, April 23, 2005, 5.

11. Gordon B. Hinckley, "The Symbol of Our Faith," *Ensign*, April 2005, 3, 6.

12. Parley P. Pratt, in *Millennial Star* 5 (March 1845): 151.

"I Knew It, and I Knew That God Knew It"

—◆—

Cecil O. Samuelson

Perhaps no event in the history of the world, since the Savior's Atonement and Resurrection, has been more important than the experience of young Joseph Smith on that early spring day of 1820. While retiring to the woods in full faith and trust that his prayer would be answered, little did he expect or anticipate what transpired.

My words cannot do justice to the occasion. Joseph's own account (see Joseph Smith—History 1:11–26) provides the critical details with which we are familiar but also should review regularly.

At a very young age, he became aware of the religious excitement in his area. He listened to various preachers and identified their differences and his resultant confusion. While troubled by these issues, he read the scriptural counsel from the book of James (see James 1:5) and concluded that he indeed lacked wisdom. He, therefore, resolved to ask God for clarification, because he had faith that his prayer would be answered. He went to a beautiful, secluded spot where he could pour out his concerns and questions and plead for guidance.

Elder Cecil O. Samuelson, twelfth president of Brigham Young University, is a member of the First Quorum of the Seventy for The Church of Jesus Christ of Latter-day Saints. Prior to his call to full-time LDS Church service, he was senior vice president of Intermountain Health Care. In addition to his career as a physician of rheumatic and genetic diseases, he served at the University of Utah as a professor of medicine, dean of the School of Medicine, and vice president of health sciences. He and his wife, Sharon Giauque Samuelson, have five children and five grandchildren.

Following a powerful struggle with the adversary, he witnessed the bright pillar of light, brighter than he could imagine, fall upon him, and within this magnificent light, he saw the Father, who called Joseph by name and introduced His Son, who instructed the boy with love and clarity. We know some, but not all, that young Joseph was told and taught that fateful day.

Likewise, we know the later response the lad received from other people. As he expected, his family believed his experience. What surprised him greatly was the reaction of others, particularly the ministers of religion. He had assumed that they would be as thrilled as was he with his remarkable interview with Deity. Their rejection and ridicule were a matter of great disappointment, confusion, and distress for this humble but honest youngster, who was only seeking a modest answer to what seemed to him to be a straightforward question.

Joseph's reflections caused him to consider the experiences of the Apostle Paul, who suffered similar persecution for his testimony of the events that occurred so long ago on the road to Damascus. He took great consolation and courage from Paul's steadfastness. In speaking of Paul's trials, Joseph reported the following:

"So it was with me. I had actually seen a light, and in the midst of that light I saw two Personages, and they did in reality speak to me; and though I was hated and persecuted for saying that I had seen a vision, yet it was true; and while they were persecuting me, reviling me, and speaking all manner of evil against me falsely for so saying, I was led to say in my heart: Why persecute me for telling the truth? I have actually seen a vision; and who am I that I can withstand God, or why does the world think to make me deny what I have actually seen? For I had seen a vision; I knew it, and I knew that God knew it, and I could not deny it, neither dared I do it; at least I knew that by so doing I would offend God, and come under condemnation" (Joseph Smith—History 1:25).

Whatever one might think of Joseph Smith, one cannot be unclear as to what he experienced or what he felt about it. Indeed, his testimony and convictions remained not only consistent but unshaken for the remainder of his tumultuous mortal days.

Our assignment today is to consider together what it is that we might ourselves do to develop testimonies similar in strength and power to the witness of Joseph Smith.

It is not likely that any of us will ever duplicate the experience of Joseph. It is not necessary, and it is not possible. We can, however, develop testimonies that will sustain us in our own lives and seasons sufficient to allow us to return with honor to our Heavenly Father and the Savior, as Joseph Smith did. Let me approach our task by asking four basic questions that will help unlock the doors of understanding essential to our being able to know as Joseph knew.

First, what is it that Joseph knew?

Second, how did Joseph know?

Third, how can we know?

And fourth, what are the implications for us when we do know?

First, What Is it That Joseph Knew?

Before going to the grove, the young boy had a strong faith in the reality of God and in the power and applicability of the holy scriptures and their counsel and promises. Without this fundamental and foundational faith, both inborn and gained from his parents, it is highly unlikely that this very young man would have presented himself and his question that was so wonderfully and unexpectedly answered in the way he reported it to occur.

From this experience, Joseph Smith learned some vital, essential truths that, at best, he had only hoped for with his limited perspective and experiences. He learned that he in reality had a vision. It was not a dream nor an imaginary thought nor some unexplained release of uncoordinated neurological impulses. He had a vision!

Through this vision he learned that God the Father lives, has a body of flesh and bones, is able and willing to speak to His children, and loves His Only Begotten Son, Jesus Christ. Joseph learned that the Savior also lives, with His wonderfully resurrected body, and acts under the direction of His Father. He learned that both the Father and the Son knew him intimately and were anxious to teach, counsel, and direct him.

Joseph learned that prayers are answered and, as in this experience, often directly and clearly. In addition, he learned that sometimes vital answers are given even when we don't know how to ask the proper question! Specifically, he learned that he was not to join any of the churches that he had been considering.

How Did Joseph Know?

On this occasion, the occasion of the First Vision, Joseph absolutely knew what he had seen, heard, and felt. It was real, and he knew that it was real. This sacred interview was so tangible, so impressive, so life-altering that Joseph Smith was never again the same, in spite of the tremendous challenges and difficulties that haunted him throughout his life. I am sure that many times he rehearsed the dilemma that I have shared from his own account, but his conclusion was always the same. He knew that he had experienced this vision.

It is appropriate to recall the importance of his preparation for what transpired in the Sacred Grove. It is clear by Joseph's own admission that he had no real idea of why he was preparing and being prepared as he was. He had faith. He not only searched the scriptures for answers but "liken[ed]" them unto himself long before he was aware of Nephi's counsel on this matter (see 1 Nephi 19:23). To understand better the intentions of God for the course of his life, Joseph was absolutely committed to following the direction or understanding that came from his faith and exercise of effort.

Moreover, although difficult, it was sustaining for Joseph to know that "God had a work for [him] to do" (Joseph Smith—History 1:33). Understanding that there is a plan, both "macro" for everyone and "micro" for each of us, gave Joseph Smith the continual confirmation that his course and responsibilities were real and approved of God.

How Can We Know?

We can obtain a testimony of surety in basically the same way that Joseph did. The basic pattern is conscientious study, deep and consistent thought, and specific, faith-sustained prayer—prayer that includes appropriate preparation, careful asking, and, particularly, concentrated listening with a firm commitment to act on the answer. At that early time,

Joseph did not have the advantage of the correcting counsel given to Oliver Cowdery but obviously intended for all of us:

"Behold, you have not understood; you have supposed that I would give it unto you, when you took no thought save it was to ask me.

"But, behold, I say unto you, that you must study it out in your mind; then you must ask me if it be right, and if it is right I will cause that your bosom shall burn within you; therefore, you shall feel that it is right.

"But if it be not right you shall have no such feelings, but you shall have a stupor of thought that shall cause you to forget the thing which is wrong" (D&C 9:7–9).

It would yet be several years after the First Vision that Joseph would translate the helpful instruction and promise of Moroni with respect to how we might really know the truthfulness of these things for ourselves:

"And when ye shall receive these things, I would exhort you that ye would ask God, the Eternal Father, in the name of Christ, if these things are not true; and if ye shall ask with a sincere heart, with real intent, having faith in Christ, he will manifest the truth of it unto you, by the power of the Holy Ghost.

"And by the power of the Holy Ghost ye may know the truth of all things" (Moroni 10:4–5).

Listen to the words and promise of the Savior: "If any man will do his will, he shall know of the doctrine, whether it be of God, or whether I speak of myself" (John 7:17).

It is very clear that we can surely know. The patterns are not ambiguous, but they require real work, real intent, real faith, real effort, and real commitment. Too often, when a desired answer seems to elude us, we may be looking in error to heaven with a questioning eye rather than looking directly into the mirror.

President David O. McKay was the Lord's prophet of my youth. Our family had a special interest in him because my maternal grandfather had served as a missionary in Scotland with Elder McKay. Thus, I have always been impacted by his example and his teachings. Let me share some of his observations and experiences that are germane to the question of how it is we can know.

Said President McKay: "If you ask me where I first received my unwavering faith in the existence of a God, I would answer you: in the home of my childhood—when Father and Mother invariably called their children around them in the morning and at night and invoked God's blessings upon the household and upon mankind. There was a sincerity in that good patriarch's voice that left an undying impression in the souls of his children, and Mother's prayers were equally impressive. . . . Before I heard my father testify that he had heard a divine voice, I knew that he lived near to his Maker. I also know," said President McKay, "through a nearness to that same Eternal Father since, that my father told the truth when he said that when he was on his mission in Scotland, in answer to fervent prayer, he received the following admonition given in audible tones: 'Testify that Joseph Smith is a prophet of the living God.'"[1]

WHAT ARE THE IMPLICATIONS FOR US WHEN WE KNOW?

This is an important query for each of us to make individually and seriously. Most of us are familiar with the initial phrase of the third verse of section 82 of the Doctrine and Covenants but may not pay as much attention to the entire verse. Let me share it for our consideration: "For of him unto whom much is given much is required; and he who sins against the greater light shall receive the greater condemnation."

It is important for us to realize that God does not bequeath His gifts to His children capriciously. While we don't know all of the reasons that each of us has the gifts that we do, we are assured that "they are given for the benefit of those who love [God] and keep [His] commandments, and [those] that seeketh so to do" (D&C 46:9). We also need to remember that with gifts, blessings, and understanding come burdens.

We know, for example, that those who die without the "law," meaning an understanding of the gospel of Jesus Christ and access to the saving ordinances (see Moroni 8:22), are eligible for the celestial kingdom. Those of us who have had the opportunity to understand and enjoy the blessings of the gospel are held to a higher standard. This is true with respect to the essential ordinances and also true concerning our conduct.

While we may be able to fool others and even ourselves on occasion, we must remember that as with the Prophet Joseph Smith, God knows each of us intimately and by name. He also knows that we have had the opportunity to know and understand these things as well. One might ask, given these considerations, wouldn't I have been better off never to have been exposed to the gospel in the first place?

If that thought occurs, then be very careful, because this may have been the exact question and conclusion of the third part of the hosts of heaven. They chose to follow Lucifer rather than accept the modest burdens—but incomparable blessings—attendant to the Father's plan that the Savior volunteered to implement (see D&C 29:36). Even for those unfortunate, lost souls, they retained their gift of agency but also the results of the poor choice that they had made. Likewise, we are responsible for our choices and inevitably live with the implications and consequences of our decisions, both good and poor.

For every challenge, problem, difficulty, or disappointment we might be called upon to endure, the evidence is clear that Heavenly Father intends for us to be not only justly recompensed but ultimately, if we do our part, to be the beneficiaries and recipients of all that the Father has (see D&C 84:38). Thus, the bounty of our gifts—our testimonies being among the chief of them—makes the ultimate choice very easy when properly considered, even when the actual implementation of what we know we need to do remains so difficult and taxing.

Just as was the case with the Prophet Joseph, we also need to know that God has important work for each of us to do. Some of that work will be specific and unique to us individually, and some will be expected of everyone. In both cases, our response needs to be as was the case with the Apostle Peter in his answer to the request of the lame beggar: "Such as I have give I thee" (Acts 3:6).

Rather than attempt to anticipate or address what specific individual expectations the Lord may require of any of us, let me attempt, in the time remaining, to focus on some responsibilities of a more general nature. Even with these, specific or customized dimensions will make each of our circumstances unique, although the principles of the general case apply.

First, with respect to those of us blessed to have solid testimonies, think of this observation made by the Lord: "It becometh every man [and woman] who hath been warned to warn his [or her] neighbor" (D&C 88:81). Obviously, missionary work is part of our responsibility. While all of us should consider how we might prepare and qualify for full-time missionary work, some of us may not have the blessing of a specific call from the prophet to serve a full-time mission. Nevertheless, the scripture reminds us that each of us, whatever our station or circumstances, is under an obligation to share the gospel with our families, friends, and neighbors. The warning we give is not necessarily confrontational or adversarial. Indeed, that should be the exception if it ever needs to occur at all. The warning is really given, almost always, in the context of sharing our testimonies and the fruits of living the gospel of Jesus Christ. How and when we do so is largely up to us, but the mandate and the expectation are clear.

Second, we are required to share the gospel and what we know with our own families. This is true when we are members of a large family, but it is also true when we, as individuals, are the only members of our family or we are a family of one.

How do we share the gospel with ourselves if this is the case? Well, we study and ponder the scriptures. We get up and go to church on Sunday, even when we may not feel like it or are even sure that we won't be missed if we are absent. We qualify for and attend the temple to the degree that we are able, and we also help our friends and neighbors in their responsibilities to share the gospel with their own families.

Let me remind you of the corrective direction given to the Prophet Joseph by the Lord. Remember, it was not a lack of testimony on Joseph's part that may have led to his distraction from this most fundamental responsibility.

"And now, verily I say unto [you,] Joseph Smith, Jun.—You have not kept the commandments, and must needs stand rebuked before the Lord;

"Your family must needs repent and forsake some things, and give more earnest heed unto your sayings, or be removed out of their place" (D&C 93:47–48).

This is sobering counsel to anyone and especially to a prophet, I must imagine! What a testimony, by the way, that Joseph really was a prophet when he had both the integrity and confidence to allow such a personal rebuke to be shared so widely. I confess that while I have not done nearly as much as I should or nearly enough in any of the important measures, this pointed counsel has been a great motivator to me as a husband, father, and grandfather.

As the years have passed and my own circumstances have changed, the Book of Mormon has taken on added significance for me. It is a model—even a manual, if you will—on how testimony-blessed parents and grandparents can fulfill their responsibilities to their families with respect to sharing and shaping the testimonies. Think of these great examples and their results.

"I, Nephi, having been born of goodly parents, therefore I was taught somewhat in all the learning of my father; and having seen many afflictions in the course of my days, nevertheless, having been highly favored of the Lord in all my days . . ." (1 Nephi 1:1).

I submit that Nephi, like other prophets and his brothers Sam and Jacob, was the product of good parenting. Likewise, you good parents, it is important to know that Lamans and Lemuels are sometimes found in even the best of families. Lehi and Sariah did their best and left the rest in the hands of the Lord.

Another example: "I, Enos, knowing my father that he was a just man—for he taught me in his language, and also in the nurture and admonition of the Lord . . ." (Enos 1:1).

Time does not permit sharing the accounts of the efforts made by Alma with Alma the Younger or King Mosiah with his children or Helaman teaching his sons or Mormon and his tutorials with Moroni. Clearly, these great prophet leaders who really knew, as Joseph Smith in our dispensation knew, also understood the necessity of working vigorously and proactively in teaching and sharing the gospel with their families. Please indulge me as I share one last example in this regard.

Mormon, the great abridger and editor of the Book of Mormon, lamented in several places that he could not include even the "hundredth part" of what was available and worth sharing (Jacob 3:13; Words of Mormon 1:5; Helaman 3:14; 3 Nephi 5:8; 26:6; Ether 15:33). Thus, we are on safe ground to conclude that what he did include he thought to be of great importance and the result of inspiration from the Lord. Let me now share with you a favorite Book of Mormon teaching experience.

Before King Benjamin gave his great address to all of his people, he gave a short, carefully crafted message to a smaller audience—his three sons. I invite you to study carefully the first several verses of Mosiah chapter 1, where you have both the words of King Benjamin and some telling editorial comments by Mormon. Let me share some of the significant statements that can help us in our teaching and helping our own family members.

"[King Benjamin] caused that [his children] should be taught in all the language of his fathers, that thereby they might become men of understanding; and that they might know concerning the prophecies which had been spoken by the mouths of their fathers, which were delivered them by the hand of the Lord.

"And he also taught them concerning the records which were engraven on the plates of brass, saying: My sons, I would that ye should remember that were it not for these plates, which contain these records and these commandments, we must have suffered in ignorance, even at this present time, not knowing the mysteries of God.

"For it were not possible that our father, Lehi, could have remembered all these things, to have taught them to his children, except it were for the help of these plates; for he having been taught in the language of the Egyptians therefore he could read these engravings, and teach them to his children, that thereby they could teach them to their children, and so fulfilling the commandments of God, even down to this present time.

"I say unto you, my sons, were it not for these things, which have been kept and preserved by the hand of God, that we might read and understand of his mysteries, and have his commandments always before our eyes, that even our fathers would have dwindled in unbelief, and we should have been like unto our brethren, the Lamanites, who know nothing concerning these things, or even do not believe them when they are taught them, because of the traditions of their fathers, which are not correct.

"O my sons," went on King Benjamin, "I would that ye should remember that these sayings are true, and also that these records are true. And behold, also the plates of Nephi, which contain the records and sayings of our fathers from the time they left Jerusalem until now, and they are true; and we can know of their surety because we have them before our eyes.

"And now, my sons, I would that ye should remember to search them diligently, that ye may profit thereby; and I would that ye should keep the commandments of God, that ye may prosper in the land according to the promises which the Lord made unto our fathers" (Mosiah 1:2–7).

Now that is a very long but very important passage that illustrates nicely the kind of responsibilities those possessing strong testimonies have to their own children and the children under their influence. Let me sum-marize what King Benjamin did with his sons. First, he saw that they were educated both in the things of the world and also in the things of God. Second, he taught them from the scriptures and also helped them under-stand why the scriptures are so important to each of us. Third, he bore specific and fervent testimony as to the truthfulness of the things that he taught. Fourth, he clearly explained the importance of keeping God's com-mandments and the absolute relationship between unrestrained obedience and receiving the blessings promised by the Lord.

If we use this same pattern in our own families, we will be well on our way to meeting the responsibilities that our testimonies confer upon us. As we meet these obligations, we in turn can enjoy the peace that the gospel brings and also know of our approval in the eyes of heaven. The Prophet Joseph Smith himself said, "An actual knowledge to any person, that the course of life which he [or she] pursues is according to the will of God, is essentially necessary to enable him [or her] to have that confi-dence in God without which no person can obtain eternal life."[2]

What a wonderful, beautiful, and necessary thing to know that Joseph Smith is in every respect a true prophet of the living God. I am grateful for my privilege and responsibility to be a witness of him and what he taught. His testimony of the Savior is foundational to my own convictions concerning the Atonement and the Resurrection of our King of Kings and Lord of Lords. Praise be forevermore to the "man who communed with Jehovah!"[3]

NOTES

1. David O. McKay, in Conference Report, April 1966, 107.
2. Joseph Smith, *Lectures on Faith* (Salt Lake City: Deseret Book, 1985), 6:2.
3. W. W. Phelps, "Praise to the Man," *Hymns of The Church of Jesus Christ of Latter-day Saints* (Salt Lake City: The Church of Jesus Christ of Latter-day Saints, 1985), no. 27.

"This Is My Beloved Son"

F. Burton Howard

To start with, I would like to pay tribute to a magnificent lady. I have loved her for more than 50 years. She personifies everything that is virtuous, lovely, and of good report. I had no idea when I met and married her how good she really was (and I thought she was perfect then). She is the self-described product of a one-bathroom home. It has been a joy for me to see how she has handled the tests and trials of our life together. One of those trials is that it's her birthday today, and she's elected to be here with us.

I have been with her in poverty and danger. I have seen her as a mother and as a daughter. I have watched her confront sickness, disappointment, and death. I have observed her in company and in solitude. I have traveled with her, studied with her, prayed with her, and lost my hair with her. Through it all I have never seen her discouraged, and I have never seen her slacken. She has supported and enhanced me in every calling I have ever had and is my equal in every way—and my better in many ways.

There has not been a day without a smile nor one without a quiet

Elder F. Burton Howard was called to the First Quorum of the Seventy of The Church of Jesus Christ of Latter-day Saints on September 30, 1978. He has served as a bishop twice and as president of the Uruguay Montevideo Mission; he is currently serving as the president of the Madrid Spain Temple. He is the author of three books. Elder Howard and his wife, Caroline Heise Howard, have five children and thirteen grandchildren.

word of encouragement. I know that her eyesight is failing a little because she continues to tell me how handsome I am, and I forgive her for that. I would not be here today were it not for her, and I want to thank her publicly for all of this and more.

Now to my subject.

A few years ago my wife and I were touring the Rochester New York Mission. The mission president asked if we would like to get up early and go to the Sacred Grove before the crowds came. We did. We drove a mile or so past the farmhouse, and he stopped the car. He said, "If you don't mind walking, I will show you my favorite way into the grove." We walked down a little grass-covered lane on the far side of the grove, and in the distance we could see tall trees. After a while we came to a small sign made of brass with gold letters, black background, mounted on two wooden posts. The sign said, "The Sacred Grove," and contained these incredible words: "God the Father and His Son, Jesus Christ, appeared to Joseph Smith in this grove." Period!

I had been intent on going into the grove and contemplating what occurred there back in 1820, but I found I could not bring myself to leave the sign. Its simple message arrested my progress. It did not say, "The Church of Jesus Christ of Latter-day Saints" or "On the morning of a beautiful, clear day, early in the spring." It didn't even purport to be a historical site. It didn't even say, "Visitors Welcome." Rather there was just the simple statement, "God the Father and His Son, Jesus Christ, appeared to Joseph Smith in this grove."

I read it again and again. My wife said, "Don't you want to go into the grove?" I said, "I need to think about the message on this sign for a moment longer. Either it is true, or it isn't. If it is, it is the greatest message in all the world. Even someone who didn't believe it could not pass by it without being profoundly changed."

President Marion G. Romney said that the Father's statement—"This is My Beloved Son. Hear Him!" (Joseph Smith—History 1:17)—"together with the Prophet's declaration that 'the Father has a body of flesh and bones as tangible as man's; [and] the Son also,' . . . (D&C 130:22), clarifies and confirms, for us of this last dispensation, all that has before been revealed and preserved for us about God. . . . Upon our acceptance and testimony to the truth of this vision and statement hangs our individual salvation."[1]

Those are strong words. To think that our own personal salvation depends upon whether we accept and have a testimony of what Joseph saw and heard in the spring of 1820!

Elder Neal A. Maxwell put it a little more softly when he wrote:

"Not understanding who Jesus really is by title and role inevitably sets up a lack of gratitude for His astonishing atonement. If we do not regard Him highly enough to pay heed to His words about *who* He is, we will pay less heed to *what* He says and requires of us. The resulting diminution of regard and comprehension will result in little faith. What 'think [we] of Christ' inevitably determines His *operative relevancy* for our lives."[2]

That is also a provocative statement. We may profess a testimony of the Prophet Joseph and what he saw in the grove, but if Joseph's experience there has no "operative relevancy" in our lives, then we are but "sounding brass" and "tinkling cymbal" (1 Corinthians 13:1). The First Vision and Joseph's statements accompanying it are the things upon which our salvation rests. And the application we make of these things and their operative relevancy to our lives are at least as important to us practically as the words that were uttered are important to us doctrinally.

Let me illustrate what I think Elder Maxwell meant by "operative relevancy." Elizabeth Claridge McCune once wrote of her father's call to go settle the "Muddy." Listen to her words:

"No place on earth seemed so precious to me at fifteen years of age as dear old Nephi. How eagerly we looked forward to the periodical visits of President Brigham Young and his company! Everything was done that could be thought of for their comfort and entertainment. And with all it was a labor of love.

"We went out with our Sabbath Schools and all the other organizations, with bands of music and flags and banners and flowers to meet and greet our beloved leader and his company. On one occasion the people were lined up on each side of the street waiting for the carriages to pass. Among them were twenty-five young ladies dressed in white who had strewn evergreens and wild flowers along the path. Bro Brigham, Bros Kimball and Wells with the entire company got out of their carriages, and walked over the flowery road . . . to our homes, [where] dinner was prepared and served.

"We all attended the afternoon meeting, the girls in white having reserved seats in front. The sermons were grand, and we were happy until President Young announced that he had a few names to read of men who were to be called and voted in as missionaries to go and settle up the 'Muddy.' This almost stilled the beating of the hearts of all present. Many of our people had been called to go to settle the Dixie country—but the Muddy, so many miles farther south! And so much worse! Oh! Oh! I did not hear another name except 'Samuel Claridge.' Then how I sobbed and cried, regardless of the fact that the tears were spoiling the new white dress. The father of the girl who sat next to me was also called. Said my companion, 'Why, what is you crying about? It doesn't make me cry. I know my father won't go.' 'Well there is the difference,' said I, 'I know that my father *will* go and that nothing could prevent him, and I should not own him as a father if he would not go when he is called.' Then, I broke down sobbing again. . . .

"We had just moved into a new house and were fixed comfortably. Many of our friends tried to persuade father to keep his home and farm; to go south a while and then come back. But father knew that this was not the kind of mission upon which he had been called. 'I will sell everything I own,' said he, 'and take my means to help build up another waste place in Zion.'"[3]

That is operative relevancy. And the individual salvation of Sister McCune and her family may well hinge on the fact that her father knew that Joseph saw what he said he saw and that Brigham Young was his divinely appointed successor and that, because of that, *nothing* could prevent him from going to settle the Muddy.

What must we do to ensure that the events of that spring morning have operative relevancy in our lives? Sister Marjorie Hinckley gave some insight into that question. In a letter to a missionary grandson, she spoke of a journey to Hawaii, where three regional conferences were held on three different islands on the same Sunday. She said it was a brutal schedule but very rewarding. Quoting now, she wrote: "The last [conference] was on Molokai. . . . [The Saints] were so excited—they piled leis on us up to our ears. We got home at 9 P.M. on Tues. and Gramps was at the office

at 7:00 the next morning. His secretary put on his desk a list of assignments for the next 60 days. Enough to give a younger man a faint heart.
There is no let-up, . . . but somehow with the help of the Lord he will
make it." Now listen to this: "Sometimes when the pressures mount I have
to remember that Joseph Smith did have a vision and though we give our
whole souls to the work we are still unprofitable servants."[4] Well, the pressures and trials of this life are enough to give any one of us a faint heart.
This Women's Conference is one way of helping all of us remember that
Joseph really did have a vision. The Lord is in His heaven, and He does
care about us. The heavens are not closed. We are in the true Church.
The blessings of the Atonement are available to all of us. There is a plan
and a timetable for all things. Knowing these things, nothing is ever
hopeless.

As we take steps to ensure that we do not forget what we have seen
and felt and what we know, it is helpful to me to recall that prior to 1820
in all of the Bible there was only one reference to a *living* God. As Jesus
taught in the synagogue in Capernaum, He referred to Himself as "living
bread" and said, "The living Father hath sent me" (John 6:51, 57). The
Jews didn't understand. Even many of His disciples complained, saying,
"This is an hard saying; who can hear it?" (John 6:60).

Before 1820 nearly everyone believed in what Elder Maxwell once
described as a "retired God whose best years [were] past. [One] to whom
[they] should pay retroactive obeisance, worshiping him for what he [had]
already done."[5]

But Joseph was introduced to a living Son by the living Father. He was
commanded to hear Him. His experience in the grove brought a comprehension that could not have been gained any other way. One of the consequences of worshiping a living God is knowing that His work is ongoing
and that He sees and hears and does that work presently.

In revelation after revelation, the Lord introduced Himself to Joseph
as "the only living and true God" (D&C 20:19) or "Jesus Christ, the Son
of the living God" (D&C 14:9; 42:1), being mere examples of many
scriptures.

The theological and personal implications of this concept were stag-
gering. For suddenly, worshiping God not only entailed remembering Him
and keeping His past commandments but also meant furthering His

present purposes, receiving additional revelation and commandments, and enlisting in His great latter-day work. Is it any wonder that the angel Moroni warned young Joseph that "those who profess to know the truth but walk in deceit, [would] tremble with anger"?[6]

Everything the Lord does has purpose and design. So it was with the First Vision. The Lord explained that, "knowing the calamity which should come upon the inhabitants of the earth," He "called upon . . . Joseph Smith, Jun., and spake unto him . . . and gave him commandments; . . . that faith . . . might increase in the earth; that [his] everlasting covenant might be established; that the fulness of [the] gospel might be proclaimed. . . . [That] they [who] sought wisdom . . . might be instructed; and inasmuch as they sinned they might be chastened, that they might repent; and inasmuch as they were humble they might be made strong, and blessed from on high, and receive knowledge from time to time" (D&C 1:17, 21–23, 26–28).

Over the course of the years following the First Vision, the beautiful, distinctive doctrines of the Restoration were revealed. Transcendent teachings, line upon line and precept upon precept, flowed from the Lord's own lips. Joseph came to know the Savior in the present tense as "the Great I Am" and not "the Great He Was." The Book of Mormon was revealed. Joseph learned about faith and how to acquire more, about prayer and asking for what is right.

He heard about and was taught his role in the great and marvelous work, which Isaiah had foretold. He learned about the gift of the Holy Ghost and what it meant always to have His Spirit be with him. He was counseled to follow the example of the Savior in all things. He restored Christ's Church and the holy priesthood. He learned about eternal marriage and the plan of happiness.

Joseph knew the Savior. He spoke with Him and, thankfully, wrote down His words. One of the greatest contributions of the Prophet Joseph has been to thereby reveal the Savior and His work, His will, and His words and the injunction to "Hear Him!"

And so it is that ultimately that vision is the test for all of us as well. It all begins and ends in a grove of trees in upstate New York, whether we will hear and whether we will *heed.* Did it really happen as Joseph said it happened?

With this question in mind, I would like to relate an experience I had as a young missionary. I was a newly appointed district president. There were six elders in our district. One day the mission president called and told me he wanted to expand the work. There was a fairly large city in our district that had never had missionaries in it before. He suggested that we go there and hold a street meeting. Having never done that, I asked him exactly what he wanted us to do.

In Uruguay, in those pretelevision days, all cities had a public square with a large park in it. There was a cathedral on one end of the square and municipal buildings on the other. In the evening the people would dress up and go for a stroll in the park. The custom was for single women to walk around the park, usually in groups, in a clockwise direction. Single men would walk in a counterclockwise direction. Everyone who wanted to see or be seen was so accommodated. Parents often sat on the benches, and children would teasingly chase one another through the parade of walkers.

The mission president said, "I want you to take your district to the park on a Friday night. Sing some hymns. When a crowd gathers I want one of you to get up on one of the benches and tell the Joseph Smith story. Take the names of any interested persons, and then we will decide whether there is sufficient potential to assign a pair of missionaries to work there permanently."

Friday came. We boarded the train and went to the city, arriving in the early evening. We went to the park. The street lights were just coming on. As a district, we had practiced a few hymns and sang them. And just as the president had promised, a small crowd gathered. Nothing like that had ever happened on their evening walk before.

We sang as long as we could. Finally one of the elders got up on the bench and began to tell the Joseph Smith story—of Joseph's experience in the grove. He told of the religious turmoil, of Joseph's desire to know which church to join, and quoted James 1:5 and spoke of how the boy Joseph decided to ask of God. People were actually listening. The young elder confidently pressed on. He told how Joseph knelt down and began to pray and how a pillar of light descended until it fell upon him, how he saw two Personages, whose brightness and glory defied description. He had just gotten to the part where one of Them spoke to him, calling him by name and saying, pointing to the other, "This is My Beloved Son. Hear Him!" (Joseph Smith—History 1:17) when the script that the mission president carefully worked out for us abruptly changed.

At the edge of the crowd, in the shadows, a group of teenage boys had gathered, and they began to throw rocks at us. I was the leader. I seemed to be the main target—although I'm sure we all felt the same way—and I had to decide in an instant whether to continue or to conclude the meeting. And that decision seemed to depend on whether Joseph really went into that grove, whether he really did see a pillar of light, and whether the Father really did say, "This is My Beloved Son. Hear Him!" But there was more: Had I really been called by a prophet? Had the mission president really been inspired to ask us to open that town? Were we really on the Lord's errand? And was knowing all of that worth more than a rock in the eye?

After the Spirit answered all of those questions, there didn't seem to be any honorable alternative. We finished the story. A few small stones found their mark. No permanent damage was done. We sang a hymn, closed the meeting, and didn't convert a soul that night. But we did open the city. Sometime later a small branch was organized. There is a prosperous ward there today. None of the members there know of that street meeting that was held in their city nearly 50 years ago, but I have never been quite the same, because on that night the absolute reality of what happened in the grove was indelibly impressed upon my mind.

It is evident that if Joseph saw what he claimed to have seen, and I testify that he did, that he did more than any man who has ever lived to reveal the nature, character, and mission of the Lord Jesus Christ to the world. As a consequence, we have some affirmative duties and responsibilities.

President Hinckley has eloquently expressed himself in this regard. Let me quote briefly from his teachings. Said he:

"I read this morning a part of Joseph Smith's testimony of the First Vision. You are all familiar with it. His going into a grove, pleading with the Lord, a light shining above him, and then the appearance of the Father and the Son. I read that testimony and thought of it. I said to myself, 'If every one of us knew in our hearts that that statement is true, then we would know that all else which follows it, which came through the restoration of the gospel, is true also.' And we would walk and live with greater faithfulness.

"Tithing would not be a problem with us. Temple service would not be a problem with us. Keeping the Sabbath day holy would not be a problem with us. We would have no inclination to go to the store and buy things on the Sabbath day. Missionary service would be no problem with us.

"All else that follows would be true. We would know it in our hearts if we had a solid, firm, immovable conviction of the truth and validity of that great vision wherein God the Eternal Father and the risen Lord Jesus Christ appeared to the boy Joseph Smith and the Father said, 'This is My Beloved Son. Hear Him!' (Joseph Smith—History 1:17)."[7]

And so it is with operative relevancy. Because of the First Vision, we do things we would not do otherwise. We teach our children because, we repent because, we pray because, we try to walk uprightly because, we keep everlastingly at it—all because of what happened in that grove.

Because of the First Vision, we know that prayer works, that the heavens are not sealed, and that the Father and the Son are separate and distinct beings.

Because of the First Vision, we have the many-splendored Restoration in all of its magnificence and variety.

Because of the First Vision, we know the great plan of happiness and our role and place as sons and daughters of God.

Because of the relevancy of that vision, eight of my great-grandparents crossed the plains in response to Brigham Young's invitation to gather to Zion, and a great-great-grandfather walked away from a 600-acre farm in what today is downtown Kansas City, Missouri, in order to stand by the Prophet.

Every Latter-day Saint knows the story of the First Vision and, to some degree or another, has faith in it. But we must take care to connect the events of the grove with real life and with present circumstance, or the result will be that the great truths of the Restoration will become something we just talk about and do not live.

The problem for most of us is that, while we dearly believe these things, the events of that day in 1820 are far away and sometimes forgotten. The wear and tear of daily living often overshadow the things we know, and we fail to heed. Without really meaning to, we sometimes find ourselves doing or saying things that are inconsistent with the voice from the grove, and Joseph's experience there ceases, for a time, to have operative relevancy for our lives.

I have always been mindful of the remarkable admonition that Moses gave to the children of Israel. He said, "Take heed to thyself, and keep thy soul diligently, lest thou forget the things which thine eyes have seen, and lest they depart from thy heart all the days of thy life: but teach them [to] thy sons, and [to] thy sons' sons" (Deuteronomy 4:9).

I have a confession to make. In an effort to ensure that I do not forget the things that my eyes have seen, I carry with me a reminder of the reality of the First Vision. I would like to show it to you. It is a leaf from a 200-year-old beech tree. I picked it myself in the Sacred Grove a few years ago. The tree, as nearly as I can tell, was in the grove on that spring morning in 1820. Perhaps some of the light Joseph saw shone on it and caused it to sink its roots deeper into the rocky soil or to claim its place among the other trees that surrounded it. Every time I open the scriptures, it helps me remember what I know.

NOTES

1. Marion G. Romney, *Learning for the Eternities* (Salt Lake City: Deseret Book, 1977), 8.
2. Neal A. Maxwell, *Lord, Increase Our Faith* (Salt Lake City: Bookcraft, 1994), 9; emphasis added.
3. Elizabeth Claridge McCune, in *Young Women's Journal*, July 1898, 292–93.
4. Sheri L. Dew, *Go Forward with Faith: The Biography of Gordon B. Hinckley* (Salt Lake City: Deseret Book, 1996), 470.
5. *The Neal A. Maxwell Quote Book,* ed. Cory H. Maxwell (Salt Lake City: Bookcraft, 1997), 135.
6. Joseph Smith, *History of The Church of Jesus Christ of Latter-day Saints*, ed. B. H. Roberts, 2d ed. rev., 7 vols. (Salt Lake City: The Church of Jesus Christ of Latter-day Saints, 1932–51), 1:79.
7. Gordon B. Hinckley, *Teachings of Gordon B. Hinckley* (Salt Lake City: Deseret Book, 1997), 225–26.

THE FIRST VISION: THE FIRM FOUNDATION FOR OUR FAITH

John K. Carmack

How does one do justice to an assignment to capture the meaning of the rapturous and seminal event of the visit of the Father and Son to the 14-year-old Joseph Smith? President Hinckley, during April conference, called it the greatest event since the birth and death of Jesus. Speaker after speaker bore personal testimony of its reality. Elder Dieter F. Uchtdorf of the Twelve built his eloquent conference address around his experience as a boy in Germany, gazing at the stained-glass window depicting the event. "I felt it was true," he said. President Hinckley returned to the subject in his closing conference words, witnessing that the Father and the Son spoke with Joseph in the Sacred Grove.

Perhaps the Tabernacle Choir best captured the sacredness of the event by opening the Sunday morning session with a moving rendition of "Oh, how lovely was the morning,"[1] accompanied by a depiction on the large conference screens of Joseph leaving his log home, walking to the grove of trees, and experiencing the sacred theophany.

This is my personal view of what that first vision means. We start with the boy Joseph and his family on a farm in Manchester near Palmyra, New York. A scene of unusual religious excitement caught the Smith family in

---

Elder John K. Carmack is an emeritus member of the First Quorum of the Seventy. His present assignment is that of managing director of the Perpetual Education Fund for the Church. In the past he served as executive director of the Church History Department.

its web. As a result of the entreaties of the various churches, some family members joined the Presbyterian church. Joseph and his father, however, stayed aloof from all of the churches. Nevertheless, young Joseph developed a deep desire to know the truth about religion. In furtherance of this desire he attended meetings, pondered the messages, and studied the Bible, but remained uneasy as he heard "some crying, 'Lo, here!' and others, 'Lo, there!'" (Joseph Smith—History 1:5).

Joseph and his father believed in God but found the teachings of the various denominations confusing, especially their conflicting claims about which church was the true church of Jesus Christ.

Another confusing matter concerned teachings about the nature of God and His relationship with men. By 1820, doctrinal beliefs about God and Jesus Christ were found in a number of creeds established by leading religious leaders during the centuries after the Apostles departed. The creeds generally settled on the belief that the Father, Son, and Holy Ghost were, in a mysterious way, different manifestations of a single God. The God of the creeds no longer spoke to men on the earth. Churches and their ministers substituted an intangible God in place of a loving and literal Father in Heaven who could hear and answer prayers. These concepts affected not only their worship of the Father but also their understanding about man's potential worth and destiny as the offspring of God.

Differences between Joseph's understanding of some Bible passages and explanations given by preachers also affected and confused him. In his state of confusion, Joseph wondered who was right and who was wrong. If Christian doctrines were at best confusing and at worst in serious error, the beliefs either needed to be corrected or true beliefs restored in some fashion.

Let's go back to the New Testament account of the time Peter spoke to Jews and others gathered around Solomon's Porch on the temple grounds in Jerusalem. After sharing his witness about the recently departed Jesus, he declared that Jesus would come to the earth again during future "times of restitution." He explained that Jesus' Second Coming would be the central event of the "restitution of all things, which God hath spoken by the mouth of all his holy prophets since the world began" (Acts 3:21). Let's look closer at this far-reaching prophecy. A *time* is the point or period when something occurs. The use of the plural *times* indicates more than one "time." The word *restitution* means restoration, or bringing back something lost. "Times of restitution," then, would be an era of restoration. During those "times," God would send His Son to earth a second time.

What does that scripture have to do with the events of 1820? Has that predicted future era of restoration begun? If so, what was the first of its "times"? Remember that we spoke about the confusing state of varying beliefs concerning the nature of the Godhead in 1820. What does the Bible teach us about the importance of knowing and worshiping the true God? Biblical prophets of God had constantly implored their people to avoid the sin of worshiping idols or false gods. A glaring example was when Israel made a golden calf out of the people's earrings and then worshiped it (see Exodus 32:2–8). That kind of sin was repeated by Israel regularly. Many of the heathens around them had never even known the true and living God but had created their own gods. In Athens, for example, Paul found a stone dedicated "TO THE UNKNOWN GOD." He declared to them, "We ought not to think that the Godhead is like unto gold, or silver, or stone, graven by art and man's device" (Acts 17:23, 29).

Further illustrating the point I make, the first of the Ten Commandments God wrote on the tablet of stone for Moses and the children of Israel was, "Thou shalt have no other gods before me" (Exodus 20:3). The second was directly related to the first: "Thou shalt not make unto thee any graven image" (Exodus 20:4). In answer to a question—"Which is the great commandment in the law?"—Jesus emphasized that the first and greatest commandment is, "Thou shalt love the Lord thy God with all thy heart, and with all thy soul, and with all thy mind" (Matthew 22:36–37). In summary, then, knowing and worshiping the true God is vitally important to mankind. How can we understand who we are and what our destiny is if we don't know that we are literally the sons and daughters of a Father in Heaven?

Now, confronted with confusion and error, even as relating to the God they worshiped, honest searchers for truth needed an authoritative voice to either correct the confusing religious differences or God needed to speak again to men. But when and how would that help come?

In view of what we have just said about loving and worshiping God, if there were to be a restoration, what would likely be the first gospel truth restored? Isn't it logical and consistent to expect that during the first "time of restitution" God would in some way reveal His true identity as our Father who created man in His own image? If so, to whom would He make His identity known? Who would believe Him and have the courage and energy to do the nearly impossible work of declaring the truth to a doubting world? Who would be able to withstand the persecution and ridicule that would surely arise?

Wouldn't God likely find a young person whose mind and heart were open to unvarnished truth? His heart had to be prepared for new revelation rather than stuck with the notion that the heavens were closed to mortals. Could young Joseph Smith fill the need? He was searching for God but hadn't accepted prevailing false concepts. He also wanted to know which church to join. He was searching for answers and direction.

Let's look a little deeper. Although he attended community meetings that were part of the religious revival around Palmyra, he was independent enough to resist the cries of "Lo, here" and "Lo, there" by preachers attempting to commit him to join one of the several churches in his community. He also lived in a community and country without a chilling official state church, as existed in most European countries. Knowing that Joseph had always told the truth, his parents would likely support him and believe whatever he told them. His father understood that God could communicate with man because he had experienced a number of spiritual dreams himself. His mother enjoyed unusual spiritual strength.

Our Heavenly Father knew that the one He chose would have to possess tremendous energy and the talent to do the great work that would be required. Looking back, we perceive that Joseph possessed amazing spiritual and energy resources.

Indeed, why not Joseph? He was searching for answers to deep religious questions. Thus in Palmyra, God had available the right person if the time had come to make Himself known again to man, as He had in the past to Abraham, Moses, Samuel, and Jesus' Apostles. Also Joseph was untouched by money, position, power, or social status.

While pondering his deep questions, young Joseph turned to the Bible for answers. In the process he came across James, chapter 1, verse 5. These words entered his mind with great power. He reflected on them over and over. He decided to put his questions and concerns directly to

God, fully expecting some kind of answer or feeling in accordance with James's promise. Accordingly, he retired to the woods to ask of God. He had never before prayed vocally. An evil power immediately seized him. Obviously Satan sensed that this prayer by Joseph was prelude to a very important event, detrimental to his evil cause. When Joseph was about to be overpowered, he cried to God for deliverance.

A light from above appeared and then descended until it fell and came to rest on him. Two brilliant and glorious personages appeared in the light. One was the Father and the other was His Son, Jesus Christ (Joseph Smith—History 1:10–20). Joseph learned very much from that pivotal morning, including:

- Satan is real and has great power.
- God is glorious beyond description, yet has a form like men.
- The Father and the Son are separate beings but work in complete unity.
- The Father knew Joseph by name; and we can love such a personal God, which we're supposed to do.
- Joseph was not to join any of the churches; their creeds were wrong.
- And finally, the existing Christian churches had a form of godliness but not His power.

The experience over, Joseph went home, overcome with exhaustion. He told his mother what had happened and she believed him. The "times of restitution" had commenced. This first "time" restored the true knowledge of God and His relationship to mankind as our Father in Heaven. We are God's potential heirs. Other "times" would continue until God restored all truths revealed in all former dispensations of the gospel.

The years ahead would test Joseph severely, but having chosen him so young, the Lord could help him avoid taking the wrong track that would lead him away from the vital task of restoration. Having the freedom to choose, Joseph could fail, but with help and proper tutoring he could and did succeed.

Thus God started the process of restoration in this direct and simple visit to Joseph. Joseph now knew God personally. Knowing and loving his Father in Heaven was a huge first step. Ahead would come the Book of Mormon, restoration of the priesthood, organization of the Church, baptism for remission of sins, the gift of the Holy Ghost, and apostles and prophets. The stone had been cut out of the mountain without hands, with the destiny to fill the whole earth.

In a revelation given to the Prophet on the day the Church was organized, the Lord commanded Joseph to record his experiences (see D&C 21:1). Those experiences included this first "time" in 1820. He started the process several times, but he was young and needed more peace, more maturity, and more insight into its significance to recount that most important event. Years passed before Joseph was able to write and dictate his history in a manner satisfactory to him. Eventually, with the help of scribes, he completed what became the official record in 1838 and 1839. That record became scripture, just as the appearance to the boy Samuel in biblical times became scripture.

The written account is both simple and powerful enough to touch humble men and women. It touched me when I first read it. Arthur Henry King, a convert to the Church steeped in literature and writing style, and incidentally a faculty member here at Brigham Young University, wrote a brief critique about Joseph's account. He had this to say about Joseph's account of the First Vision:

"When I was first brought to read Joseph Smith's story, I was deeply impressed. . . . As a stylistician, I have spent my life being disinclined to be impressed. So when I read his story, I thought to myself, this is an extraordinary thing. This is an astonishingly matter-of-fact and cool account. This man is not trying to persuade me of anything. He doesn't feel the need to. He is stating what happened to him, and he is stating it, not enthusiastically, but in quite a matter-of-fact way. He is not trying to make me cry or feel ecstatic. That struck me, and that began to build my testimony, for I could see that this man was telling the truth."[2]

Brother Hugh Nibley said this:

"Even more outrageous was his vision of the Father and the Son: the mere idea of it was astoundingly original, but again, the simple, straight-forward, noble manner in which he reported it left no room for con-tention; it was 'yea, yea, and nay, nay,' for as the only witness to the most astonishing of his experiences, Joseph could not be confounded by any contrary evidence; and by the same token neither could anyone be asked to take him seriously were it not that he came before an unbelieving world with boundless riches in his hands."[3]

I think that brings us to an important question, and that question is: What does this sacred event mean to you and me? No one has answered that question more clearly and succinctly than our present prophet, and he's answered it many times. Recently he said:

"A most remarkable manifestation occurred on a spring morning in the year 1820 when the Father and the Son appeared to the boy Joseph Smith. All of the good we see in the Church today is the fruit of that remarkable visitation, a testimony of which has touched the hearts of millions in many lands. I add my own witness," he said, "given me by the Spirit, that the Prophet's description of that marvelous event is true, that God the Eternal Father and the risen Lord Jesus Christ spoke with him on that occasion in a conversation as real and personal and intimate as are our conversations today. I raise my voice in testimony that Joseph was a prophet, and that the work brought forth through his instrumentality is the work of God."[4]

Thus, brothers and sisters, the era of restoration began in 1820 with that remarkable appearance of the Father and the Son. What began as an answer to the prayer of a young man who was uneasy and confused about religion and who found unsatisfactory the creeds and teachings of the Christian sects ended up being the start of something big—something amazing and far-reaching. He probably had little idea that his experience was one of the "times of restitution" that Peter prophesied would precede the Second Coming of Christ. He just knew that God had spoken to him and further that none of the existing churches were on the right track. What revolutionary knowledge was his!

Elder Neal A. Maxwell summed it up succinctly. Said he: "His prayer was for personal and tactical guidance. The response, however, was of global and eternal significance."[5] Joseph indeed received personal guidance that 1820 spring morning. The event served as his own focus and foundation for life. On the other hand, the global meaning was that the "times of restitution" had begun. That has affected all of us.

In what ways has it affected us? What difference does it make—that visitation to young Joseph—what difference does it make to you and me? Through Joseph we know that the true and living God is tangible, personal, knows us, and is a distinct personage from His Son, Jesus Christ. We can be certain He hears and answers our prayers in accordance with His plans and our needs, provided we ask in faith and trust His timing and method of answering our pleadings. When we know these things, we also know that we are part of the "times of restitution." Just as Joseph's experience with God placed on him a great responsibility, our exposure to and understanding of these things places on us a similar burden—to share the responsibility of building the kingdom of God on earth. What a glorious burden, and what a majestic and special relationship with God is ours! And because we are the children of our Heavenly Father, then we are also His heirs. That opens breathtaking new vistas in our lives. Have you ever thought of it that way?

One thing more needs to be mentioned. If we know that God is personal, knows our names, and is guiding the affairs of men and women, consistent with our agency, it is easier to know and love Him. And to love Him is the first and great commandment (see Matthew 22:36–38). Loving Him can start by reading Joseph's great experience in the spring of 1820. Thus the Lord told Joseph, "This generation shall have my word through you" (D&C 5:10).

Now, conclusion. In addition to the initial strong testimony I gained reading Joseph's account, I add a special experience. When I served as the Idaho Boise Mission president, I suggested to my missionaries that they memorize Joseph's story, found in the Pearl of Great Price, Joseph Smith—History, verses 1–20. I wanted them to memorize it all. To demonstrate my sincerity and unity with them, I told them I would also memorize those verses. Not the smartest thing I've done. It was not easy for me, but I kept working on it. One day, while driving alone from Boise to Idaho Falls, I was quoting the verses aloud. About the time I reached the little town of Fairfield on Highway 20, I was nearly overcome by the Spirit. It was as if I had the same experience Joseph had. I had to stop beside the highway to compose myself before driving on. I had a tremendous feeling of love for the Father and the Son that almost overcame me. I knew through the Spirit more intensely than I can describe that Joseph's account was true.

NOTES

1. George Manwaring, "Joseph Smith's First Prayer," *Hymns of The Church of Jesus Christ of Latter-day Saints* (Salt Lake City: The Church of Jesus Christ of Latter-day Saints, 1985), no. 26.

2. Arthur Henry King, *The Abundance of the Heart* (Salt Lake City: Bookcraft, 1986), 200–201.

3. Hugh Nibley, *Nibley on the Timely and the Timeless* (Provo: BYU Religious Studies Center, 1978), 3.

4. Gordon B. Hinckley, *Be Thou an Example* (Salt Lake City: Deseret Book, 1981), 10.

5. Neal A. Maxwell, "My Servant Joseph," *Ensign*, May 1992, 37.

RESTORATION: PROPHETS AND KEYS

Andrew C. Skinner

"Joseph Smith, the Prophet and Seer of the Lord, has done more, save Jesus only, for the salvation of men in this world, than any other man that ever lived in it" (D&C 135:3). This statement, though stunning (even shocking to some), is no exaggeration. It is absolutely true. Joseph Smith is the one who, more than any other, has made known to us the full and complete saving and exalting potential of Christ's atoning power. But we are not the first group of people to know about the greatness of Joseph Smith.

From the beginning of time, God and His many prophets have known of and declared the coming of Joseph Smith to inaugurate and establish this, the dispensation of the fulness of times. President Brigham Young's statement on this topic is mind-expanding!

"It was decreed in the councils of eternity, long before the foundations of the earth were laid, that he, Joseph Smith, should be the man, in the last dispensation of this world, to bring forth the word of God to the people, and receive the fulness of the keys and power of the Priesthood of the Son of God. The Lord had his eyes upon Joseph, and upon his father, and upon his father's father, and upon their progenitors clear back to

Andrew C. Skinner is a professor of ancient scripture at Brigham Young University. He has served as Dean of Religious Education (2000–2006) and currently is executive director of FARMS-ISPART. He is married to Janet Corbridge Skinner and they have six children.

Abraham, and from Abraham to the flood, from the flood to Enoch, and from Enoch to Adam. He has watched that family and that blood as it has circulated from its fountain to the birth of that man. He was fore-ordained in eternity to preside over this last dispensation."[1]

Therefore, it is not surprising that Joseph Smith was personally tutored in mortality by the Lord as well as the many prophets who foreknew of him. Many of the ancient prophets and dispensation heads appeared to Joseph and laid their hands upon his head and bestowed *keys,* powers, and knowledge they had gained from Deity themselves.

Who else among all the world's leaders and so-called power brokers have stood in the presence of God the Eternal Father; His Son, Jesus Christ; Adam; Noah; Raphael; Moses; Elias; Elijah; John the Baptist; Peter; James; John; Moroni; and many, many more and received the power to bring salvation to *all* of Heavenly Father's children? We can document at least 59 nonmortal beings who appeared to, or were seen by, Joseph Smith in vision.

President John Taylor, beloved friend and trusted associate of the Prophet Joseph Smith, summed up the matter in these words:

"Joseph Smith in the first place was set apart by the Almighty according to the councils of the Gods in the eternal worlds, to introduce the principles of life among the people, of which the gospel is the grand power and influence, and through which salvation can extend to all peoples, all nations, all kindreds, all tongues, and all worlds. It is the principle that brings life and immortality to light, and places us in communication with God. God selected him for that purpose, and he fulfilled his mission and lived honorably and died honorably. I know of what I speak, for I was very well acquainted with him and was with him a great deal during his life, and was with him when he died. The principles which he had placed him in communication with the Lord, and not only with the Lord, but with the ancient apostles and prophets; such men, for instance, as Abraham, Isaac, Jacob, Noah, Adam, Seth, Enoch, and Jesus, and the Father, and the apostles that lived on this continent, as well as those who lived on the Asiatic continent. He seemed to be as familiar with these people as we are with one another. Why? Because he had to introduce a dispensation which was called the dispensation of the fulness of times, and it was known as such by the ancient servants of God."[2]

Joseph Smith is one who seems to have lived life every day guided by the lodestar of revelation. This is impressive enough, but one of the reasons we have come to appreciate Joseph and his ministry so much is the assurance we have been given from him that the same principle of revelation by which he lived and restored so much truth is available to each of us. The Prophet Joseph Smith and all the prophets since his inaugural ministry have constantly preached that revelation is an "equal opportunity" doctrine. Said Joseph, "The best way to obtain truth and wisdom is not to ask it from books, but to go to God in prayer, and obtain divine teaching."[3] "It is the privilege of the children of God to come to God and get revelation. . . . When any person receives a vision of heaven, he sees things that he never thought of before."[4] Joseph also said that it is the privilege of any officeholder in this Church to obtain revelations so far as it relates to his or her particular calling and duty in the Church.

Both men and women share equally in the glorious flood of light, knowledge, and power restored through the Prophet Joseph Smith. As Joseph found out when translating the Book of Mormon, God "imparteth his word by angels unto men, yea, not only men but women also. Now this is not all; little children do have words given unto them many times, which confound the wise and the learned" (Alma 32:23). From Joseph's interactions with Gods and angels, there have come to us keys to perform the ordinances of exaltation for both the living and the dead. This is true for the sisters as well as the brethren.

KEYS

Keys are conduits of power and information. The revelations of the Restoration speak of keys in two major senses: one is the power and authority to *direct* the priesthood and the Church; the other sense is the means to reveal, to discover, to bring to light things unknown or hidden. In this second sense, for example, "Joseph Smith and Oliver Cowdery were given the *keys* to translate and bring hidden scriptures to light"[5] (see D&C 6:24–28). For our discussion, we will define the keys of the kingdom of God in the first sense, as the right and power to direct and govern the Lord's affairs on this earth. Joseph Smith taught that "the fundamental principles, government, and doctrine of the Church are vested in the keys of the kingdom."[6] These keys are part of the higher, or Melchizedek, Priesthood. As revealed to the Prophet Joseph Smith, this higher priesthood, which comprehends or encompasses the Aaronic and Levitical priesthoods,[7] holds "the keys of all the spiritual blessings of the Church" and "the mysteries of the kingdom of heaven" (D&C 107:18–19); it "holds the right of presidency, and has power and authority over all the offices in the church in all ages of the world" (D&C 107:8). Like God Himself, the Melchizedek Priesthood is eternal. The Prophet Joseph Smith said, "The priesthood is an everlasting principle, and existed with God from eternity, and will to eternity."[8]

The Melchizedek Priesthood was instituted "prior to the foundation of this earth," said the Prophet Joseph, and "is the channel through which the Almighty commenced revealing His glory at the beginning of the creation of this earth, and through which He has continued to reveal Himself . . . and through which He will make known His purpose to the end of time."[9] In premortality, priesthood organization existed and priesthood keys operated, as President Joseph Fielding Smith made clear in a 1966 general conference address: "With regard to the holding of the priesthood in the preexistence, I will say that there was an organization there just as well as an organization here, and men there held authority. Men chosen to positions of trust in the spirit world held the priesthood."[10]

The priesthood will continue to operate in the *post*-mortal spirit world, or the world of spirits after death. As the Savior passed through the veil into the spirit world, He was met by such noble and great leaders in mortality as Adam and Eve, Abel, Seth, Noah, Shem, Abraham, Isaac, Jacob, Moses, Isaiah, Ezekiel, Daniel, Elias, Malachi, all the prophets who dwelt among the Nephites, and many, many more, as we are told in Doctrine and Covenants 138:38–49. These formed part of the missionary force organized to teach the gospel to those in spirit prison. They were delegated keys of power and authority to do so by the Savior. Note the language of the vision of President Joseph F. Smith: "But behold, from among the righteous, he organized his forces and appointed messengers, clothed with power and authority, and commissioned them to go forth and carry the light of the gospel to them that were in darkness, even to all the spirits of men; and thus was the gospel preached to the dead" (D&C 138:30). Of the authorized ministers in the spirit world, President Joseph F. Smith further said, "They are there, having carried with them from here the holy Priesthood that they received under authority, and which was conferred upon them in the flesh."[11]

Priesthood holders are not the only ones involved in this work among the dead. President Smith offered this truly profound and important insight about sisters involved in the work of salvation in the spirit world:

"Now, among all these millions of spirits that have lived on the earth and have passed away, from generation to generation, since the beginning of the world, without the knowledge of the gospel—among them you may count that at least one-half are women. Who is going to preach the gospel to the women? Who is going to carry the testimony of Jesus Christ to the hearts of the women who have passed away without a knowledge of the gospel? Well, to my mind, it is a simple thing. These good sisters who have been set apart, ordained to the work, called to it, authorized by the authority of the holy Priesthood to minister for their sex, in the House of God for the living and for the dead, will be fully authorized and empowered to preach the gospel and minister to the women while the elders and prophets are preaching it to the men. The things we experience here are typical of the things of God and the life beyond us. There is a great similarity between God's purposes as manifested here and his purposes as carried out in his presence and kingdom. Those who are authorized to preach the gospel here and are appointed here to do that work will not be idle after they have passed away, but will continue to exercise the rights that they obtained here under the Priesthood of the Son of God to minister for the salvation of those who have died without a knowledge of the truth."[12]

Just as sisters in this life are called and authorized to preach the gospel in the earth, often working among other women, so sisters in the next life are called and authorized to be messengers of the Lord's gospel, ministering specifically among women. It will be remembered that President Joseph F. Smith made it a point of stating explicitly in his vision of the spirit world that he saw "our glorious Mother Eve, with many of her faithful daughters who had lived through the ages and worshiped the true and living God" (D&C 138:39). It is to be assumed that these were the ones mentioned by President Smith, part of the Savior's "forces and appointed messengers, clothed with power and authority, and commissioned . . . to go forth and carry the light of the gospel to them that were in darkness"

(D&C 138:30). It should be remembered that sisters are delegated specific authority to minister to women who enter the Lord's house to receive temple ordinances—all under the direction of the Melchizedek Priesthood.

Before the time of the Old Testament patriarch Melchizedek, the higher priesthood was called "the Holy Priesthood, after the Order of the Son of God." But out of respect or reverence for the name of Deity, its name was changed to the Melchizedek Priesthood in honor of the great patriarch (see D&C 107:2–4). All the prophets in ancient times held the Melchizedek Priesthood.[13] The Melchizedek Priesthood is the power by which men and women become like our heavenly parents, heirs of our Heavenly Father's kingdom and joint heirs with Jesus Christ, possessing every power and every blessing the Father and the Son possess.[14]

The first person on this earth to possess the keys of the priesthood was Adam. In fact, our first father holds the keys of presidency over *all* dispensations and eras of the gospel. He is the presiding high priest, under Christ's direction, over all the earth. Noah stands next to Adam in priesthood authority,[15] and "after these two come all the heads of the different gospel dispensations, together with a host of other mighty prophets."[16] Not the least of these are Elijah, who held the keys of the sealing power in ancient Israel (see D&C 27:9; 110:13–16), and Nephi the son of Helaman, who held the keys of the sealing power among the Nephites (see Helaman 10:4–10).

The scriptures speak of others who hold keys. Another Book of Mormon prophet, Moroni, holds "the keys of the record of the stick of Ephraim" (D&C 27:5). The prophet Moses holds the keys of the gathering of Israel and the leading of the ten tribes from the lands of the north (see D&C 110:11). A prophet named Elias holds the keys of the Abrahamic covenant (see D&C 110:12).[17] An angel named Raphael holds the keys of his dispensation (see D&C 128:21). The chief Apostles—Peter, James, and John—held the keys of the kingdom of God on earth in their day (see D&C 27:12–13; 128:20).

All of these specific keys we have mentioned constitute the keys of the kingdom of God. And all of these prophets who held keys, and many other "divers angels, from Michael or Adam down to the present time," have all returned in these latter days to the Prophet Joseph Smith and "declar[ed] their dispensation, their rights, their keys, their honors, their majesty and glory, and the power of their priesthood," according to D&C 128:21. Joseph Smith and his successors have been and now are the possessors of all the keys and powers of the kingdom of God that are possible for mortal men to possess. Note this qualifier, for there are some keys of power and knowledge that we do not yet possess in mortality, but will someday possess. President Brigham Young provided this insight:

"It is supposed by this people that we have all the ordinances in our possession for life and salvation, and exaltation, and that we are administering in these ordinances. This is not the case. We are in possession of all the ordinances that can be administered in the flesh; but there are other ordinances and administrations that must be administered beyond this world. I know you would ask what they are. I will mention one. We have not, neither can we receive here, the ordinance and the keys of the resurrection. They will be given to those who have passed off this stage of action and have received their bodies again, as many have already done and many more will. They will be ordained by those who hold the keys of the resurrection, to go forth and resurrect the Saints, just as we receive the ordinance of baptism, then the keys of authority to baptize others for the remission of their sins. This is one of the ordinances we cannot receive here, and there are many more. We hold the authority to dispose of, alter and change the elements, but we have not received authority to organize native element, to even make a spear of grass grow."[18]

Closer to our day, President Spencer W. Kimball, in a general conference address in April 1977, confirmed that no one now living holds the keys of resurrection. And that is *not* because we lack the desire to possess them. President Kimball said: "Do we have the keys of resurrection? . . . I buried my mother when I was eleven, my father when I was in my early twenties. I have missed my parents much. If I had the power of resurrection as did the Savior of the world, I would have been tempted to try to have kept them longer. . . . We do not know of anyone who can resurrect the dead as did Jesus the Christ when he came back to mortality."[19] Nevertheless, President Kimball promised, the faithful will receive not only the keys of resurrection but also the power of godhood in the resurrection.

The keys of the kingdom of God are, in a sense, "on loan" to mortals and will someday be given back to their owner and originator. That is to say, "when the Lord comes to reign personally upon the earth during the millennial era, he will take back the keys. Those who have held them will make an accounting to him of their stewardships at the place called Adam-ondi-Ahman at which gathering Christ will receive 'dominion, and glory, and a kingdom, that all people, nations, and languages, should serve him' (Dan. 7:13–14). Eventually in the celestial day, 'the keys of the kingdom shall be delivered up again unto the Father' (Inspired Version, Luke 3:8)."[20]

KEYS AND SEALING POWER

Among the keys of authority and power bestowed upon the Prophet Joseph Smith, none are of greater or more far-reaching significance than those given by Elijah.[21] This ancient prophet held the keys of the kingdom in his day; he held the keys of presidency and the keys of the sealing power that constitute the fulness of the Melchizedek Priesthood. President Joseph Fielding Smith said that "it is that sealing power which gave [Elijah] the right and authority to officiate. And the Lord said unto him, 'That which you bind on earth shall be bound in heaven.' That is how great his power was, and in that day Elijah stood up and officiated for the people in the sealing power."[22]

So great and important are the keys of the sealing power that sometimes we equate the keys of the kingdom with the keys of the sealing power. The "sealing power puts the stamp of approval upon every ordinance that is done in this Church and more particularly those that are performed in the temples of the Lord."[23] And as the revelation states, "All covenants, contracts, bonds, obligations, oaths, vows, performances, connections, associations, or expectations, that are *not* made and entered into and sealed by the Holy Spirit of promise, of him who is anointed, . . . whom I have appointed on the earth to hold this power . . . , and there is never but one on the earth at a time on whom this power and the keys of this priesthood are conferred . . . , are of no efficacy, virtue, or force in and after the resurrection from the dead; for all contracts that are not made unto this end have an end when men are dead" (D&C 132:7; emphasis added).

The keys of the priesthood, including the keys of the sealing power, are for the blessing of both the living and the dead. Said President Smith: "Some members of the Church have been confused in thinking that Elijah came with keys of baptism for the dead or of salvation for the dead. Elijah's keys were greater than that. They were the keys of sealing, and those keys of sealing pertain to the living and embrace the dead who are willing to repent."[24]

The sealing powers for the living and the dead constitute the fulness of the priesthood. We can only receive a fulness of the priesthood in the temples of the Lord. The Prophet Joseph Smith declared, "If a man gets a fullness of the priesthood of God, he has to get it in the same way that Jesus Christ obtained it, and that was by keeping all the commandments and obeying all the ordinances of the house of the Lord."[25]

Commenting on the Prophet's words, President Joseph Fielding Smith further stated: "Let me put this in a little different way. I do not care what office you hold in this Church—you may be an apostle, you may be a patriarch, a high priest, or anything else—you cannot receive the fulness of the priesthood unless you go into the temple of the Lord and receive these ordinances of which the Prophet speaks. No [one] can get the fulness of the priesthood outside of the temple of the Lord."[26] But the fulness of the priesthood *is* available to anyone who is worthy to enter the house of the Lord.

There is no exaltation in the kingdom of God without the fulness of the priesthood. Thus, the fulness of the priesthood, obtainable only in the house of the Lord, might also be termed the keys of exaltation. Again, President Smith said: "Only in the temple of the Lord can the fulness of the priesthood be received. Now that temples are on the earth, there is no other place where the endowment and the sealing powers for all eternity can be given. No man [or woman] can receive the keys of exaltation in any other place."[27]

In the houses of the Lord, these beautiful temples that now dot the earth, men and women can go and be sealed as husbands and wives for eternity. Children can be sealed to parents in family units forever. "What a glorious privilege it is to know that the family organization will remain intact."[28] What value can be put on this knowledge? There is great comfort in knowing this. There is great security. There is great stability. There is a great anchor that comes to the soul in knowing this.

My father died when I was young. I idolized my dad. Those were dark days. But tremendous peace, security, and the motivation to carry on came from my knowledge that we had been to the temple and had been sealed as a family for time and eternity. I wonder if there would not be significant value in having mothers and fathers spend some time with their children talking about the ordinances of eternity and the sealing power that binds families together forever. I believe our children would be more secure in their faith, be better prepared to face life's challenges, and come to regard living prophets with a new love and appreciation if they could understand the incomparable sealing power found in the temples of the Lord.

Conclusion

There are invaluable, even incomparable benefits that come from having the keys of the kingdom on the earth, *and* from knowing about them. First, we see that God is consistent. He has had a plan for His children from the beginning, and that plan has been administered through prophets who have held priesthood power and priesthood keys.

Second, we see that God is fulfilling His prophecies concerning the restoration of all things in this, the dispensation of the fulness of times. We may have perfect confidence and trust in Him. He has the power to fulfill all His purposes, which are perfectly just and fair.

Third, our gratitude for the Prophet Joseph Smith will increase manyfold as we begin to comprehend the magnitude of his prophetic office and calling and the significance of the keys and powers bestowed upon him from all past ages.

Fourth, our gratitude and respect for all of Joseph's successors will increase profoundly as we are able to understand the nature of the power and authority held by all the Presidents of the Church up to the current day.

Fifth, knowing that the keys and fulness of the priesthood are upon the earth, and available to all who desire them, gives us security and stability in a world that is not, much of the time, very stable. It gives us assurance of the continuation of the bonds of love and association with friends and family through the eternities.

All of this is made possible by the Father and the Son through the great prophet of the Restoration. God be thanked for Joseph Smith and his successors.

NOTES

1. Brigham Young, *Discourses of Brigham Young,* comp. John A. Widtsoe (Salt Lake City: Deseret Book, 1954), 108.

2. John Taylor, in *Journal of Discourses,* 26 vols. (London: Latter-day Saints' Book Depot, 1854–86), 21:95.

3. Joseph Smith, *History of The Church of Jesus Christ of Latter-day Saints,* ed. B. H. Roberts, 2d ed. rev., 7 vols. (Salt Lake City: The Church of Jesus Christ of Latter-day Saints, 1932–51), 4:425.

4. Joseph Smith, *Words of Joseph Smith,* ed. Andrew F. Ehat and Lyndon Cook (Provo: BYU Religious Studies Center, 1980), 13–14.

5. Bruce R. McConkie, *Mormon Doctrine,* 2d ed. (Salt Lake City: Bookcraft, 1966), 410; emphasis added.

6. Joseph Smith, *Teachings of the Prophet Joseph Smith,* sel. Joseph Fielding Smith (Salt Lake City: Deseret Book, 1972), 21.

7. Smith, *Teachings,* 166.

8. Smith, *Teachings,* 157.

9. Smith, *Teachings,* 167.

10. Joseph Fielding Smith, in Conference Report, October 1966, 84.

11. Joseph F. Smith, *Gospel Doctrine* (Salt Lake City: Deseret Book, 1939), 471–72.

12. Smith, *Gospel Doctrine,* 461.

13. Smith, *Teachings,* 181.

14. Smith, *Teachings,* 308–9, 322.

15. D&C 78:16; Smith, *Teachings,* 157.

16. McConkie, *Mormon Doctrine,* 412.

17. Joseph Fielding Smith, *Doctrines of Salvation,* sel. Bruce R. McConkie (Salt Lake City: Bookcraft, 1956), 3:126–27.

18. Young, *Discourses of Brigham Young,* 397–98.

19. Spencer W. Kimball, in Conference Report, April 1977, 69.

20. McConkie, *Mormon Doctrine,* 413.

21. Smith, *Doctrines of Salvation,* 3:126.

22. Smith, *Doctrines of Salvation,* 3:127.

23. Smith, *Doctrines of Salvation,* 3:129.

24. Smith, *Doctrines of Salvation,* 3:130.

25. Smith, *Teachings,* 308.

26. Smith, *Doctrines of Salvation,* 3:131.

27. Smith, *Doctrines of Salvation,* 3:133.

28. Smith, *Doctrines of Salvation,* 3:129.

"A Good Heart and a Good Hand"

Heidi S. Swinton

Picture with me the last hours of Joseph Smith's life, on June 27, 1844. It was a sultry summer day in Carthage, Illinois. The Prophet Joseph, his brother Hyrum, John Taylor, and Willard Richards were locked in a room on the second floor of the Carthage County Jail. On request, John Taylor sang a favorite hymn of the Prophet Joseph. His clear tenor voice filled the room. Outside and fast approaching was an evil mob bent on murder.

We have all sung this hymn, but pay attention to the words as I read them:

> A poor wayfaring Man of grief
> Hath often crossed me on my way,
> Who sued so humbly for relief
> That I could never answer nay.
> I had not pow'r to ask his name,
> Whereto he went, or whence he came;
> Yet there was something in his eye
> That won my love; I knew not why.[1]

Heidi S. Swinton is an award-winning author and screenwriter of LDS life and history, including America's Choir: A Commemorative Portrait of the Mormon Tabernacle Choir; American Prophet: The Story of Joseph Smith; Sacred Stone: Temple on the Mississippi; *and* Trail of Hope: The Story of the Mormon Trail. *She is a wife, mother, and grandmother and currently serves as a member of the Relief Society general board.*

I have asked myself the question, "Why that song?" Why not a stirring melody hailing the glory of God, like W. W. Phelps's words, "We'll sing and we'll shout with the armies of heaven"?[2] Or one with the promise of peace like "Abide with me"?[3] It was, for Joseph, most certainly, eventide. These would have been fitting conclusions to Joseph's ministry. Yet, he sought comfort in words that spoke of charity.

The ancient prophet Mormon described charity as "the pure love of Christ, and it endureth forever; and whoso is found possessed of it at the last day, it shall be well with him" (Moroni 7:47).

This was Joseph's last day. He possessed charity. And, it was well with him.

The Bible Dictionary defines charity as "the highest, noblest, strongest kind of love, not merely affection; the pure love of Christ. It is never used to denote alms or deeds or benevolence, although it may be a prompting motive" (LDS Bible Dictionary, s.v. "charity," 632). Think of it this way: Charity is not something we do; it is something we feel.

Mormon, when addressing those "of the Church," those he called "the peaceable followers of Christ," outlined in detail how to receive charity. He said: "Wherefore, . . . pray unto the Father with all the energy of heart, that ye may be filled with this love, which he hath bestowed upon all who are true followers of his Son, Jesus Christ; that ye may become the sons of God; that when he shall appear we shall be like him, for we shall see him as he is" (Moroni 7:48).

For Joseph, that pattern was part of him.

Joseph possessed "the pure love of Christ"; he was clothed in the bonds of charity in a very bitter world. When Joseph was asked why scores followed him and stayed with him through severe trial, why they left their farms, homelands, and even families to join what he called "the cause of Christ," his answer was simple: "It is because I possess the principle of love. All I can offer the world is a good heart and a good hand."[4]

Yet, we see Joseph Smith as bigger than life. He spoke with God the Father and the resurrected Lord Jesus Christ face-to-face; he translated ancient records given him by an angel; he received the priesthood of God from heavenly messengers; he built temples that proclaimed "Holiness to the Lord." These were not everyday contributions; this prophet was not an everyday man.

He bore witness "concerning Jesus Christ, that He died, was buried and rose again the third day, and ascended into heaven."⁵ Boldly, he testified that "salvation could not come to the world without the mediation of Jesus Christ."⁶

In Ether we read Moroni's plea to the Lord: "Thou hast loved the world, even unto the laying down of thy life for the world, that thou mightest take it again to prepare a place for the children of men. And now I know that this love which thou hast had for the children of men is charity" (Ether 12:33–34).

In the Garden of Gethsemane the Lord atoned for our sins; it was the singular act of charity in the history of all mankind. To partake of this gift, we are expected to live righteously, repent—and forgive others. The Lord said, "Of you it is required to forgive all men" (D&C 64:10).

President Boyd K. Packer has taught: "For some reason, we think the Atonement of Christ applies *only* at the end of mortal life to redemption from the Fall, from spiritual death. It is much more than that. It is an ever-present power to call upon in everyday life. . . . The Lord promised, 'A new heart . . . will I give you, and a new spirit will I put within you' (Ezekiel 36:26)."⁷

Joseph Smith learned that truth in Liberty Jail. Some of the darkest days of Joseph's ministry were spent in the dirty prison at Liberty, Missouri. He was incarcerated in a room not tall enough for him to stand up straight. The food was horrid, what little there was. It was bitter cold and he had no blanket. He wrote Emma and asked her to bring him one, and she wrote back that the mob had stolen all the blankets. Where was the charity of one human soul for another? The fiends had stripped his family of the simple necessities for facing the winter. Imagine how he felt.

For four and a half months he suffered in that cell below ground, betrayed by his onetime friend and brother in the gospel, William Wines Phelps.

We all know that name. Phelps wrote the hymn "The Spirit of God." It was sung at the dedication of the Kirtland Temple, when the glory of God poured down from the heavens and angels were seen on the roof in the middle of the day. Phelps had been a stalwart in the Church. He was called as one of the first Church leaders in Missouri, the "center stake of Zion." But something happened in his heart. It hardened. He turned from his responsibilities, his friends, and God. Phelps and others signed a damaging affidavit against the Prophet Joseph, who was then sentenced to a public execution set for November 2, 1838. The brave intervention, the charity, of Missouri General Alexander Doniphan saved the Prophet's life. Joseph and a handful of other Church leaders spent the next months, November to April, in prison.

Did Joseph demand the Lord send down punishments on the former Church member, W. W. Phelps? Did he shake his fist at the sky and say to the Lord, "How could you let this happen to me? This is your Joseph, here in this jail. And it's cold"?

That was the setting for the Prophet's oft-quoted petition to the Lord, "Where is the pavilion that covereth thy hiding place?" (D&C 121:1).

Have you felt like that? Have you called out to the Lord in grief, disappointment, pain, or despair and said, "What's going on here?"

The Lord responded, "Let thy bowels also be full of charity towards all men" (D&C 121:45). Even towards W. W. Phelps.

Would your thought have been, "Charity, at a time like this?" How about thunderbolts from the sky on Phelps's house? Or a torrent flooding his property? Or how about boils?

We often quote the Lord's response: "Know thou, my son, that all these things shall give thee experience, and shall be for thy good" (D&C 122:7). In other words, "Think of what you can learn from this, Joseph." That's hard, sometimes, when we hurt so very much.

But the Lord continued: "The Son of Man hath descended below them all. Art thou greater than he?" (D&C 122:8). Such counsel! Jesus Christ had passed through tribulation far in excess of Joseph's; He had been cast into the pit, given up to the hands of murderers, faced the sentence of death, fierce winds, blackened skies. The very jaws of hell had gaped open wide to consume Him.

That verse points to the atonement, to the pure love of Christ. The Lord had already paid for Phelps's betrayal and had known such betrayal Himself; He had experienced the anguish of the Saints seeking refuge in Illinois; He had felt the loss of their lands and their lives at the hands of the mob while He was in Gethsemane.

"Charity never faileth" takes on new meaning when put in those terms. Sobering, isn't it? The pure love of Christ manifest by the

Atonement was taught in Liberty Jail. And so it is with us. We turn to the
Lord in our extremities. Things are not going well and we ask Him to
move a mountain from here to there. The Lord can do that. But more
important than a change in the landscape is the change in our hearts.

The Lord concluded His comfort—His tender mercies—to Joseph
with "Hold on thy way" (D&C 122:9). I love that. Joseph Smith was no
stranger to Jesus Christ. He knew the way. This was a time for the Lord's
promise, "A light shall break forth" (D&C 45:28). And it did. Joseph was
allowed to escape from jail. He made his way to Quincy, Illinois, where
the Saints had taken refuge. The 1,500 residents of Quincy had taken in
the 5,000 religious refugees who had straggled into their fledgling little
community. (Do the math.) The Lord provided the Saints with rescuers
whose hearts were larger than their homes. Their hearts and hands
reflected, "I was a stranger, and ye took me in" (Matthew 25:35).

Can't you hear John Taylor singing:

> *Stript, wounded, beaten nigh to death,*
> *I found him by the highway side.*
> *I roused his pulse, brought back his breath,*
> *Revived his spirit, and supplied*
> *Wine, oil, refreshment—he was healed.*[8]

Not long after, in the midst of the building of the Nauvoo Temple,
came a letter from W. W. Phelps:

"Brother Joseph: . . . I am as the prodigal son. . . . I have seen the folly
of my way, and I tremble at the gulf I have passed. . . . I know my situation, you know it, and God knows it, and I want to be saved if my friends
will help me. . . . I have done wrong and I am sorry. . . . I ask forgiveness.
. . . I want your fellowship; if you cannot grant that, grant me your peace
and friendship."[9]

What would you have done? Would you have said, "Are you kidding?
Do you know what I went through in Liberty Jail?"

But not Joseph. He knew the pure love of the Christ. He understood
the Atonement. He knew that the Lord had already atoned for Phelps's
transgressions. Now it was Joseph's responsibility to forgive Phelps in his
repentant status and to exercise charity. Joseph's response to Phelps is a
profound lesson in charity for each one of us:

"Dear Brother Phelps: . . . We have suffered much in consequence of your behavior—the cup of gall, already full enough for mortals to drink, was indeed filled to overflowing when you turned against us. . . . Having been delivered from the hands of wicked men by the mercy of our God, we say it is your privilege to be delivered from the powers of the adversary. . . . Again take your stand among the Saints of the Most High, and by diligence, humility, and love unfeigned, commend yourself to our God, and your God, and to the Church of Jesus Christ. . . .

> "'Come on, dear brother, since the war is past,
> "'For friends at first, are friends again at last.'
> "Yours as ever,
> "Joseph Smith, Jun."[10]

Four years later, W. W. Phelps gave a stirring eulogy at the Prophet's funeral. He had come to stand by Joseph with firm conviction. And then in tribute he wrote the much-loved hymn "Praise to the man who communed with Jehovah!"[11]

"Cleave unto charity," we read from Moroni (Moroni 7:46), who was the grand tutor to the Prophet Joseph Smith. Joseph had learned that lesson well. Forgiveness in our hearts invites charity.

The Lord Jesus Christ had experienced, firsthand, treachery of the vilest degree. On the day of His trial, an Apostle and a witness of Him turned traitor. Enemies had stalked this man who shunned violence, who never cursed or lifted His voice or hand, who ate with sinners and the poor as well as those recognized as important. Finally, those on the errand of the evil one took him prisoner. They subjected him to a mock trial and crowned His head with thorns; they made a mockery of justice. He stood silent, knowing of a far greater plan than His trumped-up crucifixion. They paraded Him through Jerusalem; they condemned Him to hang on a cross, among thieves.

Yet, He was calm. His Father's ways were His ways. He intended to fulfill His Father's plan because He knew, with Godlike knowledge, that charity never faileth. Even with those who reviled and abused Him, spat at Him, He remained steadfast and immovable. His doctrines and teachings were so secure in His heart that He submitted to their cruelties. On many previous occasions, He had stopped or been stopped in those same streets to help those seeking blessings, healings, counsel, and faith. He had taught multitudes and performed miracles. Now, in His most desperate hours, He stood alone—able and qualified. Hanging from the cross, in agony unspeakable, His words were cryptic and telling: "Father, forgive them; for they know not what they do" (Luke 23:34).

Father, forgive them. That statement says it all.

Charity forever changes those who receive it. It isn't the way of the world. "If it is going to bother me, it's going to bother you" is the standard on the street. But the words of John connect charity to divinity: "Peace I leave with you, my peace I give unto you" (John 14:27).

The First Presidency said as the Salt Lake Temple neared completion in the early 1890s:

"We feel now that a time for reconciliation has come; that before entering into the Temple to present ourselves before the Lord in solemn assembly, we shall divest ourselves of every harsh and unkind feeling against each other; that not only our bickerings shall cease, but that the cause of them shall be removed, and every sentiment that prompted and has maintained them shall be dispelled; that we shall confess our sins one to another, and ask forgiveness one of another; that we shall plead with the Lord for the spirit of repentance, and, having obtained it, follow its promptings; so that in humbling ourselves before Him and seeking forgiveness from each other, we shall yield that charity and generosity to those who crave our forgiveness that we ask for and expect from Heaven."[12]

The Atonement does more than pay for our sins. It is also the agent through which we develop a saintly nature. When the Savior accepts our repentance and pours down charity, His pure love, He restores our spiritual balance.

We can ask the Lord for strength to forgive—it may not be easy, and it may not come quickly. If we will seek it with sincerity, it will come. "If you wish to go where God is," Joseph taught, "you must be like God."[13] "Love is one of the chief characteristics of Deity," he said, "and ought to be manifested by those who aspire to be the sons [and daughters] of God."[14]

Joseph extended charity to all the world; it was the signature of his ministry. He taught charity. He lived charity. At the end, he demonstrated that he was possessed of charity, the pure love of Christ.

Let's return to John Taylor, who later would serve as God's chosen prophet. He, like Joseph, found charity in jail. The words of the last verse he sang before the death of the Prophet Joseph are so significant:

> *The Savior stood before mine eyes.*
> *He spake, and my poor name he named,*
> *"Of me thou hast not been ashamed.*
> *These deeds shall thy memorial be;*
> *Fear not, thou didst them unto me."*[15]

I bear my testimony of the doctrine of charity. "One touch with the finger of his love"[16] is assurance beyond mortal expression. I know that. I have felt His charity, that pure love; there is nothing like it. May we seek this Jesus, may we receive His love in our hearts, and may it fill our souls. May we turn to His atoning sacrifice as the strength we need to "hold on" our way.

NOTES

1. James Montgomery, "A Poor Wayfaring Man of Grief," *Hymns of The Church of Jesus Christ of Latter-day Saints* (Salt Lake City: The Church of Jesus Christ of Latter-day Saints, 1985), no. 29.
2. W. W. Phelps, "The Spirit of God," *Hymns,* no. 2.
3. Henry F. Lyte, "Abide with Me!" *Hymns,* no. 166.
4. Joseph Smith, *History of The Church of Jesus Christ of Latter-day Saints,* ed. B. H. Roberts, 2d ed. rev., 7 vols. (Salt Lake City: The Church of Jesus Christ of Latter-day Saints, 1932–51), 5:498.
5. Smith, *History of the Church,* 3:30.
6. Smith, *History of the Church,* 5:555.
7. Boyd K. Packer, "'The Touch of the Master's Hand,'" *Ensign,* May 2001, 23, 24.
8. *Hymns,* no. 29.
9. Smith, *History of the Church,* 4:141–42.
10. Smith, *History of the Church,* 4:162–64.
11. *Hymns,* no. 27.
12. James R. Clark, comp., *Messages of the First Presidency of The Church of Jesus Christ of Latter-day Saints,* 6 vols. (Salt Lake City: Bookcraft, 1965–75), 3:243.

13. Smith, *History of the Church,* 4:588.
14. Smith, *History of the Church,* 4:227.
15. *Hymns,* no. 29.
16. *Latter-day Saints' Messenger and Advocate,* vol. 1 (October 1834): 16.

In the World but Not of the World

Julie B. Beck

Learning to be in this world and not of this world is not easy, and as we discuss this subject today, I hope that you will listen with the Spirit to the things the Spirit wants to teach you and write down an action list that the Lord gives you that is personal and directed to you. That should be part of our learning in any situation of this kind. In my current calling as a counselor in the Young Women general presidency, I hear daily of the challenges that our youth and their parents are facing in living gospel standards. It might be easy for us to get discouraged about this and the conditions we live in, but I also hear of much good that is happening with our youth in these days. President Hinckley has complimented them twice in recent conferences. He said, "We commend our wonderful youth who for the most part stand up to the evils of the world, who push these evils aside and live lives pleasing to the Lord."[1]

Our youth do have many questions regarding standards. They are in a season of asking why: "Tell me why. Give me a reason why I should do these things." They need good reasons to make good choices, and the choices they make must be based on gospel standards. I would like to share with you the dialogue from a short video[2] that teaches how the

---

Julie B. Beck is currently serving as first counselor in the Young Women general presidency. She is a graduate of Dixie College and Brigham Young University. She and her husband, Ramon, have three children and five grandchildren.

standards are bedrock. As you read this, you might want to list the doctrines that are talked about in the video. This focuses on the words of two latter-day prophets and helps answer the questions some of our youth have regarding standards:

> **Young woman:** Why are there so many rules?
>
> **Young man:** Yeah, why do we have to have standards?
>
> **Young woman:** What's wrong with my shirt? It's not that tight!
>
> **Young man:** Can't I make my own decisions? It's my life.
>
> **Young woman:** My boyfriend says I should prove to him that I love him. I'm scared. What should I do?
>
> **Young man:** So I make a mistake. No big deal. I'll just repent—later.
>
> **President Boyd K. Packer:** It is my purpose to explain to the youth and young adults, and to their parents, why we hold so rigidly to high standards of moral conduct; why we avoid addictive drugs and tea, coffee, alcohol, and tobacco; why we teach standards of modesty in dress, grooming, and speech. You need to know where our standards came from and why we cannot loosen up and follow what the world does.
>
> **Narrator:** Our standards are grounded in eternal truths, which come from an Eternal Father.
>
> **President Gordon B. Hinckley:** I know that God, our Eternal Father, lives. He is the great God of the universe. He is the Father of our spirits, with whom we may speak in prayer.
>
> **President Packer:** Before we came into mortal life, we lived as spirit children of our Father in Heaven. All human beings—male and female— are created in the image of God. Each of you is a beloved spirit son or daughter of heavenly parents, and as such, you have a divine nature and destiny.
>
> **Narrator:** You are choice spirits who have come forth in this day when the responsibilities and opportunities, as well as the temptations, are the greatest. You are at the beginning of your journey through this mortal life. Your Heavenly Father wants your life to be joyful and to lead you back into His presence.
>
> **President Packer:** We came to earth to be tested and to gain experience, with a promise that "through the Atonement of Christ, all mankind may be saved, by obedience to the laws and ordinances of the Gospel" (Articles of Faith 1:3).

Narrator: Heavenly Father has given you agency, the ability to choose right from wrong and to act for yourself. You have been given the Holy Ghost to help you know good from evil. While you are here on earth, you are being proven to see if you will use your agency to show your love for God by keeping His commandments.

Narrator: Look to the Savior as your example. Although He came to earth as the Son of God, He humbly served those around Him. Jesus Christ gave His life for us and suffered for our sins. Through the Atonement, you can receive forgiveness and be cleansed from your sins when you repent.

President Hinckley: Like the polar star in the heavens, regardless of what the future holds, there stands the Redeemer of the world, the Son of God, certain and sure as the anchor of our immortal lives. He is the rock of our salvation, our strength, our comfort, the very focus of our faith. In sunshine and in shadow, we look to Him, and He is there to assure and smile upon us.

President Packer: The great plan of happiness enables family relationships to last beyond the grave. Sacred ordinances and covenants, available only in the temple, make it possible for individuals to return to the presence of God and for families to be united eternally.

Narrator: Our family is what makes the standards we live and keep so important, not only our earthly families, but also our eternal family with our Heavenly Father. The standards will help you make correct choices that lead you back into His presence.

President Packer: We do not set the standards, but we are commanded to teach them and maintain them. However out of step we may seem, however much the standards are belittled, however much others yield, we will not yield—we cannot yield.

Young man: As I live the standards of this Church, I feel good about myself. I love our Savior, and the Spirit touches me so much when I think of Him and all that He has done for me.

Young woman: Especially after I've had a hard time and I just go and pray and ask for His help, and immediately I feel that He's there with me.

Young woman: You sort of have this warm feeling come over you, and you just know that everything's going to be okay, and without Him, nothing would be possible.

President Hinckley: We must stand firm. We must hold back the world. Live by your standards. Pray for the guidance and the protection of the Lord. He will never leave you. He will comfort you. He will sustain you. He will bless and magnify you and make your reward sweet and beautiful.

Don't you love the testimony of our prophet and his affirmation that we can stand firm? "Faithful and true we will ever stand!"[3] That is a confident statement, and the prophet knows we live in a world that has ever-changing standards. President Packer has said recently that "society is on a course that has caused the destruction of civilizations and is now ripening in iniquity."[4] That's sobering.

But we also have always had prophets to counsel us and strengthen us. The scriptures are full of teachings from prophets, such as Alma, that say, "Follow the voice of the good shepherd, come ye out from the wicked, and be ye separate, and touch not their unclean things" (Alma 5:57).

Every boy and girl needs parents and leaders who follow the Good Shepherd, who know how to be separate from the world. Young people need adults in their lives who live and teach the Lord's standards without equivocation.

I would like to explore with you three ways we can help uphold the counsel of the prophets. These are things we can implement in our lives to be separate from the world and not to be in the world.

First, *avoid* and *resist* evil; second, *prune* out the bad things and *graft* in things that will bear good fruit in our lives; and third, *teach the doctrine* that was taught by our prophets in this short example, doctrine that is the basis for our standards.

First of all, avoiding and resisting evil.

The scriptures say: "Go ye out . . . from Babylon, from the midst of wickedness" (D&C 133:14). We have to do that.

President Hinckley just said recently to the young women: "Modesty in dress and manner will assist in protecting against temptation. . . . Stay away from sleazy entertainment. . . . I plead with you to avoid disfigurement. . . . I again mention drugs. . . . Stay away from them as if they were a foul disease."[5] Avoid temptation—that's what the prophet is telling us.

Avoiding is much easier than resisting, I can tell you that. Elder Lynn Robbins taught me an example of avoiding and resisting. He said: "Picture yourself walking into a warm kitchen that smells of the aroma of freshly baked chocolate chip cookies. There in front of you is a plate of cookies.

The chocolate is still warm and melting a little bit. How hard is it to resist eating one?"

Can you do it? I don't know about you, but I don't think I have ever passed up that opportunity. It is just too much to resist, and if there is a glass of milk handy, I have to eat more cookies to go with the milk until it comes out even. So it isn't just one cookie, it has to come out right. If there is a reason I should not eat chocolate chip cookies, I resist following that aroma and avoid the kitchen altogether. That's something I know about self-mastery, that it is much harder resisting temptation than avoiding it. We must do both.

In the *For the Strength of Youth* pamphlet, it talks about this in the section about entertainment and the media. It gives counsel about avoiding. For instance, here's an avoidance phrase: "Do not attend, view, or participate in entertainment that is vulgar, immoral, violent, or pornographic in any way."[6] Avoid it.

And then here is something about resisting: "Have the courage to walk out of a movie or video party, turn off a computer or television, change a radio station, or put down a magazine if what is being presented does not meet Heavenly Father's standards."[7]

Now the first option is to avoid. Don't go to the bad movie in the first place. Be ye separate, or go out from Babylon.

Resisting is possible, but imagine how much more difficult it is when you go to a movie with a group of friends. You buy a ticket and popcorn and a soda, and you sit down through the previews, and the movie begins, and you realize you should not be there. Do you have the courage to stand up, walk past your friends, go out into the lobby, and wait for them until the movie is over? That is powerful resisting. It is much easier not to have gone to the movie in the first place, to have avoided it, as the counsel has been given.

We need to learn to avoid as much as possible the people, the places, and the things that pull us down. Our youth need help with that. They need restraints to help them avoid. The scriptures say—this is in 2 Corinthians—"Wherefore come out from among them, and be ye separate, saith the Lord, and touch not the unclean thing; and I will receive you. And will be a Father unto you, and ye shall be my sons and daughters, saith the Lord Almighty" (2 Corinthians 6:17–18). That is counsel and a promise about avoiding that is centuries old. It's not a new idea to resist temptation.

Now pruning and grafting.

Young people are active. They are loaded with energy, ideas, imagination, enthusiasm. They have to be doing something. It's not fair to expect them to sit home in a stark room, doing nothing, learning nothing, experiencing nothing, merely to avoid being exposed to bad things.

So I call this the Jacob 5 principle of grafting and pruning. Think of our lives and our youth as the trees as spoken of in Jacob 5, and we can learn a lesson from these verses that tell us about changing for the good: "And as they [the trees] begin to grow ye shall clear away the branches which bring forth bitter fruit. . . . For it grieveth me that I should lose the trees of my vineyard; wherefore ye shall clear away the bad according as the good shall grow, . . . and the bad [shall] be hewn down and cast into the fire. . . . And the branches of the natural tree will I graft into the natural branches of the tree" (Jacob 5:65–66, 68).

Pruning is a concept that I think that most of us understand. We say things like, "I'm not going to do that!" or "I'm going to stop that bad habit!" or "It's time to make a change!" We want to cut things out of our life that aren't productive. Often we work very hard at stopping bad behaviors. But change is always much easier if, along with the pruning, we graft in something good to take its place. Pruning leaves a gap, so what will we replace that will bear good fruit? President Hinckley suggested a few things we can graft into our lives just this last conference in the priesthood meeting when he was speaking about the evils of gambling:

"There are better ways to spend one's time. There are better pursuits to occupy one's interest and energy. There is so much of wonderful reading available. We are not likely to ever get too much of it. There is music to be learned and enjoyed. There is just having a good time together—in dancing, in hiking, in cycling, or in other ways—boys and girls together enjoying one another's company in a wholesome way."[8]

Five suggestions from a prophet of good things to graft into your lives—that's a great list. There are myriad activities that all of us can take part in that will bear good fruit, and the Holy Ghost is the one who inspires us with these ideas. This concept is taught to us in Moroni, chapter 7. You've heard these verses before, but think of these in terms of grafting in good things:

"For behold, my brethren, it is given unto you to judge, that ye may know good from evil; and the way to judge is as plain, that ye may know with a perfect knowledge, as the daylight is from the dark night.

"For behold, the Spirit of Christ is given to every man, that he may know good from evil; wherefore, I show unto you the way to judge; for every thing which inviteth to do good, and to persuade to believe in Christ, is sent forth by the power and gift of Christ; wherefore ye may know with a perfect knowledge it is of God" (Moroni 7:15–16). You will have ideas of things to graft into your lives which will bear good fruit if you think and pray about them.

Now the third idea is teaching the doctrine, which goes back to the words of the prophets.

I began with a video that taught some of those doctrines upon which our gospel standards are based. I hope you wrote a list of what some of those were.

Parents and leaders could strengthen themselves and our young people morally if they answered questions—those whys—with true doctrinal principles from the scriptures. The scriptures are a great untapped resource for us in teaching about standards.

Not long ago, I spoke to a father about his son and his son's appearance, which did not meet the gospel standard. In a way, he did not want his son to be different from the other teen boys in his school, but he was wondering if "fitting in" with friends was more important for the young man than looking the part of someone who held the priesthood of God.

As we talked, the father said that he had often spoken with his son about his appearance, but they had not spent time in conversations that involved deeper understanding and testimony that changes behavior. So together we identified some of the doctrine found in the scriptures that might strengthen that son and his testimony:

• His identity as a child of God. Does he have a testimony of that? Do you talk about that with regard to dress and appearance?

• How about the body as the temple of your spirit?

- Another one: qualifying for and utilizing the Holy Ghost. There is much teaching in the scriptures on those principles.
- The doctrine of the priesthood. The young man held the priesthood. What did that mean in his life? Did he have a testimony of that?
- How about the sacrament and the sacredness of the sacrament as that young man represented the Savior at the sacrament table?

All those teachings are found in the scriptures, and when we open the scriptures and teach from them, the Spirit attends our teaching, and we have a powerful partner.

Not long ago, I was with some young women and their leaders, having a discussion with regard to Sunday dress and the girls' appearance at Church meetings. The leaders were concerned that casualness had become the fashion, and most of you understand what that means—everything from hairstyles to footwear becomes extremely casual sometimes. They were hoping that I would be able to settle their dilemma and answer the girls' questions and tell them exactly what they should wear to church. I quickly pondered, wanting to do something, teach something, that would have meaning and not just recite the rules again. And with a prayer in my heart, I turned to some scriptures. I said, "Please open your scriptures with me." Turning to Doctrine and Covenants 19, we began reading:

"For behold, I, God, have suffered these things for all, that they might not suffer if they would repent;

"But if they would not repent they must suffer even as I;

"Which suffering caused myself, even God, the greatest of all, to tremble because of pain, and to bleed at every pore, and to suffer both body and spirit—and would that I might not drink the bitter cup, and shrink—

"Nevertheless, glory be to the Father, and I partook and finished my preparations unto the children of men" (D&C 19:16–19).

After reading those verses, we had a short discussion. We talked about who the voice was in the scripture. It's the Savior, Jesus Christ, speaking about His atoning sacrifice. We talked about the intensity of His suffering as He atoned for our sins and His promise to us that we don't have to suffer as He did if we repent. We talked about sacrament meeting as being the place where that repentance takes place week after week and what a gift that is in our lives.

Then I bore my testimony to those young women that when I partake of the sacrament, I am serious. It's a serious occasion for me. I go to sacrament meeting to repent, because I've been commanded to do so, and because it's my great privilege, the gift of the Lord to me. And when I go, I dress in a serious fashion. Now there are times when I dress casually—which means nonchalant, unplanned, offhand—and I go to places that are casual places. But when I go to Church to take the sacrament, I go with a serious purpose, and I dress in a serious way in order to honor the Atonement of the Savior. That was my testimony to those young women about dress and appearance at church.

A few months later, the Young Women leader found me, and she told me that, following our conversation, the girls gathered together, and they said: "We didn't understand. We're going to establish our own guidelines for Sunday meetings." And they changed the way they dressed based on an increased understanding of the sacrament. Doctrinal principles matter to these young people.

President J. Reuben Clark Jr. has said, and this is still a true statement:

"The youth of the Church are hungry for the things of the Spirit; they are eager to learn the gospel, and they want it straight, undiluted. . . .

"You do not have to sneak up behind [them] and whisper religion in [their] ears. . . . You do not need to disguise religious truths with a cloak of worldly things; you can bring these truths to [them] openly."[9] The doctrine is important in their lives.

It is possible to be in this world and not of this world. We can do this if we avoid and resist evil. As the scriptures say, we have to be separate from it. We can prune out the bad in our lives and graft in the good by seeking after "anything virtuous, lovely, or of good report or praiseworthy" (Articles of Faith 1:13).

Then we can also teach the doctrine. That is important. Those principles have to be in our lives. Now President Hinckley gave us this strong teaching: "While standards generally may totter, we of the Church are without excuse if we drift in the same manner. We have standards—sure, tested, and effective. To the extent that we observe them, we shall go forward. To the extent that we neglect them, we shall hinder our own progress and bring embarrassment to the work of the Lord. These standards have come from [the Lord]. Some of them may appear a little out-of-date in our society, but this does not detract from their validity nor diminish the virtue of their application. The subtle reasoning of men, no matter how clever, no matter how plausible it may sound, cannot abridge the declared wisdom of God."[10]

My friends, this is the restored gospel of Jesus Christ. We are children of our Heavenly Father, who loves us. Our Savior, Jesus Christ, atoned for our sins and gave us the example of His perfect life. That "His way is the path that leads to happiness in this life and eternal life in the world to come"[11] is my testimony.

NOTES

1. Gordon B. Hinckley, "Closing Remarks," *Ensign,* May 2005, 102.
2. *Standards and Eternal Truths* (Salt Lake City: The Church of Jesus Christ of Latter-day Saints, 2003).
3. Evan Stephens, "True to the Faith," *Hymns of The Church of Jesus Christ of Latter-day Saints* (Salt Lake City: The Church of Jesus Christ of Latter-day Saints, 1985), no. 254.
4. Boyd K. Packer, "'The Standard of Truth Has Been Erected,'" *Ensign,* November 2003, 26.
5. Gordon B. Hinckley, "Stay on the High Road," *Ensign,* May 2004, 114.
6. *For the Strength of Youth* (Salt Lake City: The Church of Jesus Christ of Latter-day Saints, 2001), 17.
7. *For the Strength of Youth,* 19.
8. Gordon B. Hinckley, "Gambling," *Ensign,* May 2005, 61.
9. J. Reuben Clark Jr., "Excerpts from *The Charted Course of the Church in Education,*" *Ensign,* September 2002, 56, 60.
10. Gordon B. Hinckley, "Pursue the Steady Course," *Ensign,* January 2005, 4–5.
11. "The Living Christ: The Testimony of the Apostles, The Church of Jesus Christ of Latter-day Saints," *Ensign,* April 2000, 2.

LIVING IN THE LIGHT OF THE TEMPLE

Janette Hales Beckham

When my youngest daughter was about four, she came into the kitchen one day and said, "Am I sealed?"

I said, "Are you what?"

She said, "Am I sealed?"

She had taken me a little by surprise. I realized that her friend, who was adopted, had gone to the temple with her family to be sealed and Mary knew she hadn't been to the temple. I explained that when a man and woman choose to be married in the temple for time and eternity, the children born to them are sealed to them. It is called being born in the covenant. She left the room looking a little less than convinced, and several times in the next few months she would ask, "Are you sure I am sealed?" I believe Mary was expressing a concern that all people have in wanting to know they will be with their loved ones forever.

About twenty years later, when Mary had just been sealed to her eternal companion, I was asked to speak at the dedication of the San Diego California Temple, and I invited her and her husband to be with me. It

Janette Hales Beckham has previously served in The Church of Jesus Christ of Latter-day Saints as general president of the Young Women, as a member of the Primary general board, and as the assistant to the matron of the Provo Temple. She currently serves as a Gospel Doctrine teacher. Sister Beckham was married to the late Robert H. Hales; they are the parents of five children. She is currently married to Raymond E. Beckham.

caused me to reflect on the commitment it takes to cause that sealing power to continue from one generation to the next.

The question asked by my daughter could be asked by many, and I realized it may just as well have been my nonmember father asking, "Am I sealed?"

I realize that the promises of the sealing power are more than we can totally understand. It may be the reason we ponder the often-quoted statement of Orson F. Whitney called "A Precious Promise," recorded from the April general conference of 1929.

He stated: "The Prophet Joseph Smith declared—and he never taught more comforting doctrine—that the eternal sealings of faithful parents and the divine promises made to them for valiant service in the cause of truth, would save not only themselves but likewise their posterity. Though some of the sheep may wander, the eye of the Shepherd is upon them and sooner or later they will feel the tentacles of divine providence reaching out after them and drawing them back to the fold. . . .

"Who are these straying sheep—these wayward sons and daughters? They are children of the Covenant."[1]

As I considered children of covenant and my assignment in the San Diego Temple, my thoughts turned to the sacred nature of our daily tasks.

I have learned that many times we see temple work in isolation. We go to the temple to be baptized for the dead. We go to the temple when we get ready to go on a mission. We go to the temple when we are ready to get married. We go to the temple to perform ordinances for the deceased. We go to the temple when it's ward temple night.

We understand the importance of temple work, but do we see the work of the temple as we go about our daily work? Do we appreciate the sacred nature of our daily tasks?

Let me give an example: When I had been called to be the Young Women president of the Church in 1992, my call had been announced and I knew I would be called on the next day to speak in general conference. I was a widow living alone, and I stood at my sink that evening, feeling a bit overwhelmed. I wondered what I might do that would make a difference for 500,000 young women. The simple line came into my head: "Turn the heart of the fathers to the children, and the . . . children to their fathers" (Malachi 4:6). I went to the Tabernacle early the next morning and added these words to my message on the teleprompter:

"Now, to every adult member of the Church, may I suggest that you learn the names of the young people in your ward or branch and call them by name. Encourage them in their work efforts. Recognize them for the good things they do. They need our support, and we need theirs."[2]

For the next five and a half years I took every opportunity to help people understand the needs of youth during their growing years. The last Worldwide Celebration planned and approved before our release was entitled "Turning Hearts of Young Women to Their Families."

Only later did I realize that I was doing the work of the temple.

If you look carefully at the handbooks, you will notice there are two purposes for all we do in our youth programs:

1. Help young people grow spiritually
2. Help strengthen families

Is that not the work of the temple?

As I meet with young women now as they come to the temple for the first time, I often repeat to them the words from the Young Women Theme: "You have prepared yourself to make and keep sacred covenants, receive the ordinances of the temple and enjoy the blessings of exaltation."

As Young Women leaders serve, is that not the work of the temple?

Let me give another example: When I was a little girl I attended the Thurber Elementary School on Main Street in Spanish Fork. It was next door to the old Second Ward building, where now is a new stake center. I often went to Primary with my friends after school. One of the traditions of that ward was to go to the home of the Primary president to pass off the Articles of Faith when we had them memorized. One day I was sitting in the living room of Sister Stewart, the Primary president. As I finished reciting what I had memorized, she reached over and took hold of my hand and said, "Janette, wouldn't you like to be baptized?"

I didn't know very much about it, but my younger sister had just turned eight and I think they realized that we were not members. I was nearly eleven. I was baptized on April 1, 1944. Sister Stewart was carrying out her responsibilities as a Primary president and making sure we learned the Articles of Faith, but I believe she also acted upon a spiritual prompting.

Is that not the work of the temple?

I'm sure that serving in the temple full time has increased my appreciation for the work of the temple that precedes temple work. I want you to go home and see the temple in the things you are doing:

- Gathering your family around the table at mealtime for family prayer
- Family home evening
- Getting little children ready for church
- Sitting with a child at the piano (did you know we have 100 organists in the Provo Temple?)
- Visiting teaching

Just like Sister Stewart reaching out to me, I see you reaching, reaching, reaching to hold on to people, to hold on to your families.

Is that not the work of the temple?

As you carry out your responsibilities from day to day, as you think about the sacred nature of your daily tasks, I would ask you to ask yourselves, "What does this have to do with the temple?"

The second part of my message I would like to call "Sacrifice Brings Forth the Blessings of Heaven."

This is the first line of the last verse of the hymn written to honor the Prophet Joseph Smith, "Praise to the Man." As we celebrate the 200th birthday of the Prophet Joseph, we will again be reminded of the sacrifices that were made to bring the blessings of the temple to the Saints of this dispensation. It is difficult to imagine how they accomplished the building of a temple, first in Kirtland and then in Nauvoo.

Section 88 of the Doctrine and Covenants was given to Joseph Smith in 1832. Its words help us see that preparing for the temple and building a temple required discipline and sacrifice. Consider words from that section and see if they don't apply to us today: "Teach one another. . . . Organize yourselves; prepare every needful thing; and establish . . . a house of learning, a house of glory, a house of order, a house of God. . . . Cease . . . from all your pride and light-mindedness. . . . Love one another. . . . Cease to be idle; cease to be unclean; . . . retire to thy bed early . . . ; arise early, that your bodies and your minds may be invigorated" (verses 118–19, 121, 123–24).

(That last line is for me in our new assignment.)

My husband was called to serve in the Provo Temple presidency and I was called to be an assistant to the matron just after October conference. We began serving there November 1. I thought about President Monson's words when he said: "Each thing we do in our lives prepares us for the next thing. We just don't know what the next thing is."[3]

Right! We didn't know what the next thing was! Ray and I thought we were retired. You might say we had other plans. Have you ever received a call when you had other plans?

I remember being touched by the words of Elder David A. Bednar. He said that life is "one drop of oil added to our spiritual lamp of preparation every day."[4] That's a nice line for the temple. "Life is one drop of oil added to our spiritual lamp of preparation every day."

I have since read many times the parable of the ten virgins in the 25th chapter of Matthew. Although some artists depict the ten virgins as women, the parable lists no pronouns, male or female. Perhaps they were virtuous people on a journey to meet the Savior, symbolically referred to as the Bridegroom. They were all good people, but some were wise and some were foolish. They were all making the journey.

What a good reminder that our spiritual preparation is ours alone. No one can do it for us. It requires us to make choices. As Elder Bednar suggested, "Life is one drop of oil added to our spiritual lamp of preparation every day." He added, "That's how it works." We have to decide to add oil to our lamps.

As Elder Bednar spoke in April conference, I felt he expanded on this theme as he talked about the tender mercies of the Lord. He told us the tender mercies of the Lord were available to each one of us, but our experiences were dependent on our choices. And he said that we have to choose to be chosen. He said, "To be or to become chosen is not an exclusive status conferred upon us. Rather, you and I ultimately determine if we are chosen."[5] He quoted the 121st section of the Doctrine and Covenants, where it states: "Behold, there are many called, but few are chosen. And why are they not chosen? Because their hearts are set so much upon the things of this world, and aspire to the honors of men" (verses 34–35).

Temple work is one of the choices that does require sacrifice. There will be distractions. President Boyd K. Packer has warned, "We should expect that the adversary will try to interfere with us as a church and with us individually as we seek to participate in this sacred and inspired work. Temple work brings so much resistance because it is the *source of so much spiritual power* to the Latter-day Saints and to the entire Church."[6]

What are the things of the world that might distract us?

Many may not be bad things, just things we need to give up. When we choose to follow the prompting of the Spirit, we usually have to turn away from something else. We may choose to leave a TV program to study for an exam, choose to delay an advanced education to have a baby, choose to give up a good job to care for a toddler. We may choose to delay time with family to serve a mission or, as some I know, choose to set the alarm for 3:30 or 4:00 in the morning and leave a warm bed to be ready and to drive from Santaquin or Heber to be at the temple to greet the patrons for the early Tuesday session.

The things we choose will be different for each of us, but I believe I am just barely coming to understand what Elder Bednar referred to as he spoke of the tender mercies of the Lord, "the very personal and individualized blessings . . . we receive from and because of . . . the Lord Jesus Christ."[7]

For years I had a personal line I used with fellow workers as we were making hard choices and experiencing change. I often said, "Remember, *growth feels like a loss!*" We have to give up something in order to grow.

I appreciated the words of Elder Robbins in April conference when he said, "The Lord often teaches using extreme circumstances to illustrate a principle. . . . The truer measure of sacrifice isn't so much what one gives to sacrifice as what one sacrifices to give."[8]

When a person is performing service it seldom feels like sacrifice because the Spirit attends the act. But at the moment of decision, when you choose to give something up or to go without something you want or something you want to do in order to respond to a call or a prompting of the Spirit, it feels like a loss. It feels like sacrifice. Then, it is the Spirit that fills the void, and good feelings follow. Blessings follow the sacrifice.

As I interact with the more than 3,000 workers in the Provo Temple, I am reassured that their calendars are as full as anyone's. They, too, have health problems, family challenges, important occasions, but they are the miracle workers. They come day after day and the patrons come day after day. When I arrive at the temple about 5:45 A.M., the lobby is filled with young students waiting for the door of the baptistry to open. And they just keep coming day after day.

I do believe that sacrifice brings forth the blessings of heaven!

To conclude my message I would like to refer to words of the prophets and the words of the hymn "More Holiness Give Me."

As we read the newspaper, watch the six o'clock news with reports of a troubled world, or just battle traffic on the freeway, we might ask, What is needful in our day, and consider the words of the hymn: "more gratitude . . . , more trust . . . , more hope . . . , more meekness."

May I suggest the last verse of the hymn:

> More purity give me, More strength to o'ercome,
> More freedom from earthstains, More longing for home.
> More fit for the kingdom, More used would I be,
> More blessed and holy—More, Savior, like thee.[9]

One year ago a letter from the First Presidency was read in sacrament meetings. I quote from that letter: "We . . . invite adult members to have a current temple recommend and visit the temple more often. Where time and circumstances permit, members are encouraged to replace some leisure activities with temple service."[10]

President James E. Faust in April conference spoke of the need to "stand in holy places." He said: "We are bombarded on all sides by a vast number of messages we don't want or need. More information is generated in a single day than we can absorb in a lifetime. To fully enjoy life, all of us must find our own breathing space and peace of mind."[11]

For each of us who is raising children, communicating with grown children, balancing Church callings and economic demands, I think we would relate to the term "bombarded." I believe President Faust is telling us that the temple can help us in our ability to handle the daily dilemmas that confront us. Listen to his words:

"Holiness is the strength of the soul. It comes by faith and through obedience to God's laws and ordinances. God then purifies the heart by faith, and the heart becomes purged from that which is profane and unworthy. When holiness is achieved by conforming to God's will, one knows intuitively that which is wrong and that which is right before the Lord. *Holiness speaks when there is silence,* encouraging that which is good or reproving that which is wrong."[12]

Every prophet has emphasized the significance of temples. Brigham Young, during times of peril and struggle for survival in the Salt Lake Valley, began plans for temple building. Wilford Woodruff announced the revelation of genealogical work. Joseph F. Smith prophesied the building of a temple in Switzerland and in 1906 said temples would one day dot the land. Harold B. Lee prophesied that the Church would one day build small temples that would dot the earth. Ten years later, in 1982, Spencer W. Kimball stated twenty-two temples were in planning and construction. Ezra Taft Benson dedicated temples in Freiberg and Frankfurt, Germany.

Howard W. Hunter was the President of the Church for only nine months. In 1994, he asked us to "establish the temple of the Lord as the great symbol of [our] membership."[13] He said, "Let us be a temple-attending and a temple-loving people. . . . Let us go not only for our kindred dead, but let us also go for the personal blessing of temple worship."[14] President Hunter felt so strongly about the importance of the temple that he had his temple message printed on his funeral program. It is the way he wanted to be remembered.

Ten years ago President Gordon B. Hinckley, when he became the President of the Church, said: "This is the greatest era in the history of the Church for temple building. Never has the construction of temples gone forward with the momentum that is now being carried forward. . . . We will continue to build temples."[15]

In 1995 there were 47 temples. Today there are soon to be 122 in 37 countries. There are 5,000 local family history centers. There are 2.4 million rolls of microfilmed records. There are 1 billion names on the Church's Internet site. But, it has been pointed out that "technology isn't at the heart of the work. . . . The *heart of the work* is the hearts of the children which are to be turned to their fathers."[16]

Have you thought about the fact that when President Hinckley one day stands before our Heavenly Father, he will be accountable, as will every prophet, for everything he was supposed to tell us. It is a reminder then, to us, that when he has told us, we are accountable.

I would like to conclude with President Hinckley's words from October conference 2004:

"I would hope that we might go to the house of the Lord a little more frequently. . . . *We have done all that we know how to do* to bring temples closer to our people. . . . In this noisy, bustling, competitive world, what a privilege it is to have a sacred house. . . . I encourage you to take a greater advantage of this blessed privilege. It will refine your natures. It will peel off the selfish shell in which most of us live. It will literally bring a sanctifying element into our lives and make us better men and better women."[17]

President Hinckley has also said: "If you are able, go to the temple on a regular basis. You will be better fathers and husbands, better wives and mothers. I know you have much to do, but I make you a promise that if you will go to the house of the Lord, you will be blessed."

And then he said, "Life will be better for you."[18] That is a promise from our living prophet: "Life will be better for you." I bear testimony that I have witnessed the joy and happiness promised to those who take advantage of the blessings of the temple.

It is wise for us to consider the *sacred nature* of our daily tasks and to recognize the opportunity we have each day to add one drop of oil to our spiritual lamp of preparation. I believe that *sacrifice* is required to realize the blessings our Heavenly Father has promised us. May we seek the *holiness* which "speaks in silence" and encourages that which is good, is my prayer.

NOTES

1. Orson F. Whitney, in Conference Report, April 1929, 110–11.
2. Janette C. Hales, "You Are Not Alone," *Ensign*, May 1992, 80.
3. Thomas S. Monson, in private meeting with the author.
4. David A. Bednar, in Julie Dockstader Heaps, "Legacy of family, faith is foundation of life," *Church News*, October 23, 2004, 6.
5. David A. Bednar, "The Tender Mercies of the Lord," *Ensign*, May 2005, 101.
6. Boyd K. Packer, "The Holy Temple," *Ensign*, February 1995, 36; emphasis added.
7. Bednar, *Ensign*, May 2005, 99.

8. Lynn G. Robbins, "Tithing—a Commandment Even for the Destitute," *Ensign*, May 2005, 34.

9. "More Holiness Give Me," *Hymns of The Church of Jesus Christ of Latter-day Saints* (Salt Lake City: The Church of Jesus Christ of Latter-day Saints, 1985), no. 131.

10. "Letter from the First Presidency," *Ensign*, March 2004, 45.

11. James E. Faust, "Standing in Holy Places," *Ensign*, May 2005, 62.

12. Faust, *Ensign*, May 2005, 62; emphasis added.

13. Howard W. Hunter, "The Great Symbol of Our Membership," *Ensign*, October 1994, 2.

14. Hunter, *Ensign*, October 1994, 5.

15. Gordon B. Hinckley, in Dell Van Orden, "Pres. Hinckley ordained prophet," *Church News*, March 18, 1995, 3.

16. Don Anderson, in John L. Hart, "Turning the hearts," *Church News*, April 2, 2005, 7; emphasis added.

17. Gordon B. Hinckley, "Closing Remarks," *Ensign*, November 2004, 104, 105; emphasis added.

18. Gordon B. Hinckley, *Teachings of Gordon B. Hinckley* (Salt Lake City: Deseret Book, 1997), 624.

A WONDERFUL FLOOD OF LIGHT

Ann Madsen

When Joseph Smith walked into the grove that spring day in 1820 he had been reading this scripture: "If any of you lack wisdom, let him ask of God, that giveth to all men liberally, and upbraideth not; and it shall be given him" (James 1:5).

He said of that experience: "Never did any passage of scripture come with more power to the heart of man than this did at this time to mine. It seemed to enter with great force into every feeling of my heart. I reflected on it again and again, knowing that if any person needed wisdom from God, I did" (Joseph Smith—History 1:12).

Have you ever felt a scripture enter with great force into your heart? Have you continued to think about it again and again? I have. I pray that today we may better understand the powerful force the scriptures can be in our lives.

How do we receive and keep the light of the scriptures each day? How do we access this powerful force that helps us discern between light and darkness in an ever-darkening world? The scriptures help us to see the contrast, and to choose the Savior's way.

"And the light which shineth, which giveth you light, is through him

Ann Madsen teaches courses on Isaiah and the New Testament at Brigham Young University. She is currently serving as a stake Relief Society president. She is married to Truman G. Madsen and they have four children, sixteen grandchildren, and five great-grandchildren.

who *enlighteneth* your eyes, which is the same light that *quickeneth* your understandings" (D&C 88:11; emphasis added).

I love the scriptures, the good word of God.

I can't remember the exact time when I began to love these words. But three experiences come to mind.

First, at a slumber party when I was 13 years old: I had been reading my father's tiny leather-bound Doctrine and Covenants. I was in a world of my own, curled up in my sleeping bag in a corner, when I came upon these words:

"Behold, ye are little children and ye cannot bear all things now; ye must grow in grace and in the knowledge of the truth. Fear not, little children, for you are mine, and I have overcome the world, and you are of them that my Father hath given me; and none of them that my Father hath given me shall be lost" (D&C 50:40–42).

Suddenly I knew that it meant me! These words were written to me! Have you felt like that?

Second, when I was 14 years old: I came upon Moroni's familiar invitation:

"Ask God, the Eternal Father, in the name of Christ, if these things are not true; and if ye shall ask with a sincere heart, with real intent, having faith in Christ, he will manifest the truth of it unto you, by the power of the Holy Ghost" (Moroni 10:4).

Those words came with "great force" into my heart and I reflected on them again and again until I had memorized them. As I knelt late that night praying, I used those precise words over and over again, fully expecting an answer. Suddenly I felt the unmistakable warmth of the Holy Ghost. It was one of the first times I had known that unique warmth. I knew beyond doubt that the Book of Mormon was true and that Joseph Smith was, indeed, a prophet. (I felt like running to my dormer window and shouting to my sleeping neighborhood. "Joseph IS a prophet! The Book of Mormon IS true!") Have you felt that way?

Third, that same summer when I spent my lunch hours on Temple Square: I would sit in the old visitors' center studying the Book of Mormon, praying that some nice tourist sitting nearby would ask me what I was reading or if I were a Mormon so that I could bear my *new* testimony to some lucky stranger. It happened one day. A woman asked me, and I told her!

I remember exactly a time much later when my ardor for scripture reading had cooled. I had been home a few weeks from our mission in New England with my family. I awoke one morning with a vague feeling that something was missing—more than those hundreds of missionaries we had loved and the wonderful members, new and old. I felt strangely cut off from the rich spiritual diet of the mission field. I wondered if this were simply inevitable.

Suddenly I realized I wasn't studying the scriptures each morning as I had those three years in the mission home. After a few days of immersing myself in the scriptures again the problem evaporated and I have been reading daily ever since. The emptiness wasn't inevitable. I had been starving. And I knew what it felt like to be nourished again. Later I heard President Spencer W. Kimball describe my situation:

"I find that when I get casual in my relationships with divinity and when it seems that no divine ear is listening and no divine voice is speaking, that I am far, far away. If I immerse myself in the scriptures the distance narrows and the spirituality returns. I find myself loving more intensely those whom I must love with all my heart and mind and strength, and loving them more, I find it easier to abide their counsel."[1]

We can't learn from a closed book. Now my scriptures are open, and as I search consistently I am gathering the truths I need to live and grow and solve my daily dilemmas. As I store these truths in my heart I am prepared for the unexpected, the unforeseen. The distance continually narrows between the Lord and me.

Do you keep your scriptures open? When I was called as a stake Relief Society president, my stake president counseled me to always stand before the sisters of our stake with my scriptures open in my hand so that they would understand that the scriptures were also theirs to search. I love to stand with these pages opened, feeling that all the words inside are available to me.

I invite you to literally leave your scriptures open as a silent reminder, beckoning you to read. Leave them open on your bedside table, on your desk, in the living room. It will symbolize your readiness to read. Open scriptures are like a treasure house with its door ajar awaiting your entry.

Like Joseph Smith, we, too can pray, read, suddenly understand, and then act on what we have learned. Living what we learn enables our horizon to broaden, our step to quicken. It is like a bright, lighted staircase. As we move up step by step we come ever closer to the Father and the Son, the same personages Joseph saw.

How does this process work? Is there a perfect way? I'm sorry. The answer has to be no.

Perhaps there is one rule: read! And then read some more.

The scriptures themselves offer this simple advice: "Treasure up in your minds *continually* the words of life, and it shall be given you in the very hour that portion that shall be meted unto every man" (D&C 84:85; emphasis added).

We can't swallow all we need to know in one giant gulp. As we hunger and thirst we must eat and drink "continually."

Jesus promised the Samaritan woman at Jacob's well: "Whosoever drinketh of the water that I shall give him shall never thirst; but the water that I shall give him shall be in him a well of water springing up into everlasting life" (John 4:14).

When we accept the water that Jesus offers us, it will eventually become a well in us "springing up into everlasting life."

Can this glorious water be stored? Yes! Find *your way* to store these words in *your mind and heart*. Replenish your own well.

Let me share a few of my ideas and experiences.

First we must **read the word.** Open the book as I did again after my mission. Read, and this will continually increase your pool of knowledge. I have the sense that whatever we read thoughtfully will be there when we need it, safely stored. That motivates me to keep stocking my mind and heart with these eternal truths for the Holy Ghost to draw upon. We receive the word by reading it.

Read aloud. Joseph Smith taught us: "Faith comes by *hearing* the word of God, through the testimony of the servants of God; that testimony is *always* attended by the Spirit of prophecy and revelation. . . . Faith comes not by signs, but by *hearing* the word of God."[2] I believe this literally. So I read the scriptures aloud. And I listen at every opportunity to the words of living prophets. General conference is my favorite fountain!

Find a time to spend with the scriptures. We get caught up in saving time, doing things faster and faster. Why? We only have now, this moment. Yet, paradoxically, we can *give* this moment to someone who needs our time. And we can *take* time to do whatever we choose. We can even choose to waste time, to squander it on inane TV programs or silly novels. (By the way, a nap is not squandering time!) We each have 24 hours a day. I asked my mathematically gifted daughter, Emily, just how many waking hours we had in a month. In a nanosecond she told me an average of 540 hours. After your family, can you think of any better use for your time each month than the 2 hours you spend visiting teaching? 2 hours out of 540! I warmed to the task. How many minutes in a day? Emily reported 1,080 waking minutes. With more than 1,000 minutes, can you find 15 to 30 uninterrupted minutes to read and ponder the good word of your Heavenly Father each day? Start with one minute and work up.

Okay, you say, when?

I believe in dovetailing activities. It seems to have caught on. They call it multitasking now. I find listening to the scriptures on CDs or tapes when I am alone in my car or walking works well. Many of us make time for exercising. I read on the treadmill. I love that treadmill bookrack!

When do you begin reading scriptures to children? Perhaps the same time that you start whispering to them of Jesus during the sacrament—on the day they are blessed. Read aloud to your nursing baby or to your toddlers. They will look at you knowingly, and you'll wonder what they know that they're not telling. Help them grow reaccustomed to these beautiful words, this godly language. This sweet familiarity will breed a burgeoning love for the good word of God, even before they can talk. It will all sound familiar.

I tried reading Isaiah to 8-month-old Ryan, who was trying to take his first steps:

"They that wait upon the Lord shall renew their strength; they shall mount up with wings as eagles; they shall run, and not be weary; and they shall walk, and not faint" (Isaiah 40:31). This scripture fit his circumstance, but I think he would have enjoyed almost anything I read to him, as long as we locked eyes.

You can **read with your family** regularly at mealtime. Dovetail. Jewish parents give a drop of honey to a child as he begins to read the Torah to insure that reading the scriptures will be sweet. Good, home cooking is like that honey. Choose a meal, any meal when you are all home, and take turns reading: before, during, or after eating. As our children began leaving home on missions and to marry, we read after dinner each evening. I remember once when our Navajo son, Larry, took his turn reading, put down the book, and exclaimed, "This is REALLY GOOD STUFF." Now that Truman and I are alone, we read the Book of Mormon right after breakfast and it's still "really good stuff." Sweet as honey!

Our daughter Mindy's family does SS&P—Scripture, Song, and Prayer—just before bedtime, at home, on vacation, or at our house. It's completely portable. Every night they sing one song or hymn and read one scripture verse or more, teaching as they go. Then they kneel in family prayer. I remember when they were all pre-baptismal age, their father asked, after reading one verse, "So what does *repent* mean?" Excited answers included: "It means turning back. It means doing good instead of bad." You could tell they had been taught. Their discussions have lengthened as their testimonies have grown.

I read with a friend early in the day. Shirley and I read on the phone 15 to 20 minutes most weekday mornings, then launch into our day. We've been doing this for more than 30 years. We visit for a moment or two. We take turns praying for the Spirit to be part of our enterprise, and then we read aloud to each other. So many times we exclaim how a scripture answers today's pressing need. One morning she told me of one of her son's questions asked the night before. Then we read D&C 124:109–116, and each of his questions was answered. I wrote his name next to each verse that had his answer in it. Coincidence? No. Miracle. Yes. We shouldn't be surprised at how often such answers have come over these many years.

Pray each time you pick up these amazing books. Ask to understand, to see your daily problems as God sees them, and to be able to liken all scriptures to yourself as Nephi directed his people. The scriptures give us a panoramic perspective: an endless, wide-angle view. You will develop a template that will help with each day's decisions. You will come to know that miracles take time, but they happen.

Learn by heart. Robert Frost speaks of learning by heart in his poem called "Choose Something Like a Star." Addressing a star, he implores:

Say something to us we can learn
By heart and when alone repeat.[3]

That idea has blessed my life. Memorize the beautiful words you just can't leave on the page.

"Peace I leave with you, my peace I give unto you" (John 14:27).

How often I have said those words to myself to find the peace I was lacking. I learned more about memorizing from Susan Tanner in her address to the BYU graduates in 2004. Following her lead, I invited our children and grandchildren to a family home evening to celebrate my husband's birthday. I asked them to each bring a memorized gift, some words that they loved. When our returned-missionary grandson Rob took his turn, he had memorized all of 1 John 4. We were riveted as he spoke with such personal understanding the words he had stored in his heart to share.

Prophecy is the poetry of God. Speak it by heart, "and when alone repeat." Like lovely strains of music calm us, so can this special poetry God has preserved for us. Why not carry it always written in your heart to draw upon in the moment when you need it?

We are all teachers. I started to say that my study of scriptures is different because teaching is my profession. But that's not so at all. We are all teachers and can be tutored daily by the greatest Teacher of all time, Jesus Christ. He taught Adam, Abraham, Moses, Isaiah, and Joseph Smith. And He teaches us. As we learn, He expects us to teach each other.

How did Jesus tutor Joseph Smith? With the scriptures. Remember in the First Vision when Jesus told Joseph, "They draw near to me with their lips, but their hearts are far from me"? (Joseph Smith—History 1:19). That was straight out of Isaiah (see Isaiah 29:13). The angel that came next to tutor young Joseph was a keeper of scriptural records; Moroni, who used the same method, quoted Malachi and Peter's words to school the youthful prophet. We can access this same process. We have the texts for the course.

What can we discover in the scriptures? What will YOU find? What you need!

I have found the Lord, Jesus Christ, and how it feels to bask in His light. We love Him more and more as we discover in the lines of His books how much He loves us without reservation and without ceasing.

"Who shall separate us from the love of Christ? . . . I am persuaded, that neither death, nor life, nor angels, nor principalities, nor powers, nor things present, nor things to come, nor height, nor depth, nor any other creature, shall be able to separate us from the love of God, which is in Christ Jesus our Lord" (Romans 8:35, 38–39).

I have learned that when we know we are beloved sons and daughters of a Heavenly Father, we learn how to see one another with new eyes as close kin, truly beloved brothers and sisters. "Beloved." Have you ever noticed how many times we are addressed as "beloved" in the scriptures? The computer counted 166 times. Mormon, Moroni, and Nephi address even their enemies as "beloved." How often do you address those around you as "beloved"? Try it; it feels good.

We learn how to talk to each other, with kindness and love, never demeaning, but seeing each other's godly capacity. Such wonderful ideas: persuasion, long-suffering, gentleness, meekness, love unfeigned, and even an increase of love to prove that our faithfulness is stronger than the cords of death (see D&C 121:41–44).

We learn how to feel Heavenly Father's love. There is a difference between knowing you are loved and feeling it. My stake president often counsels us in these words: "Never begin your day without first coming to our Heavenly Father in prayer, and stay on your knees until you feel the arms of His love around you." I testify that such a feeling is real, tangible, and possible for each of us. We can seek it each morning of our lives. What a sweet quest each day as we remain on our knees until we feel God's love.

We can learn how to forgive. Jesus taught us volumes in His few words from the cross: "Father, forgive them; for they know not what they do" (Luke 23:34). How grateful I am that someone wrote that down. The scriptures are the gateway, the key to personal revelation. When we need to know, we must go through the gate and use the key.

May I conclude with a personal experience and testimony.

Realizing that all of us are constantly in the process of forgiving, I posted a sign on my refrigerator:

FORGIVE EVERYONE, EVERYTHING, EVERY TIME.
LET IT GO!

But the sign didn't work! Sometimes I still fail to forgive. Others seldom realize how they have hurt us. But we know. We can jettison those feelings, helping to heal our own hurt, subtracting it from our hearts, making room for Christ's love that can complete the healing process. It is always our turn where forgiveness is concerned. There are people right now, some even in the spirit world, whom I am in the process of forgiving. A few weeks ago I was searching the scriptures for help. I was a bit abashed when I came upon Moroni 7:44 and read again that a man or woman must have charity—perfect love—or he or she is nothing: zero. So I searched more earnestly to see what having charity really meant, and it suddenly seemed vitally important to know each detail. I love that feeling of immediacy that comes when I realize that a scripture is written just for me. I read slowly, carefully unpacking the words as I went along.

"And charity suffereth long, and is kind, and envieth not, and is not puffed up, seeketh not her own, is not easily provoked, thinketh no evil, and rejoiceth not in iniquity but rejoiceth in the truth" (Moroni 7:45).

The word *truth* jumped off the page. I could see that I had been collecting grievances, rejoicing in iniquity, but I should have been rejoicing in the truth. Then another scripture came brightly to mind:

"Truth is knowledge of things as they are, and as they were, and as they are to come; and whatsoever is more or less than this is the spirit of that wicked one who was a liar from the beginning. The Spirit of truth is of God" (D&C 93:24–26).

And the voice in my heart was saying, "Truth is things as they are now! 'That wicked one' tries to hide our present truth from us. Live in the now, Ann; you're different than you were when you felt that pain and blame. You're stronger now. You're different. That pain is ancient history. The people you blamed are also different, probably better."

Nearly 50 years ago I embroidered a sampler as I awaited the birth of our youngest daughter. It now hangs in her home. "Look not sorrowfully into the past, it comes not back again. Wisely improve the present, it is thine." I've watched her live that. Signs do work! So discard the past, things "as they were." Painful wounds can be healed. Christ is the physician here. You are His fully participating patient. Your forgiveness becomes a bridge over which you will one day walk to meet those whom you have forgiven, and you will greet them in love. Look up, Ann, with "a perfect brightness of hope" (2 Nephi 31:20). See yourself whole and holy. See those you seek to forgive whole and holy, meeting you on that bridge. Trust and have faith in things "as they are to come." Hope and faith in the Lord Jesus Christ walk hand in hand. They are our tools for shaping the future.

In this process of forgiveness and repentance I rejoice in the words of Moroni, which instruct me perfectly:

"Wherefore, my beloved [there it is again] brethren [or sisters], pray unto the Father with all the energy of heart, that ye may be filled with this love, which he hath bestowed upon all who are *true followers* of his Son, Jesus Christ; that ye may become the sons [or daughters] of God; that when he shall appear we shall be like him, for we shall see him as he is; that we may have this hope; that we may be purified even as he is pure" (Moroni 7:48; emphasis added).

When our minds are stocked with scriptures, they become the language of our revelations. Do you see? Scriptures stored in our hearts enter our prayers effortlessly. We speak God's language back to Him.

The scriptures fill us with God's love. When we are "true followers" of Jesus Christ we provide a loving context, a circle of love, for those whose lives touch ours, and our own love level is increasing. We become each other's safe place. We learn to love better by loving better. Ever so slowly we are filled to overflowing. There is not room enough to receive. This is charity, the pure love of Christ. Once in a quiet garden I knew this feeling in a remarkable way. I testify it is real! As Alma knew and taught, "[It] is sweet above all that is sweet, and . . . white above all that is white, yea, and pure above all that is pure; and [we can] feast upon this . . . even until [we] are filled, [and never] hunger [or] thirst [again]" (Alma 32:42). It has become "a well of water springing up into everlasting life" (John 4:14). I cannot say the smallest part that I feel.

I know "that which is of God is light" (D&C 50:24). Keep looking up to that light—to Christ. Look inside by that light. Look away from darkness and despair towards that perfect brightness of hope, which can light your way.

We each need our own light. Ask for it, plead for it, not just in your extremity but daily. Keep your scriptures open. Let the scriptures shine their flood of light into your life.

NOTES

1. Spencer W. Kimball, *The Teachings of Spencer W. Kimball,* ed. Edward L. Kimball (Salt Lake City: Bookcraft, 1982), 135.

2. Joseph Smith, *History of The Church of Jesus Christ of Latter-day Saints,* ed. B. H. Roberts, 2d ed. rev., 7 vols. (Salt Lake City: The Church of Jesus Christ of Latter-day Saints, 1932–51), 3:379.

3. Robert Frost, *Robert Frost's Poems* (New York: St. Martin's Press, 2002), 257.

"I Tried to Do Everything Right But . . ."

Nora Nyland

Almost ten years ago, a distraught father came into my office. He was distressed because his daughter had not been accepted into our dietetics program. After a long discussion of why he felt this was unfair to his daughter, he said, "We've always taught our children that if they do *a* and *b* they'll get *c*." Now, I can't remember what I said to him, but it was far more polite than what I was thinking. Because I was thinking, "And on what planet does that work?"

As I thought about this father's statement, I finally realized what was so faulty about it—he was talking about little *a*, little *b*, and little *c*. You really don't have to live very long to realize that doing *a* plus *b* often doesn't equal *c* in this mortal existence. Lest you think me a pessimist, let me assure you that I am chronically optimistic—I truly expect good outcomes most of the time. I am also, though, chronically realistic, which means I know that sometimes outcomes are far different from what we expected or wanted.

I want to assure you, however, that I know with every fiber of my being that big A plus big B equals big C. In other words, in the grand and eternal plan of happiness, I have no doubt whatsoever that $A + B = C$;

Nora Nyland is the director of the dietetics program at Brigham Young University and an associate professor in the Department of Nutrition, Dietetics, and Food Science. She serves as a Relief Society teacher and enjoys gardening, sewing, and kaleidoscopes.

that our thoughts, choices, attitudes, and actions will be rewarded in exactly the appropriate and fair manner. Only in the next life will justice and mercy be perfectly applied by our perfect Savior.

"And now, the plan of mercy could not be brought about except an atonement should be made; therefore God himself atoneth for the sins of the world, to bring about the plan of mercy, to appease the demands of justice, that God might be a perfect, just God, and a merciful God also. . . . What, do ye suppose that mercy can rob justice? I say unto you, Nay; not one whit. If so, God would cease to be God" (Alma 42:15, 25).

I've observed that, as mortals, we tend to want perfect mercy exercised in our behalf and perfect justice in everyone else's. No one in this mortal sphere has the ability to judge perfectly; therefore justice and mercy will seldom be perfectly meted out—either by ourselves or by others. This is just one reason that little a plus little b sometimes equals q instead of c.

In the larger equation, big C is celestial life, the outcome we want to attain. Big A is our antemortal existence, our pre-earth life, or our first estate (see Abraham 3:26). We know we made some correct choices then because we are here now. Your patriarchal blessing is about the only place, outside of scriptures and prophetic statements, where you get a glimpse of that premortal life. For many years I typed patriarchal blessings for my father, and phrases such as "because of your diligence in defending truth," or "you stood squarely on the side of the Savior," or "you have proved faithful before coming to this earth" often preceded a statement about a blessing or opportunity in this life.

Back to the equation, where the big B stands for body time, our mortal existence, or our second estate (see Abraham 3:26). This is such a small piece in the entire spectrum of our existence, but how large it seems and how important it is. It is in big B that we make covenants and receive ordinances. It is in big B that we demonstrate our worthiness to live with Heavenly Father again, and it is in big B that we develop the attributes of godhood by how we deal with the fact that little a plus little b doesn't always equal little c.

One of the best ways to make ourselves miserable is to expect that we can protect ourselves from the experiences of mortality by doing little a and little b just right. Abraham learned that life on earth was intended to

be a test: "We will go down, for there is space there, and we will take of
these materials, and we will make an earth whereon these may dwell; and
we will prove them herewith, to see if they will do all things whatsoever
the Lord their God shall command them" (Abraham 3:24–25). Now, what
kind of a test would it be if every good act were immediately rewarded and
every evil act immediately punished? It would require no determination,
faith, or, frankly, many brains, to do everything we are commanded to do
in that system. If it were fair, it wouldn't be a test!

Apparently, we really liked this plan—enough to shout for joy (see Job
38:7)—and thought that the opportunity to be tested would be wonderful.
So why do we have such a hard time with the concept now? I think we
are a little bit like my darling 6-year-old great-nephew, Sam. Sam's family
had a family home evening lesson about the blessing of having bodies.
About a week later, Sam smashed his fingers in the sliding patio door. His
screams of pain brought his mother, Lynnette, running from the basement.
Amidst his tears he cried, "Why did I tell Heavenly Father that I wanted
a body?" Lynnette replied that if he didn't have a body he wouldn't be in
their family. To which Sam exclaimed, "I know, but I didn't know about
doors and owies!"

Owies! Life is full of them. A friend and I frequently joke that as spirit
beings who had never had a clock and never felt pain, we may have been
a bit naïve when we said, "Eighty years of mortal challenges? Sure, I can
do that. Piece of cake!" Perhaps we didn't really understand about doors
and owies.

For just a moment, please close your eyes and complete this sentence:
"I tried to do everything right, but . . . (now fill in the blank)." You may
have finished the sentence with something inconsequential but still irk-
some, like the recipe didn't turn out, or the computer program wouldn't
work, or the plant died. You may have finished with something far more
painful, such as I'm still not married, I have no children, my child left the
Church, my marriage fell apart, I have cancer, or I lost my home. If we
really got to choose, we wouldn't ask for any of those or the myriad other
things that might have completed the sentence.

It is very natural to feel a bit put upon or let down when our best,
righteous efforts do not result in what we perceive as the prize. Somehow,
we think something must be wrong; that someone or something is against

us personally. Peter's response to that is "Think it not strange concerning the fiery trial which is to try you, as though some strange thing happened unto you: but rejoice, inasmuch as ye are partakers of Christ's sufferings; that, when his glory shall be revealed, ye may be glad also with exceeding joy" (1 Peter 4:12–13). Little *a, b,* and *c* subsumed in big *B.*

I love the account of Brigham Young's secretary asking him, "President Young, why is it that the Lord is not always at our side promoting universal happiness and seeing to it that the needs of people are met, caring especially for His Saints? Why is it so difficult at times?" Before I give you Brigham Young's answer, think for a moment about what the people had been through. They had been in the Salt Lake Valley about ten years. Remember all the problems they had with building the temple. What endeavor could have been more righteous than that? Remember the persecutions in Ohio, Missouri, and Nauvoo. Remember the treacherous trek across the plains. Remember that all these things were happening to people who were trying their best to live the gospel. The secretary's question, "Why is it so difficult at times?" seems a very logical one to me. President Young responded, "Because man is destined to be a God, and he must be able to demonstrate that he is for God and to develop his own resources so that he can act independently and yet humbly. . . . It is the way it is because we must learn to be righteous in the dark."[1]

Joseph Smith was certainly in a dark place when from the depths of Liberty Jail he asked, "O God, where art thou? And where is the pavilion that covereth thy hiding place?" (D&C 121:1). His impassioned prayer was answered: "My son, peace be unto thy soul; thine adversity and thine afflictions shall be but a small moment; and then, if thou endure it well, God shall exalt thee on high" (D&C 121:7–8). In the next section, Joseph is told, "Know thou, my son, that all these things shall give thee experience, and shall be for thy good" (D&C 122:7).

I hope I'm not the only one who sometimes thinks, "I don't really want this much experience, thank you." Or, "This small moment is dragging on forever!" But the truth is, once they're over, I wouldn't trade any of my trials because of things I learn and ways I grow in getting through them.

Several years ago I asked a psychologist to speak to my class about stress management. She said something very simple but very profound,

"Life isn't fair, but it's real." I've thought about that a lot, and I realize that if we spend all of our energy railing against the unfairness, we have no energy left to deal with the reality. How much happier and more productive we can be if we simply let go of the fact that there will be unfairness and inequities in life and focus instead on how we will deal with the various circumstances of our lives.

In a conference address in 1989, Elder Ronald E. Poelman said:

"Adversity in the lives of the obedient and faithful may be the consequence of disease, accidental injury, ignorance, or the influence of the adversary. To preserve free agency, the Lord also at times permits the righteous to suffer the consequences of evil acts by others."[2]

None of the causes of adversity Elder Poelman lists is fair, but each is real. Each can disrupt the little *a* plus little *b* equals *c* scenario. Especially painful are the times when the difficult circumstances we face, despite our best efforts, are the result of someone else's agency. How ultimately fair it is, however, that the Lord does not restrict anyone's agency. Each person has the opportunity to prove him or herself faithful or not, true or not, worthy of eternal life and exaltation or not.

Let me interject something here. I am in no way suggesting that planning and working for things we want to attain in this life are futile. The most likely way to reach goals and accomplish many good things is to attend to *a* and *b*. We simply need to stop assuming that we can control every outcome by our own efforts. Our efforts are often tempered by the decisions, actions, and choices of others—and those decisions, actions, and choices don't have to be evil or wrong to affect us. For instance, too many good candidates for graduate school or the plum job means that some very fine people won't be accepted or get the job. Our efforts are also affected by physics (two objects can't occupy the same space at the same time, hence a crash), by laws of genetics (most people won't be 6-foot, 7-inch basketball stars; others will be prone to certain diseases), by physiology (chemicals can become unbalanced, arteries can clog, and joints can wear out), and by human nature (people can wrong us). The issue isn't that these things happen; it is how we deal with them when they do.

I wish I had a succinct, foolproof list of how to deal with life's unfairness, but I don't. Here are a few thoughts, though. One thing that may help us deal with life is avoiding the tendency to assume that when life gets hard, it's because we did something wrong. Now, occasionally that is the case, and the principle of repentance can help us remedy the situation. Guilt is an extraordinarily useful tool. Its function is much like the function of physical pain—it's intended to stop us. The pain of touching a hot stove causes us to pull back and, hopefully, avoid that action in the future. Guilt, too, should make us pull back and repent. Wallowing in guilt or self-doubt, however, is like leaving our hand on the stove indefinitely—not its intended purpose and far more painful than necessary.

I hadn't intended to be this personal, but a personal example illustrates what I mean. When I was fourteen years old, I received my patriarchal blessing. In that blessing I am told, "Through your faith and your devotion and your worthiness, you will find a suitable companion and receive a beautiful temple marriage. . . ." I am now fifty-two years old, and I have never been married. In the thirty-eight years since receiving my blessing, I simply have not met my suitable companion. First let me tell you that it would be dishonest to say that my marital status has never bothered me or that it hadn't occurred to me that I did *a* and I did *b,* but I haven't got *c.* It would also be dishonest to say that my marital status has bothered me a lot or that I think I've been cheated. I told you I'm an optimistic, happy person, and I simply have too many blessings to spend time focusing on the ones I don't have.

Anyway, the real point I want to make is this: I could have spent the last twenty-five years endlessly worrying about whether I was lacking faith, devotion, and worthiness—the three attributes mentioned in connection with temple marriage. I certainly know women who have literally paralyzed their progress agonizing over the reason they're not married. I didn't want to do that. Instead I have carefully pondered about faith, devotion, and worthiness and prayed earnestly that I would incorporate them fully in my life and be aware of anything that needed changing. Then I went about using them, not worrying about them. Picking at scabs doesn't help anything heal.

Another important thing we can do is remember that when seen in its entirety, life *is* fair: the big A (premortal life) plus a righteously lived big B (mortal life) really does equal big C (celestial life). In the short term, *many* things work together for our good, but ultimately, Paul tells us, "we know that *all* things work together for good to them that love God"

(Romans 8:28; emphasis added). All of our efforts to keep the commandments, be true to our covenants, and follow the Savior will be rewarded with eternal life, however hard the struggle here.

In Lehi's vision of the tree of life, he saw "a tree, whose fruit was desirable to make one happy" (1 Nephi 8:10). He also saw an iron rod and a straight and narrow path by the rod leading to that tree. Later, Nephi learned that the tree represented the love of God, which "is the most desirable above all things" (1 Nephi 11:22), and that the iron rod was the word of God, which we obtain from the words of the prophets—ancient or modern (see 1 Nephi 11:25). Lehi further saw "a mist of darkness; yea, even an exceedingly great mist of darkness, insomuch that they who had commenced in the path did lose their way, that they wandered off and were lost" (1 Nephi 8:23). From Nephi we learn that "the mists of darkness are the temptations of the devil, which blindeth the eyes, and hardeneth the hearts of the children of men, and leadeth them away into broad roads, that they perish and are lost" (1 Nephi 12:17).

Satan's goal is to disrupt our grasp on the rod and our trip on the narrow path. It really makes no difference to him how he does that. The mega sins are certainly flashy and eternally lethal, but he doesn't need to use them if smaller things like disillusionment, discouragement, or despondency over life's difficulties will accomplish the same thing.

We simply cannot lose sight of the eternal nature of our mortal tests. In Romans 8 we read:

"Who shall separate us from the love of Christ? shall tribulation, or distress, or persecution, or famine, or nakedness, or peril, or sword? . . . Nay, in all these things we are more than conquerors through him that loved us. For I am persuaded, that neither death, nor life, nor angels, nor principalities, nor powers, nor things present, nor things to come, nor height, nor depth, nor any other creature, shall be able to separate us from the love of God, which is in Christ Jesus our Lord" (Romans 8:35, 37–39).

That says to me that the only thing that will keep us from the love of God, that most precious and desirable of all things, is ourselves. No life circumstance is powerful enough to draw us away unless we let go of the rod.

Even knowing that, though, doesn't make life a snap. We often find ourselves in need of hope and peace when we might be discouraged by life's events. Placing our trust firmly in the Lord helps. In the October 2004 general conference, President James E. Faust said:

"In an increasingly unjust world, to survive and even to find happiness and joy, no matter what comes, we must make our stand unequivocally with the Lord. We need to try to be faithful every hour of every day so that our foundation of trust in the Lord will never be shaken. . . . The way to find joy in this life is to resolve, like Job, to endure all for God and His work. By so doing we will receive the infinite, priceless joy of being with our Savior in the eternities."[3]

That trust can increase our patience. Elder Neal A. Maxwell said:

"Patient endurance is to be distinguished from merely being 'acted upon.' Endurance is more than pacing up and down within the cell of our circumstance; it is not only acceptance of the things allotted to us, it is to 'act for ourselves' by magnifying what is allotted to us. (See Alma 29:3, 6.)

"If, for instance, we are always taking our temperature to see if we are happy, we will not be. If we are constantly comparing to see if things are fair, we are not only being unrealistic, we are being unfair to ourselves."[4]

C. S. Lewis's observation captures this realistic trust: "We are not necessarily doubting that God will do the best for us; we are wondering how painful the best will turn out to be."[5]

One reason we have trouble with life's difficulties is that we think we should somehow be exempt from them. A friend of mine overheard an exchange between an Asian student and a department secretary regarding some department policy. Each time the secretary tried to explain what the rule was, he countered with what he wanted to do instead. She finally said that this was simply the policy, to which he replied, "Yes, but I am looking for exception." Heavenly Father loves us too much to let us be exceptions—He won't let us skip the very experiences that will develop our faith, refine our characters, and teach us celestial lessons. He didn't exempt Nephi, who said, "And I did not murmur against the Lord because of mine afflictions" (1 Nephi 18:16); He didn't exempt Paul, who noted, "I reckon that the sufferings of this present time are not worthy to be compared with the glory which shall be revealed in us" (Romans 8:18); and He won't exempt you.

Elder Joseph B. Wirthlin in October 2004 general conference said:

"The question 'Why me?' can be a difficult one to answer and often leads to frustration and despair. There is a better question to ask ourselves. That question is 'What could I learn from this experience?' The way we answer that question may determine the quality of our lives not only on this earth but also in the eternities to come. Though our trials are diverse, there is one thing the Lord expects of us no matter our difficulties and sorrows: He expects us to press on."[6]

Elder Wirthlin said, "Knowing who we are, we should never give up the goal of achieving our eternal destiny."[7] He then suggests that three things to help us press on are testimony, humility, and repentance.

Humility is crucial to learning from our experiences. Recognizing our dependence on the Lord for strength and deliverance is probably the first step in receiving them. We can't very well feel humble and angry at the same time. I love this story shared by Elder Maxwell several years ago:

"The spiritual submissiveness which is central to the blessings of the Atonement was well exemplified by Melissa Howes as she led her family in prayer a short while before her father died of cancer. Melissa was only 9 and her father 43. Consider unselfish Melissa Howes's pleading, in her own words as reported to me by her mother: 'Heavenly Father, bless my daddy, and if you need to take him and need him more than us, you can have him. We want him, but Thy will be done. And please help us not to be mad at you.'"[8]

What a beautiful, simple, and honest prayer—"Help us not to be mad at you." I can't imagine that Melissa's prayer for perspective went unanswered, and I can't imagine that similar pleadings from our lips would go unanswered. That type of prayer allows us, regardless of circumstances, to have "the peace of God, which passeth all understanding" (Philippians 4:7). That peace is one of the miracles of the Spirit, and I think it is reserved for our humble and meek moments.

Sisters, mortal life isn't fair, but it's real. When we understand things as they really are, though, real in the sense of divine destiny and eternal expectations, we can weather the unfairness. Because pain is part of the process of perfection, we can expect that we will experience pain of various kinds in this life. I've spoken a lot about the fact that in the eternities we can expect complete fairness and ultimate rewards for our righteous behavior. Paradoxically, we can still be happy, cheerful, pleasant, and joyful right now despite the pains. Our hope for a brighter day should never cloud the view of this day. We live in a beautiful world full of opportunities and challenges, promises and perils. The gospel of Jesus Christ and His Atonement hold the keys for happiness now and happiness eternally. King Benjamin points this out when he says, "And moreover, I would desire that ye should consider on the blessed and happy state of those that keep the commandments of God. For behold, they are blessed in all things, both temporal and spiritual; and if they hold out faithful to the end they are received into heaven, that thereby they may dwell with God in a state of never-ending happiness. O remember, remember that these things are true; for the Lord God hath spoken it" (Mosiah 2:41).

The Savior has overcome the world so that we can overcome the world. I testify with Alma "that whosoever shall put their trust in God shall be supported in their trials, and their troubles, and their afflictions, and shall be lifted up at the last day" (Alma 36:3).

NOTES

1. Brigham Young's Office Journal, 28 January 1857.
2. Ronald E. Poelman, "Adversity and the Divine Purpose of Mortality," *Ensign*, May 1989, 23.
3. James E. Faust, "Where Do I Make My Stand?" *Ensign*, November 2004, 18, 21.
4. Neal A. Maxwell, "Endure It Well," *Ensign*, May 1990, 33–34.
5. C. S. Lewis, *The Quotable Lewis* (Wheaton, Ill.: Tyndale House Publishers, Inc., 1989), 469.
6. Joseph B. Wirthlin, "Press On," *Ensign*, November 2004, 101.
7. Wirthlin, *Ensign*, November 2004, 104.
8. Neal A. Maxwell, "Testifying of the Great and Glorious Atonement," *Ensign*, October 2001, 14.

Facing Economic Challenges with Provident Living

Jan R. Van Orman

I am pleased to speak to you today on a topic that has deeply affected my belief and my life. During all of my professional and Church service I've worked closely with people who face economic challenges. I've faced a few challenges of my own. As I've studied and pondered the plight of poverty and hardship I've come to believe that we really don't understand economic adversity and what it is supposed to teach us. Because there is so much adversity, it ought to be good for something! I find answers in the doctrine of provident living.

I say this is a doctrine of belief because provident living establishes principles and practices that are fundamental to our becoming like Christ. Indeed, the Savior's life epitomized this lifestyle. Living providently means simply to live as the Lord intends. Obviously—and worth remembering—is that if we learn the right lessons, happiness will follow. To me the term provident living is more encompassing and whole than a term we hear a lot today—self-reliance. Self-reliance is confusing because life isn't about "self"—it's about family and community; and we all rely greatly upon one

Jan R. Van Orman is the assistant international vice president at Brigham Young University and a former field officer of the Inter-American Foundation, a U.S. government foreign assistance agency. He has been a consultant to various international development organizations, including the World Bank and U.S. Agency for International Development. He and his wife raised their family of five daughters and a son in Washington, D.C. He has also served as a mission president in Brazil.

another, and especially upon the Lord. A privilege of mortality is to learn how to share our life with others. So, I would like to share some powerful lessons that I have learned through unique experience. They show that many of life's challenges can be overcome by following a simple formula of actively enlarging[1] what we have, then giving it away. The trick is to understand this equation and to keep it in balance.

Well-being is really about perspective. It isn't a state that we attain, but a purposeful way of living that *can* change our circumstances, and surely *will* change who we are. It changes our attitude and our heart to become more like Heavenly Father's. And this is the real objective of provident living.

Let me give you an example told to me by Tim Sloan, the director of LDS Employment Resources Services. As a missionary, Brother Sloan was sent to take the gospel to the indigenous people of Bolivia. He and his companion were blessed to see many converts among the believing Quechua Indians, who live about as modest a lifestyle as any people on earth. As they embraced the Church, Brother Sloan and his companion, who served as the branch president, noted that these impoverished Saints not only faithfully paid their tithes, but also donated fast offerings. The first reaction of the young elders was to tell these poor new members, "It's okay, you don't need to pay fast offerings." They thought, "You're the ones who should be receiving fast offerings." Then the missionaries realized that these humble people didn't know they were poor! Sharing what they had with others was the way they lived. Even though they had so little material wealth, they made do and—this is the important point—they were united and happy.

Perhaps this is a secular version of Zion. Do you know that the richest Americans donate, on average, less than two percent of their income to charity, while people who live below the poverty line donate, on average, more than six percent of their meager means?[2] It seems an irony that those who are most concerned for the poor are poor people themselves. Clearly, giving has less to do with what we have than with how we feel and act toward others in our daily lives.

Most of my career I worked with the poor in Latin America and the Caribbean. It is probably no surprise to you that women were the inspiration and energy behind many of the hundreds of self-help projects that I visited and tried to assist. Women often see brighter possibilities and are willing to strive for them with great courage. They certainly exemplify the exalting traits of perseverance and sacrifice. Perhaps women understand intuitively what is really important in life.

In my work in foreign aid I was not an administrator, but worked directly with poor, grassroots community groups of all kinds. I became well acquainted with slums and rural villages and met people in their hovels and huts. I sat on their dirt floors and ate modest meals with them. I saw how they lived and worked together. I listened to their stories and saw how they deal with hardship. I learned from them. What they taught me was profound.

Let me show you four pictures to share some of the important things I learned from sisters who get along while living at the bottom of society. These are real pictures, not glamour shots. For each of these people this was the first time anyone had ever taken their picture.

This photo is stark in its appearance and indicates the conditions in which these Queché women live. But the photo is powerful in its meaning. These women live in mud huts, as you see. They have no electricity or running water, no stores or grocery supply. However, you can see that they are burying a loved one in a rather fancy coffin. There are seven bouquets of flowers around it. In front you see the ceremonial altar they made.

One of the early lessons I learned in visiting poor communities to discuss their self-help projects was about "the burial fund." I could easily see the merit of buying pipes for water, or getting seeds to plant, or starting a revolving credit fund. But the first group that asked me to help them begin a small burial fund must have wondered at my incredulity. I thought, "There's no return on that investment! That doesn't improve anyone's life! You can't help the dead!" What I didn't understand is that what poor people value most is people. Like the pharaohs of old, they make great sacrifice to send loved ones from this world with dignity and tribute, anticipating a praiseworthy reuniting one day. One of the few things poor people possess that the world cannot take from them is their dignity and honor. To them a person's honor is their wealth. Their stature and value grows from respect they show to relatives and friends. Burial is the last earthly sacrifice they can make to affirm and dignify this relationship.

I learned from these humble Queché that every soul has dignity and that we are all equal. Among the poor, there is a willingness to sacrifice for others that is uncommon in wealthy society. For the poor, life is not about one's temporal condition, but how we act our part. These illiterate women instinctively know that family is enduring and their relationships are eternal. Although they do not know of the restored gospel, they honor to the fullest their personal relationships. This respect grows from a powerful faith in a divine Father, which faith gives them power.

This young Ecuadorian mother is working on a loom practicing an art that dates back thousands of years. Notice the pride she takes in her task and the detail of her work. She is a talented artisan whose trade honors her traditions and earns a little income for her family. You see her daughter learning from her—watching and working alongside. Where there are few schools and life is hard, parents teach their children who they are and how to work. Children learn to contribute to the well-being of their family. Even though life is challenging, they get by. They are proud of their heritage and enjoy a harmonious life.

This woman is disciplined and skilled. She works very hard, like most women. I don't know how women, even in the best of circumstances, bear the multiple and neverending burdens placed upon them. But I do know that hard work is a founding principle of mortality—the second principle the Lord taught Father Adam and Mother Eve. This photo shows a sweet relationship between a parent and child. That relationship develops when parents teach their children to work and of their heritage. We all need to know who we are and to be taught how to fit meaningfully into our community. People who gain a sense of tradition and purpose gain beauty and meaning in their lives.

Here is a group of Mayan women—most of them are only about four feet tall. They are surrounded by the chickens that now provide them a living. See each woman lovingly holding a chicken? Except those who are afraid of the chickens—they're holding the eggs! This association of forty women started four years ago with 500 chicks. Today they have over 5,000 chickens and are known for producing top-quality eggs and for their traditional recipes. These women didn't know how to take care of chickens and had no idea how to collect or sell eggs. But, they relate, "With a little help, we learned."

Here's the story behind this poignant scene. For more than twenty years the Mayan villages in highland Guatemala were persecuted by para-military groups, and virtually all of the adult men were killed. The only people left in entire villages, like this one, were the very young and very old and the widows. Culture didn't prepare these women to head their households. It was their fathers, brothers, and husbands who had raised the crops, managed the money, and interacted with people outside the vil-lage. Women were not even taught Spanish because it was never imag-ined they would engage the outside society. Unexpectedly, they were caught in a devastating conflict between culture and calamity.

A few very sensitive local organizations gradually helped many of the isolated widows of the Guatemalan highlands. They were able to commu-nicate with these women through their children, who had learned Spanish in school. Little by little the widows organized self-help activities like this one and began to create a livelihood for themselves. If you look carefully, you can almost see a few smiles, even though it is quite unlike Indian women to be so demonstrative in public.

These women faced their adversity with great courage and creativity. They proved that even the most devastating tragedy can be overcome with sensitive cooperation. As they took responsibility for their predica-ment and learned new things, their efforts generated energy and lifted their confidence and self-esteem. They began to look to their future with new hope.

We all belong to a community—in reality, more than one. We need to learn to work together for what we need. Somehow people's efforts multiply when they're joined. By working together, many enterprising people accomplish miracles. Together they achieve dreams they scarcely dare to dream.

Lastly, this Haitian woman worked with her community to build the canal she now proudly crosses. It's one of the few functioning canals today in desperately poor Haiti. The project was planned and carried out by the people of her village—men, women, and children working side by side. It channels precious water for cooking, bathing, irrigation, and storage in a small reservoir.

She is wearing the only dress she owns. Note that it is clean and proper, as is she. Disadvantaged does not mean dirty or undignified. Although she is very poor, you can see her self-respect. To me, this is a classic photo of human dignity. Clearly this woman possesses courage and strength. She does not lament her life, but rejoices in improving it. She is the better for having contributed to this project. Together, her little community created new conditions that improve everyone's standard of living and open new possibilities. They learned the power of self-help and began a process that has generated momentum of its own. In the development vernacular, we say they have become "empowered."

Had some well-meaning international welfare or government group come in to build the canal, I don't think this Haitian woman would be standing quite so tall or would feel as confident about taking her future into her own hands. We see the positive result of her exercising her agency.

So, we learn that people don't need wealth to be dignified and take charge of their future. People gain courage and competence as they exercise their will and work together. In the end, we are each responsible for our own happiness. We come to realize that happiness is less dependent upon material things than we sometimes imagine.

Let me refer again to the doctrine of provident living. It can be described in a simple formula of receiving and giving. To use this formula for our benefit—that is, to overcome life's challenges—we must first understand perfectly the "receiving" part of the equation. Here are its principles:

• We depend upon God for our well-being (see Mosiah 4:5; 2 Nephi 2:5–7).

• Everything we have is the Lord's. He shares His creations with us (see D&C 104:14–15).

• We have not earned the things we enjoy; they come as gifts and blessings (see Mosiah 2:23–24; Alma 22:14; James 1:17).

• Since God gives us blessings freely, we should share them freely with others (see Matthew 10:8; Mosiah 18:28).

• God gives us blessings so we can learn wise stewardship and show our will to be like Him (see D&C 44:6; 52:40; 104:13; Mosiah 4:26).

Sisters, we don't control what we receive, but we are stewards of what we have. And everyone has valuable things to give—time, talents, our creativity; things we have learned; emotional support; sincere prayers. God has given us these resources and so much more, all so that we might share with others. Eternal blessings and happiness come as we willingly give what we have away. What we need to learn is to pass the gifts on. When we do, we build a bridge of charity and love within our families and neighborhoods. We link together.

So many women do this intuitively and with unceasing generosity. Bless you for this! I recognize that too often women receive too little appreciation for their gifts. However, let me observe that in the Lord's ledger a lack of recognition makes one's sacrifice more pure; therein, it becomes more perfecting. As people give, their worth is enlarged. They are not poor, because they have given to another. Giving is an act of charity that, by its very offering, affirms our worth.

Charity is a behavior that transforms us. Mormon called it "the pure love of Christ" (Moroni 7:47). Being charitable, we become more like our heavenly parents. Charity is serving our fellow woman, which is to serve God. It is being the good neighbor and Good Samaritan. Our pioneer forbears gave us such great examples of service and sacrifice. After all their hardship, they testify of gaining joy.

What I am trying to say is that "giving" is a key to facing economic challenges. It is easy in circumstances of need to focus on "receiving." But giving brings more happiness and is so much more useful. Another mistake we can make when facing economic challenges is, in our pridefulness, to take the attitude that we can go it alone. We don't invite others to help us. When we do this, we make it hard for others to give and for us to receive. Giving is the vital part of the perfecting formula—to receive and to give. This sanctifying exchange develops an attitude and lifestyle—in both the giver and the receiver—that counters the focus of today's world, which is far too much on physical things and personal needs. The world shines a glared focus on self. When we look at ourselves, we often stare at blemishes in the mirror. However, when we look away, it becomes possible to see others' needs. Without others, we cannot prosper.

I greatly respect the courageous women whose photos I have shown you. These are four among thousands upon thousands of similar stories. Do you know that approximately half of the earth's population lives in poverty today? These brothers and sisters have had to learn how to live in poverty and to "be well," simply because this is their life. There is no glamour in living simply. But there can be honor and even fulfillment in it. The great principles that edify and perfect can be practiced whatever a person's economic situation. I have been generously taught this by people who have so much less than I, but who give much more. They show us the basics of living providently. To be poor is not necessarily to be unhappy or unfulfilled. You have seen that those who have little are quite capable of progressing. Thus, happiness and progression become, in large part, a matter of one's perspective and expectations.

I really hope you can understand what I am trying to say—what these women have taught me about the process of living and improving one's life, even when circumstances are grim and unfair. Struggle gives us something in common with others who struggle—with the meek who inhabit and will inherit the earth. It brings us closer to compassion. It teaches the essence of charity.

Today many of you will participate in the great welfare projects of this conference. Many of you have and will participate in local church efforts to help the poor. What a wonderful gift you give. I hope your service will be especially meaningful to you. Let me urge you to also look close to home to find people *with* whom you can give—to reach out to your extended family and neighbors and to service groups in your community.

There is great personal growth and reward in helping people close around you, because with them—face-to-face—you must share a part of yourself.

I conclude by summarizing some simple wisdom—fundamental principles—taught by the world-class experts in provident living whose pictures we have seen.

1. Acting with noble dignity and courage, we gain respect for ourselves and others. Each of us is a child of God. He has given each of us unique and precious qualities with which we can prosper in our earthly sojourn. It is liberating to recognize that we don't have to be like someone else. It is comforting to remember that happiness comes from within.

2. We own and control our personal agency. What we do with what we have is up to us. We can usually do a lot more than we imagine. Work and struggle are not necessarily sorrow, but can be a pathway to discovery and self-esteem.

3. We can resolve many problems by working together. Where family is an incubator in which we learn the important things of life, community can be a catalyst for changing life's circumstances. To work together productively, we must esteem every person as ourselves; that is, treat everyone as equal, truly be our sister's sister. This is the wellspring for growth and perfection.

4. An abiding faith in a loving God brings strength to carry on. Let me quote a prophet, President Ezra Taft Benson, for you to understand how following Christ can bring perfection out of hardship:

"When you choose to follow Christ, you choose to be changed. . . .

"Can human hearts be changed? Why, of course! It happens every day in the great missionary work of the Church. It is one of the most widespread of Christ's modern miracles. . . .

"The Lord works from the inside out. The world works from the outside in. The world would take people out of the slums. Christ takes the slums out of people, and then *they take themselves* out of the slums."[3]

The Lord does not view hardship or poverty the way the world does. Neither does the Lord solve problems like many well-intended, but often misdirected, social intervention programs. God's ways are not our ways; and it is His way we are here to learn. There is great power that comes from exercising God-given agency and stewardship, from expanding our talents and gifts, and from learning to work in unity, as equals. One of the grounding scriptures on overcoming challenges is Doctrine and Covenants 104, where the Lord says, "It is my purpose to provide for my saints, . . . but it must needs be done in mine own way." And what is the Lord's way? He says "that the poor shall be exalted, in that the rich are made low" (verses 15–16).

Let me ask, are you "poor," or are you "rich"? I have pondered what you might be feeling today. I suspect that some have come to this session seeking help with large burdens. I can tell you that those women whose pictures you've seen have found blessings in struggling with and in overcoming their burdens. They found self-respect, purpose, and personal strength. They found unity and support. They are progressing. They are exercising their will and improving conditions for their own development and that of their families and neighbors. Somehow, they have risen above the things of the world and are bringing about good works, even in their humble circumstances. Their "being is well."

These women have balanced the equation of well-being by living providently. They give as much as they receive—maybe more. I sincerely believe that as we focus on giving we overcome many earthly challenges and temptations. I cannot explain how this happens with any worldly logic. But I can sincerely testify to you that this does happen, somehow, through the Lord's divine calculus.

May He bless you with burdens and opportunities, and in your efforts to overcome them majestically.

NOTES

1. "Enlargement" relates to fundamental principles taught in the Lord's parable of the talents (Matthew 25:14–30) and doctrine of perfection (Matthew 5:48), which directs us to magnify our gifts from God, to increase in learning, and to grow in wisdom.
2. Annual ranking of top philanthropists, *Business Week*, November 29, 2004, 90.
3. Ezra Taft Benson, "Born of God," *Ensign*, November 1985, 5–6; emphasis added.

"Bright As the Sun, This Heavenly Ray Lights Ev'ry Land Today"

Harriet Uchtdorf

My dear sisters, I love to attend the BYU Women's Conference. During *last* year's conference, I made plans to attend every session *this* year. I wanted to relax and listen and be uplifted. It never was part of my plan to be a presenter. But in the Church we learn to be flexible and learn to adjust *our* plans, right?

During general conference of October 2004, I had to learn not to make any more detailed plans for the rest of my life. In 1999 my husband and I were transferred from Europe to Church headquarters in Salt Lake City. I used to call our assignment in Salt Lake City our "overseas assignment," because I was expecting soon to go back to our homeland, Germany, back to our children and grandchildren, back to our longtime friends, back to our familiar environment, and back to our home, which we still kept.

In my mind's eye, I can see Heavenly Father smile down at me as I was making detailed plans for our future, not considering *His* timetable and *His* plans for us.

That October, on the Friday before general conference at about noon,

Harriet Uchtdorf received her bachelor's degree in business administration in Frankfurt, Germany, and worked with the public transportation department until she married Dieter Uchtdorf. Sister Uchtdorf has served in many callings in the Church and as an Institute teacher in Frankfurt. She and her husband have two children and five grandchildren.

my husband surprised me with a visit at home. He normally doesn't come home for lunch, but he called and said that he could be with me in a few minutes. I quickly prepared a light lunch. When my husband entered our house and looked into my eyes, he did not say one word, but I could feel in my heart and in my mind that he had been called to the holy apostleship. At this moment, the Spirit bore a strong testimony to me that this was the will of the Lord, and that our life would be changed forever. We spent a very special hour together in our home, sharing our innermost feelings, which included also moments of sacred turmoil. These were tender moments we enjoyed at our wonderful place of refuge and of defense. When my husband left for his office again, I knew with all my soul that he was truly called to be an Apostle of the Lord Jesus Christ.

Only a few days before, we were on our daily walk in our neighborhood and shared our thoughts that two new Apostles would be called during the upcoming general conference. We were curious who they might be. In our evening prayers, we asked Heavenly Father to bless and protect these new Apostles and their families and help them in this great transition. Little did we know or even guess who we were praying for. But I know of the power of prayer, and I know that your prayers have blessed us since this change came into our lives.

Alone at home I reflected on my life, our plans, the Lord's plan, and His timetable. My thoughts went back to when I was 12 years old. It was a sad time in my young life. My father had passed away from cancer. He was a great father, a loving husband—just a good man. He was very educated, spoke five languages, played professionally four different musical instruments in a symphony orchestra, and came from a prominent family of Frankfurt.

My parents had great plans for us. The future had looked bright and promising, even after many destructive years of war. But these two years— terrible years—of my father's illness turned our home into a place of suffering and sadness. After my father's death, my mother was extremely depressed. We went every Sunday to our Protestant church service, but there was no balm of Gilead. There was nothing and nobody who could comfort my mother.

Well, not quite! Our Heavenly Father, in His great love, had not forgotten us.

Eight months after the passing of my father, two American missionaries knocked on our door in Frankfurt, Germany. Those two missionaries, guided by the Spirit and well prepared, knew exactly what our little single-mother family needed. After a short and pleasant conversation, they handed my mother the Book of Mormon, with some marked verses to be read before their return in a few days. My mother loved to read the Bible, and she was immediately interested in this new book, curious about its content. When she started to read the Book of Mormon, she could not stop until she had read the whole book. She was so excited about the message that often my sister and I had to sit down and listen as she read to us some verses which impressed her so much that she felt they were written just for her.

Those two inspired missionaries came back after a few days and taught us the plan of salvation. It was like a miracle. Our eyes and hearts were opened to an, until then, unknown vision of our earthly existence. We learned about the purpose of life, where we came from, why we are here, and where we will go after this life. We learned that we truly were children of our Heavenly Father and that He loved us and cared for us. We learned that families could be together forever, even beyond this life.

When these two young men, serving the Lord far away from their own families, testified with power and conviction of this glorious truth, memories came back to me of the last weeks of my father's life and his suffering. I had stood and prayed often at the window of our apartment, looking out to see when the doctor would come to bring relief for my father's pain. How I loved these two young missionaries, well prepared by the Lord and by their parents, teachers, and friends, teaching us the principles of eternal families. On this day, there was no darkness in our home, because light and darkness cannot occupy the same space at the same time. We felt the Spirit, we knew the message was true, and on this day tears flowed freely and hope came back to our home. This was a true miracle for our family; it was as if angels had been sent to us. Those two missionaries were the angels of glory who brought us the restored gospel.

There is a beautiful hymn of the Restoration that reflects very much how we felt at this time. In some ways, we considered it our "German hymn." We sang it whenever possible, and every time it touched our hearts deeply. It is a powerful, uplifting, and joyful hymn. I quote:

Hark, all ye nations! Hear heaven's voice
Thru ev'ry land that all may rejoice!
Angels of glory shout the refrain:
Truth is restored again!

Oh, how glorious from the throne above
Shines the gospel light of truth and love!
Bright as the sun, this heavenly ray
Lights ev'ry land today.[1]

The missionaries invited us to attend church on Sunday. We were a little late and had to squeeze into a filled chapel when the opening hymn was sung. The members were singing this beloved hymn of the Restoration with great enthusiasm and joy. I felt like I was sitting among an angels' choir. I had never heard any of our Protestant congregations sing with such power and volume.

Today I know this was the first time in my 12-year-old life that I felt the Spirit of God testifying of the truth of the Restoration. I felt as if I were being wrapped up in a warm and secure blanket of divine love.

The members of the Church welcomed us warmly; they were true friends. We felt immediately part of the family of Saints. We loved to go to church, and we felt at home!

Finally, on a cold winter day, my mother, my nine-year-old sister, and I were baptized, and we stepped through this marvelous gate on our journey from darkness into the light toward eternal life. And we rejoiced, as verse two of this great hymn proclaims:

Searching in darkness, nations have wept;
Watching for dawn, their vigil they've kept.
All now rejoice; the long night is o'er.
Truth is on earth once more!

We loved our new life. My sister and I couldn't believe how my mother was changing. She smiled again. We talked together; we prayed together; we laughed together. There was that spark back in her eyes, a desire to learn. There was new hope and a joyful heart and face.

My mother radiated what Alma referred to in the precious Book of Mormon when he asked the people of the Church: "Have ye spiritually been born of God? Have ye received his image in your countenances?" (Alma 5:14).

Yes, she had become a new person!

Such a life-changing decision was not unnoticed by our extended family. My grandmother felt that we had become unfaithful to the faith of our fathers. My Aunt Lisa thought we were out of our minds. She announced that she would search out the missionaries in her town and convince them of their wrong ways. She found the meetinghouse; she found the missionaries; she talked to them; and she got baptized. It was much more difficult for my grandmother to make this important but huge change in her life. It took many years of watching us and observing how the gospel and the Church influenced our lives before she had a firm testimony of her own and became a member. Now we are all sealed together forever.

As the blessing of the restored gospel came to our country, it is now spreading throughout the world. Last month my husband and I were on an assignment in Chile and Peru. As we met with the wonderful members and missionaries, the hymn "Hark, All Ye Nations!" was sung in the beautiful Spanish language. Members of various cultural and ethnic backgrounds bore their witness of the restored gospel of Jesus Christ. It touched my heart when a newly baptized, humble brother bore a sincere testimony of the Prophet Joseph Smith in a remote chapel in Peru.

> Oh, how glorious from the throne above
> Shines the gospel light of truth and love!
> Bright as the sun, this heavenly ray
> Lights ev'ry land today.

How grateful I am for the many wonderful missionaries who are serving in all the world today. They are bringing heavenly light into a dark world. As our hymn proclaims:

> Chosen by God to serve him below,
> To ev'ry land and people we'll go,
> Standing for truth with fervent accord,
> Teaching his holy word.

My dear sisters, you are the women who will prepare these young men and women to serve missions. You will help them to bring the gospel light to every land today. You will serve a mission with your husband or as a mature single sister and bless the people of the world. You will be an example to our youth—an example in decency and quality in everything that affects our lives. You will teach our youth to pray and to study. You will teach them to be confident and have faith in Jesus Christ. You will teach them leadership and humility, and you will help them to claim the gift of discernment through their own righteousness. You will teach them that the truth will not always be popular but that it will always be right. And after all of this, you can promise them:

"That which is of God is light; and he that receiveth light, and continueth in God, receiveth more light; and that light groweth brighter and brighter until the perfect day" (D&C 50:24).

My dear sisters, thank you for being such a wonderful influence for good! I love you! May God bless you!

NOTE

1. Based on German text by Louis F. Mönch, "Hark, All Ye Nations," *Hymns of The Church of Jesus Christ of Latter-day Saints* (Salt Lake City: The Church of Jesus Christ of Latter-day Saints, 1985), no. 264.

"When the Light Had Departed . . . I Went Home"

Susan W. Tanner

My dear brothers and sisters, I am so happy to be here with you today. I feel of your spirits. I don't know specifically what your need is today. I hope, though, that you are here with a certain question or a specific desire, because when you come hungry, you are more likely to be fed. I know that the Holy Ghost is the true teacher. So what you learn today may not be anything that I say, but rather something that the Spirit teaches you in response to your questions and desires. As it says in the Doctrine and Covenants, if I preach by the Spirit and you receive by the Spirit, then we can be "edified and rejoice together" (D&C 50:22).

Last summer I began personally preparing for this year's remembrance and celebration of the "great and marvelous work" of the Restoration. I reread Joseph Smith's history, I read Lucy Mack Smith's history of her son, and I was able to visit historical sites in Palmyra where many of the Restoration events unfolded.

I realized the profound influence Joseph's home life had upon him. After the most glorious vision in this dispensation occurred, the boy Joseph "went home." His mother immediately sensed his contemplative

Susan W. Tanner is currently serving as the general president of the Young Women. She graduated from Brigham Young University in humanities. Sister Tanner is a former president and counselor in all of the women's auxiliaries, on both the ward and stake levels. She has also been a curriculum writer for the Primary organization. Sister Tanner and her husband, John S. Tanner, have five children and five grandchildren. Her favorite roles are wife, mother, and homemaker.

spirit and asked "what the matter was" (Joseph Smith—History 1:20). Joseph knew that his home was a place of trust and acceptance, of safety and refuge.

As I entered that small, humble log home, I felt its holiness. I could envision Joseph leaning on the fireplace pondering the visit from Heavenly Father and His Son. I also went to the upstairs bedroom, shared by six brothers, where the angel Moroni came to Joseph in response to his penitent prayer.

What happened in this home to prepare this young boy to be the prophet of the Restoration? I think that Joseph came already prepared in his heart. He was innately, deeply spiritual; he had a bright mind and a pleasing personality. But in addition to that, he learned much from his parents. They taught him to work hard and to shoulder responsibility, to be obedient and to have faith, to turn to the scriptures and to the Lord in prayer for every need.

They modeled how to live. When Lucy Mack Smith had problems in her life, she went to the scriptures. When her sister Lovina died, Lucy was particularly downhearted. She said, "I did not feel as though life was worth seeking after, and in my reflections I determined to obtain that which was spoken of so frequently from the pulpit, namely a change of heart. In order to accomplish this, I perused the Bible and prayed incessantly."[1] Another time she "retired to a grove . . . not far distant and prayed to the Lord" to help her solve a problem.

Little Joseph was only about seven years old when Sophronia, his older sister by about three years, suffered from typhoid fever. After 90 days of illness, the attending doctor said there was no hope for her life. Lucy said, "My husband and I clasped our hands together and fell upon our knees by the bedside and poured our grief and supplications into his ears. . . . Did the Lord hear our petition? He did hear us. And I felt assured that he would answer our prayers."[2] Later that night Sophronia began breathing freely and continued to heal from that time forward. Joseph witnessed this constant reliance upon the Lord for help and guidance in every situation. He had learned from the faithful examples of his parents this paraphrased message of the 23rd Psalm:

My Shepherd will supply my need:
Jehovah is His Name;
In pastures fresh He makes me feed,
Beside the living stream.[3]

What is it that made his home or any home a safe haven? And what is lacking in our society to provide such homes? Two contrasting experiences come to my mind, both in third-world countries and conditions. I visited a young woman in a home with very little furniture or space and open sewage running on the premises. Although the girl and her mother were members, they had not come to church for a long time. After some visiting, I asked the young woman what her hopes and dreams were. She hesitated, then she said, "My greatest hope is that my father would not drink." That comment has haunted me. I continue to be far more concerned by her *hopeless* home situation than her *impoverished* one. In a sense she is spiritually homeless.

In contrast to the spirit of that home, my daughter visited a Relief Society woman who lived high on the Altiplano of La Paz, Bolivia. A small group of young adults was taking food to this poor woman, who lived in a one-room shack with her children and grandchildren. The cold air of the high plains whipped through the insecure roof. There was not room to invite these young adults into her humble home, but her smile and her loving spirit welcomed them anyway. She thanked them profusely and then began enumerating God's many blessings to her. Before they left, she asked if they would sing a hymn with her—"Because I Have Been Given Much."[4] Her so-called home was a spiritual sanctuary.

Making a home a place of refuge has much less to do with temporal arrangements than with the Spirit. I felt this in Joseph Smith's small and humble log home. When we don't have a spiritual retreat where we can find sanctuary, we feel an emotional homelessness much like street homelessness. In an article entitled "HomeLess America," Bryce Christensen discusses this issue:

"For since when did the word *home* signify merely physical shelter, or *homelessness* merely the lack of such shelter? . . . Home [signifies] not only shelter, but also emotional commitment, security, and belonging. Home has connoted not just a necessary roof and warm radiator, but a place

sanctified by the abiding ties of wedlock, parenthood, and family obligation; a place demanding sacrifice and devotion, but promised loving care
and warm acceptance."[5]

In this sense, the young woman I visited was emotionally and spiritually homeless, while the impoverished Relief Society sister was rich in
spirit in her little home.

Each of us has a need within us to be loved, accepted, and trusted.
We seek a safe place to go where these needs are met. When I speak to
young women, I always ask them what their challenges are. Invariably one
of the top problems is a feeling of loneliness or a lack of belonging. They
have this need to belong. Many feel this isolation in high schools where
they are one of the only members of the Church. Also, unfortunately,
many others feel it because they do not have a home where they feel nurtured and protected.

Even in the safest of homes, we have moments of eternal longing, of
homesickness for our heavenly home. C. S. Lewis said:

"If I find in myself a desire which no experience in this world can satisfy, the most probable explanation is that I was made for another world.
. . . If that is so, I must take care, on the one hand, never to despise, or be
unthankful for, these earthly blessings, and on the other hand, never to
mistake them for the something else of which they are only a kind of copy,
or echo, or mirage. I must keep alive in myself the desire for my true country, which I shall not find till after death."[6]

Safe homes on earth foster the Spirit by modeling Christlike virtues,
thus helping to satisfy those feelings of heavenly homesickness. The family
proclamation teaches that "the family is central to the Creator's plan,"
and "happiness in family life is most likely to be achieved when founded
upon the teachings of the Lord Jesus Christ."[7]

That statement teaches us precisely what makes a home a sanctuary
from the world. It is a home that is founded upon the teachings of Jesus
Christ. He must be the rock upon which our foundation is built. As it says
in one of my favorite scriptures, in Helaman 5:12:

"And now, my sons, remember, remember that it is upon the rock of
our Redeemer, who is Christ, the Son of God, that ye must build your
foundation; that when the devil shall send forth his mighty winds, yea, his
shafts in the whirlwind, yea, when all his hail and his mighty storm shall

beat upon you, it shall have no power over you to drag you down to the gulf of misery and endless wo, because of the rock upon which ye are built, which is a sure foundation, a foundation whereon if men build they cannot fall."

This scripture suggests that the storms of life are inevitable. It does not say *if* but rather "*when* the devil shall send . . . winds [and] hail [and] storm [to] beat upon you." Joseph Smith faced mighty storms, but his early beginnings in a home that had been built upon the sure foundation of Jesus Christ had taught him whom he could trust.

I know neighbors, friends, and relatives who have had wind and hail beating upon them. I have personally seen in their lives the ravages of abuse, out-of-wedlock pregnancies, depression, divorce, debilitating accidents, death, same-gender attraction, sickness, suicide, stillborn babies, and wayward children. If these, my loved ones, knew how to turn to the Savior for strength and sustenance, they were able to weather the storms, though still not without some hurt and heartache. One friend said to me:

"These last years have been especially difficult ones for us, as you know. We have felt the mighty winds and storms beat against us. I do not know what I would have done without the safe arms of the Savior around us to protect us from being dragged down to the gulfs of misery. I have been grateful over and over for the home that I was raised in, for the principles I was taught by my parents, who probably didn't even realize they were doing so. They were wonderful examples of Christlike people. That safe haven of childhood helped bring 'safety to our home this past year as the storms descended.'"[8]

> When I walk through the shades of death
> Thy presence is my stay;
> One word of Thy supporting breath
> Drives all my fears away.[9]

This friend found profound strength even while facing her trials. Joseph Smith had great fortitude amidst constant persecution. How? They both had learned in their homes to lean on the Savior. Their homes were refuges of righteousness.

Recently I learned of a home that has been ravaged by a great storm. It is obvious that the Christlike faith and characteristics that have been taught by the parents are deeply embedded in the hearts of the children, because they are responding with complete trust and selflessness. The mother writes:

"In August of 2004 our then 18-year-old son, Seth, was injured in a falling accident at a party with friends from the Church and sustained a broken neck and a C5 spinal cord injury, which has left him with limited arm movement and no feeling below his chest area. This has been a life-changing experience for our entire family. Even during his three-month stay in the hospital, my children were actively involved in his care, coming to stay with him so my husband and I could have a break. . . . Since his homecoming they have continued to play a very active role in his daily care. . . . His brothers and sisters are fulfilling a labor of love for their brother that has forged a strong bond between them that I am sure will last through eternity.

"Let me tell you specifically about his younger sisters. Rachel has been involved with Seth's care both at school (he returned to finish his senior year in January) and at home. She leaves her classes early so she can ride home on the bus with him (this is somewhat of a sacrifice for her since she has choir in the last period and she loves to sing with the choir). At home she also helps . . . bathe and dress him and helps with home therapy.

"Liesl helps Seth with eating and . . . face washing and teeth brushing. She gives up her precious sleep time every morning during the week to help him eat before he goes to school. There are countless other tasks that the girls perform for Seth on a daily basis, but the most impressive thing to me is the incredible moral support they provide for him and their ready willingness to help him. I have never heard them complain about helping him, even when I know they would rather be doing something else. They are truly learning firsthand what it means to bear one another's burdens. . . . I feel it is a great blessing and honor to be their mother. The good news in the story of Seth is the promise that he has received in many priesthood blessings that he will recover and live a normal life. Fortunately, his injury was incomplete, which means that, medically speaking, he has a higher chance of recovery. But we are setting our trust in the Lord in this matter. Seth's faith is especially exemplary to all of us."[10]

This home is a holy sanctuary. It has been built on the foundation of Jesus Christ—the principles He taught, the pattern He modeled. Christ taught selfless service. He taught that we serve one another even when the load seems unfair or unbalanced. He demonstrated pure love, love that never faileth, love that "suffereth long, and is kind, . . . seeketh not her own, . . . beareth all things, believeth all things, hopeth all things, endureth all things" (Moroni 7:45).

I grew up in such a home. Like Nephi, I was born of goodly parents and was "taught somewhat in all the learning of my father [and mother]," and therefore I came to have a "great knowledge of the goodness . . . of God" (1 Nephi 1:1). Recently my healthy 80-year-old father had a medical emergency. He is doing much better now, but during those days and weeks of uncertainty, I thought a lot about what he and my mother have meant to me through the years. The home they made for my brothers and me, like Joseph Smith's home, was a place of refuge, protection, and sanctuary. Because they verbalized and exemplified their love for and reliance upon the Lord daily, we knew and loved Him too. We felt that climate of trust, mutual respect, and love that armed us to face the inevitable challenges of life.

Early in their marriage, my parents made the temple their model for the kind of home they wanted to establish. To be a holy place where children could feel the Spirit, it needed to be a house of "prayer, . . . fasting, . . . faith, . . . learning, . . . glory, . . . order, a house of God" (D&C 88:119). I remember family prayer twice a day as a happy time—a time when we talked and laughed, shared frustrations and challenges, and then prayed in faith. My father always said, and still does, "Heavenly Father loves us, and things will all work out, but we must do our part." My mother always said, "Be wise and careful about what you pray for, because Heavenly Father will answer your prayers. Look each day for the little miracles in your life."

When my husband and I started our own home, we learned from the homes where we grew up. We remembered working side by side with parents in the kitchen, in the garden, and in Dad's office. We hiked mountains, did homework, went to general conference, ate breakfast and dinner daily together. We looked to our parents' examples of disciplining strong-willed children and prioritizing busy schedules. In these later years, we marvel at their untiring devotion and sacrifice to serve Heavenly Father, to build His kingdom, all the while continuing to support and love and build unity within the family.

My husband and I are now the parents of young adults who are no longer living at home. How can we best provide refuge for them in the trials they face or give appropriate love and guidance in decisions they must make? We hope they have built their own foundation upon Jesus Christ and that they will turn to Him when the storms beat upon them. We have tried to teach them faith, which is represented in the words of the hymn "Be Still, My Soul": "Thy God doth undertake to guide the future as he has the past."[11] We know from countless past blessings that we can continue to trust Him in our futures.

Also, the door to our home is always open to our dear children, both figuratively and in actuality. Even Joseph sought comfort in his parents' home in later years. He again returned there during the gloomy period of sin and repentance after Martin Harris had lost the translated manuscript from the gold plates. His parents' home was ever a place of refuge amidst all of life's storms.

I invite each of us to remember and model righteous examples from our growing-up homes. While many of us will have positive reflections, some will need courage, knowledge, and strength to improve upon past situations. As we continue to learn how and diligently strive to make our environments stronger and more spiritual, I know Heavenly Father will bless us in this most important endeavor. President James E. Faust recently taught about the need for righteous homes. He said: "If we really want our homes to be places of holiness, we will try harder to do those things that are conducive to the Spirit of the Lord. . . . May the Lord bless each and all of us in our special responsibility to find holiness to the Lord by standing in holy places. That is where we will find the spiritual protection we need for ourselves and our families."[12]

It is my hope that these righteous refuges that we build on earth—like the homes where my husband and I grew up, like Seth and Rachel and Liesl's home, and like Joseph Smith's home—will prepare us to finally return to our eternal sanctuary. There our eternal longing will be satisfied:

> *There would I find a settled rest,*
> *While others go and come;*

No more a stranger, nor a guest,
But like a child at home.[13]

After the glorious First Vision, Joseph Smith "went home." After his participation in the great unfolding of the Restoration of the gospel of Jesus Christ, Joseph Smith again "went home." The same morning that Joseph and Hyrum went to Carthage they had read this passage from Ether in the Book of Mormon:

"And it came to pass that I prayed unto the Lord that he would give unto the Gentiles grace, that they might have charity.

"And it came to pass that the Lord said unto me: If they have not charity it mattereth not unto thee, thou hast been faithful; wherefore, thy garments shall be made clean. And because thou hast seen thy weakness thou shalt be made strong, even unto the sitting down in the place which I have prepared in the mansions of my Father" (Ether 12:36–37).

Once again Joseph "went home"—this time to a "settled rest . . . like a child at home," to the place prepared for him in the mansions of his Father.

I testify that the family is ordained of God and is central to His plan. I know that we are about Heavenly Father's work as we provide earthly refuge in strong, Spirit-filled homes for His children. May we be diligent, joyful, and unwavering in this endeavor and then ultimately find final refuge, safety, and sanctuary in His mansions above.

NOTES

1. Lucy Mack Smith, *History of Joseph Smith, Revised and Enhanced,* ed. Scot Facer Proctor and Maurine Jensen Proctor (Salt Lake City: Bookcraft, 1996), 40.
2. Smith, *History of Joseph Smith,* 69.
3. Issac Watts, "My Shepherd Will Supply My Need," in his *Psalms of David,* 1719.
4. Grace Noll Crowell, "Because I Have Been Given Much," *Hymns of The Church of Jesus Christ of Latter-day Saints* (Salt Lake City: The Church of Jesus Christ of Latter-day Saints, 1985), no. 219.

5. Bryce Christensen, "HomeLess America: What the Disappearance of the American Homemaker Really Means," *The Family in America* 17, no. 1 (January 2003): 1.
6. C. S. Lewis, *Mere Christianity* (New York: HarperCollins, 2001), 136–37.
7. First Presidency and Quorum of the Twelve Apostles, "The Family: A Proclamation to the World," *Ensign*, November 1995, 102.
8. Letter in author's possession.
9. Watts, "My Shepherd Will Supply My Need."
10. Letter from Jayne Belle Coyne, March 21, 2005, in author's possession.
11. Katharina von Schlegel, "Be Still, My Soul," *Hymns*, no. 124.
12. James E. Faust, "Standing in Holy Places," *Ensign*, May 2005, 68.
13. Watts, "My Shepherd Will Supply My Need."

HOME AS SANCTUARY: ONE MOTHER'S JOURNEY

Betsy VanDenBerghe

Joseph Smith's home offered him sanctuary from bitter trials and public persecution, yet his Palmyra cabin was primitive and rustic, with no traces of professional interior decorating. The cleaning challenges of constantly tracked-in mud, lack of indoor plumbing, soot and smoke from the fire, and, above all, a large family housed in small quarters must have been insurmountable. But the sanctuary didn't exist inside the four walls of a boyhood home; it lay in the hearts of believing, loving parents—parents whose reaction to their teenage son's problems consisted not of embarrassment but of unconditional acceptance and a firm belief in his mission. The sanctuary of a home in which parents offer trust, hope, forgiveness, and unconditional love transcends physical space and endures beyond childhood. It becomes a life-sustaining force, helping children to suffer, grow, and overcome throughout their lives.

I've read biographies of people nurtured in this love who find that even life's most harrowing circumstances cannot extinguish its power. Gerda Weissman Klein, a Jewish concentration camp survivor, describes it well in her biography, *All But My Life*. "Love is great, love is the foundation of nobility, it conquers obstacles and is a deep well of truth and

---

Betsy VanDenBerghe writes for Church and BYU publications, and continually struggles toward sanctuary in her imperfect home. She is grateful for the patience of her husband, Jed, and children John, William, Christian, Grace, Anika, Benjamin, Samuel, and Andrew in making this journey with her.

strength," she observes. "The greatness of [my parents'] love . . . ignited within me a spark that continued to glow through the years of misery and defeat. The memory of their love—my only legacy—sustained me in happy and unhappy times in Poland, Germany, Czechoslovakia, France, Switzerland, England. It is still part of me, here in America."[1]

My husband and I are grateful for the sanctuary of our childhood homes; however, we're even more thankful for our parents' unconditional acceptance during our years as single adults, many of which were spent away from home. The refuge of my parents' love took on a life of its own through telephone wires as I called home for comfort, confirmation, and direction from various college dormitories and roommate-filled apartments. The most important of those phone calls happened when, after Mom and Dad had helped me move across the country for a job, I called to say the Spirit was prompting me to go on a mission. Their support of that particular decision has been one of their greatest gifts to me.

With examples like these—combined with a wonderful husband and professional experience writing about family issues—you would think creating a sanctuary for my own children would come naturally. It has not. My personality is headstrong, demanding, and easily exasperated. My children are closely spaced and not perfect. What comes naturally to me are unrealistic expectations, shrieks of agitation, overdramatic looks of disapproval, and long-winded lectures.

Far less easy for me to achieve have been the fruits of the Spirit mentioned in the New Testament: "joy, peace, longsuffering, gentleness, [and] meekness" (Galatians 5:22–23)—the divine love so well described in 1 Corinthians. Charity and unconditional love involve a willingness to "suffereth long" through children's never-ending mistakes and lapses in judgment. It requires the ability to "envieth not" other families and other children. A home of refuge avoids being "puffed up" and "seeketh not her own" in worrying more about what the world thinks than what God thinks. Hardest for me is not being "easily provoked," because a sanctuary home "beareth all things, . . . hopeth all things, [and] endureth all things" (see 1 Corinthians 13:4–7).

I know I am not alone in having difficulty creating this charitable refuge with my very human disposition. Hearing other mothers relate what pushes their tolerance to the limit is a source of consolation to me.

One friend asked her older, competent kids to prepare the younger ones for church and, when it was time to go, found them all still in pajamas playing a board game. Thanks. Another painstakingly and meticulously readied her daughters for a picture-taking session and, upon arriving at the studio, discovered the girls had been playing with a pen in the car and had covered their dresses with ink. I have a particularly hard time with teenagers—already late for school, slowly eating their breakfast while they read the cereal box, gradually bringing each spoonful to the mouth as the carpool honks outside.

I relate to an incident described several years ago in a *New York Times* feature article on large families. In it a Minnesota mother of 3 biological and 14 internationally adopted children describes her family-trip fiasco: "There were two kids in the way back fighting, they wouldn't stop, we were on the highway and I yelled, from the front seat: 'That's IT. I've HAD it. I'm coming back!'" Mrs. Kayes made it almost to the back seat before getting a paralyzing leg cramp, which resulted in her children having to hoist her hand-over-hand back to the front. At least, noted the reporter, this mother had "gotten the attention of the squabbling pair in back, who shut up, awestruck, to watch."[2]

With the passage of time, anecdotes like these seem funny. Other mistakes our children make involve too much disappointment, sometimes, to laugh about. The challenge then is to discipline and set limits, of course, but to do so using the Doctrine and Covenants' admonitions of "love unfeigned, . . . showing forth afterwards an increase of love toward him whom thou hast reproved, lest he esteem thee to be his enemy" (D&C 121:41, 43).

I cannot accomplish this kind of sanctuary with willpower, goal setting, and especially my myriad shortcomings combined with the frustrations of child rearing. However, I can accomplish it grace by grace through faith in the Lord Jesus Christ. As mothers we cannot rear our children in love and righteousness without relying on the merits of the Savior to compensate for our inevitable failings (see 2 Nephi 31:19). His love fills the void when ours is lacking. His Atonement helps us overcome, or at least improve on, so many weaknesses—that I know firsthand, "I can do all things through Christ which strengtheneth me" (Philippians 4:13). Further encouragement comes from Moroni, who assures us that charity is a gift from God. We don't need to be born with it; we need to pray for it "with all the energy of heart, that ye may be filled with this love" (Moroni 7:48).

Before the Savior makes "weak things become strong" (Ether 12:27), however, He shows us our weaknesses. Still, the realization that my home had become less than a sanctuary took a while to sink in. After all, I am a conscientious mother who doesn't spank, reads bedtime stories, chauffeurs eight kids around in a big van, and wears out every pair of pants at the knee playing on the floor. But as my kids had gotten older, I had become too intent on their achievements, too discouraged by their normal growing pains and mistakes, and too addicted to my day-planner to make time to listen to their needs or participate in the "wholesome recreational activities" encouraged by the proclamation on the family.

A turning point occurred several years ago when our family went to Temple Square and happened upon a display featuring the Church's Home Front commercials. Scene after scene showed parents defusing tense, frustrating, and potentially anger-filled situations with patience, humor, attention, and playfulness. Kids are fighting in the car, endlessly calling, "Where are we?" and Mom hunts frantically for the exit. Dad doesn't scream, though. Instead, he quips, "We're . . . on vacation!" A mother tries to shove clothes in a dryer, but when her toddler comes up waving toys in her face, she doesn't brush him away. She puts down the clothes and starts playing with him. A father discovers a potato chip trail that leads to his child in the closet, munching chips. He joins her inside for a brief picnic, only to have a chagrined mother open the closet door to exclaim, "I cannot believe you two. . . . You forgot the dip!"

Those commercials switched on a tiny microchip in my brain. Perhaps *switched on* is even too drastic a phrase. A vague sensation of wanting to change, of wanting not to get mad all the time, flickered through my mind, almost subconsciously. But it was enough.

Not all of us experience a mighty change of heart dramatically or instantaneously. "For every Paul, for every Enos, and for every King Lamoni," said President Ezra Taft Benson, "there are hundreds and thousands of people who find the process of repentance much more subtle, much more imperceptible."[3] *Subtle* and *imperceptible* describe the changes I've undergone at the hands of a Father in Heaven who requires my willingness, however faint, before He can begin a true change of heart. And it seems those changes need to take place many times throughout my life.

How does He do it? How does He lead our homes toward sanctuary? I can share my journey, but I can't offer a formula for anyone else. Many different kinds of mothers, I'm sure, benefit from many different ways of being led by the Spirit. The Book of Mormon explains that when God communicates with men, He does it "according to their language, unto their understanding" (2 Nephi 31:3). For some He sends inspiration through feelings; for others, guidance through people; and for others, enlightenment through music, art, or dreams. The way He often directs me is through books. They may not be the books others need and may not point in the direction others need to take, but in my case, over several years Heavenly Father put some pivotal authors in my path who helped me recognize my personal mothering weaknesses and repent.

BYU philosophy professor Terry Warner wrote a book, *Bonds That Make Us Free*, which pulled the rug of all my self-justifications out from under my feet. After reading it I knew I had to abandon certain tendencies: my sense of self-pity and martyrdom as a mother at having to actually suffer, work hard, and grow; my sense of anger that everyone in the family didn't always live up to my expectations; my tendency to manipulate husband and children into doing things the way I wanted them done; and my tendency to love with strings attached, rather than loving fully and unconditionally. Former justifications for these and other mind-sets seemed neither rational nor righteous after I read this book.[4]

Another BYU educator, Catherine Thomas in the religion department, wrote a book called *Spiritual Lightening*, which infused the doctrines of the Restoration into my understanding of motherhood. Prime among those doctrines: God is the one who is omnipotent—not you, the mother. Your children are here for His purposes and to fulfill the missions He has given them—not to make you, the mother, look good. Your job is to guide, help, suffer, and grow with your children—not to try to remove all suffering from their lives or to control their agency. Other insights from Sister Thomas include the revelation that anxiety over your children is not perceived by them as unconditional love. Also, when you, the mother, improve, the entire family improves spiritually. And this—like a lifeline

tossed to discouraged mothers everywhere—it's never too late! With
teenagers, with grown children, with all of our imperfections, it's never
too late to let the Atonement work its way into our hearts and create a
sanctuary. Remember, you are not omnipotent, but Heavenly Father is.[5]

Another book appeared on my kitchen table: *Mitten Strings for God:
Reflections for Mothers in a Hurry* by Katrina Kenison. I almost tossed it
aside because it looked too packaged and cute. Instead I opened it and let
the author's gentle, comforting, real-life anecdotes enfold me as I drifted
into her home's peaceful sanctuary—quiet mornings with sleepy children
crawling into Mom and Dad's bed for hugs; summer days spent digging in
sandpiles and wading in streams; dinners cooked alongside one child peel-
ing potatoes and another arranging an awkward centerpiece using twigs
and wildflowers; meandering conversations on a porch between mother
and child as Mom knits mitten strings. The child pretends to knit, finger-
ing imaginary yarn in the air, after a while declaring, "I'm knitting mitten
strings for God." It didn't matter that my bustling household couldn't
exactly replicate those scenes; what mattered was the love and serenity
behind them.[6]

Books like these, spiritual impressions, and scripture study took my
flickering awareness to an overwhelming desire for change. Viewing
myself, like King Benjamin's people, in my own carnal state—controlling,
humor deficient, and stressed out—I returned once again to an intense
study of the Atonement, ready to beg the Lord: "Change me. My heart is
broken. We both know I can't do this alone." He gave me hope by helping
me feel my family *had* done some things right, especially in focusing our
gospel study on a core doctrine found in the Doctrine and Covenants:
"This is the gospel, . . . that he came into the world, even Jesus, to be cru-
cified for the world, and to bear the sins of the world" (D&C 76:40–41).
Through our family nights, scripture study, and especially in observing
Easter, we had tried to "talk of Christ, . . . rejoice in Christ, . . . preach of
Christ" (2 Nephi 25:26). And it was through the Savior that the sanctuary
in my heart and in our home began to germinate and, month by month,
year by year, grow stronger.

But change comes slowly. I always want the Lord to perfect me minutes after the first heartfelt prayer. Instead, as the gospel reference *True to
the Faith* well explains, conversion is a process, not an event—a quiet

miracle that, in my case at least, brings about change over years rather than weeks or even months. And those years are often fraught with setbacks. Just when it seemed peace and sanctuary had reigned in our home for a while, a combination of sick kids, too many science-fair projects, and a teenager's sarcastic comment would send me into a tirade that made someone or even the whole family feel worthless. Then I'd return to my room and pray, mad to be so human. But in my room hangs a picture of Christ in Gethsemane. It helps me remember: "He did this for me. My faith is in Him, not in my limited abilities."

For my part I had to find time for deeper scripture study and prayer, which, in my particular circumstances, translated into sacrificing much of my beloved reading of other things. But I'll have time someday for many activities I yearn for; in the meantime, when I need it most, my breakdowns are gradually becoming the exceptions more than the rule. Several milestones have let me know that the fruits of the Spirit are appearing with greater frequency in our home. Please allow me to share some of them.

First, the fruit of *peace,* marked by a definite drop in temper tantrums. One night I left for a meeting, giving husband and children the usual list: do the dishes, finish all homework, pick up the house. When I got back, of course, the house was still a mess, but somehow the anger didn't rise. Instead I noticed that at least the dinner dishes were mostly done, a few kids were working on homework, and the baby was in his pajamas. I didn't start "silently" crashing the remaining dinner dishes into the dishwasher or sulk around picking up toys. With genuine cheerfulness, I said, "Okay, let's finish what's been started!" While this may seem insignificant to every other inhabitant on the face of the planet, what a victory for me!

Second, the fruit of *longsuffering,* marked by a sincere feeling of sympathy when my children are goofing up. An interesting phenomenon has started to occur: sometimes when I'm looking at a missing-assignment report, sometimes when a child has just fought with every possible sibling within a half-hour period, I recall quite vividly dumb things I did as a child, adolescent, and even grown-up. I remember the feelings of frustration and discouragement those actions brought on and sense that my children need to know I too falter and must change. Before discussing problems, I often hear myself saying to the guilty party, with true empathy, "You know, I've done worse things than this." Discipline must sometimes take place, but the long-winded lectures replete with their litany of the children's past mistakes are diminishing. They may someday disappear altogether.

Third, the fruit of *temperance,* marked by self-restraint in not overprogramming my family to the breaking point. I have not yet been inspired to drop all music lessons, though it would probably help, and I can't control the number of parent-teacher conferences, Church meetings, and kids' programs coinciding on a given day. But I have felt inspired to scale back what I can and not to get so pessimistic when everything, as usual, can't get done. I've tried to remember Elder Richard D. May's observation that "we may find we have crowded our lives with too many good things and not left sufficient time for weightier matters."[7] A physical component of temperance has also emerged as I feel renewed respect for my body's need for sleep, exercise, and not to run faster than it has strength.

The fruits of *hope* and *faith* have brought on the realization that the Lord wants the success of my family even more than I do. I used to pray with fervor every morning and then, like the old saying goes, work as if everything depended on me—and ultimately as if God didn't exist. Now I find I'm able to maintain faith throughout the day, asking Heavenly Father for help in my heart when I'm supposed to be three places at once or when I feel like exploding after a child rolls her eyes at me. Sometimes I still do explode, but I get over it quicker and don't spend hours ruminating over "the sins which . . . so easily beset me" (2 Nephi 4:18). I wholeheartedly agree with Elder Dallin H. Oaks that, in progressing toward conversion, "our family relationships—even more than our Church callings—are the setting in which the most important part of that development can occur."[8] Thus, hope and faith compel me to believe that the same Savior who empowers people to recover from addictions, from sins of the flesh, from diseases and all powers of evil will surely help me become a better mother.

Finally, that ever-precious fruit of the Spirit, *joy,* has rebounded in my heart and in my home. I realized this one night when the kids were supposed to be getting ready for bed at the end of a long, tiring day. Anxious to get to sleep, I discovered a herd of the younger ones collected in the girls' room. They were jumping and dancing on the bed with music blasting from the CD player. I walked in on their party and suddenly found myself picking up the three-year-old and dancing. Everybody started laughing. We kept dancing. There was a great, great feeling in the room. It reminded me of something I couldn't pinpoint—until I recognized it. We had become a real-life Church commercial!

In moments like these, the words of Jesus Christ ring true: "My yoke is easy, and my burden is light" (Matthew 11:30). He will ultimately create sanctuary in our homes if we turn our hearts over to Him. The refuge Jesus Christ creates is not contingent on our disposition, our children's behavior, our family size, or ideal circumstances. My sister has to work full time, and my neighbor's chronic health problems restrict her to mothering flat on her back from the living room couch. Both mothers, with their attitudes of genuine love and acceptance, are examples of sanctuary to me.

The hymn "How Firm a Foundation" describes a promise to everyone "who unto the Savior for refuge have fled": "I'll strengthen thee, help thee, and cause thee to stand, . . . upheld by my righteous, omnipotent hand."[9] When we flee to the Lord for refuge, He creates sanctuary not only for our children's sake, not only for our husband's sake, but also for our *own* sake. I bear testimony that Jesus Christ can and will lead us beside the still waters and restore our souls.

NOTES

1. Gerda Weissman Klein, *All But My Life* (New York: Farrar, Straus, and Giroux, 1957), 86.
2. Melissa Fay Green, "The Family Mobile," *The New York Times Magazine*, August 19, 2001, 33.
3. Ezra Taft Benson, "A Mighty Change of Heart," *Ensign*, October 1989, 5.
4. C. Terry Warner, *Bonds That Make Us Free: Healing Our Relationships, Coming to Ourselves* (Salt Lake City: Shadow Mountain, 2001).
5. M. Catherine Thomas, *Spiritual Lightening* (Salt Lake City: Bookcraft, 1996).
6. Katrina Kenison, *Mitten Strings for God: Reflections for Mothers in a Hurry* (New York: Warner Book, 2000).
7. Richard D. May, "Book of Mormon Principles: They Think They Are Wise," *Ensign*, August 2004, 66.
8. Dallin H. Oaks, "The Challenge to Become," *Ensign*, November 2000, 33.
9. Attributed to Robert Keen, "How Firm a Foundation," *Hymns of The Church of Jesus Christ of Latter-day Saints* (Salt Lake City: The Church of Jesus Christ of Latter-day Saints, 1985), no. 85.

WOMEN—THE LORD'S CROWNING CREATION

Dieter F. Uchtdorf

You women are special in the eyes of the Lord. My wife and I love to be with the members of the Church all around the world. Tender feelings come back as we meet with you here at BYU.

Our daughter studied at BYU, and we attended her graduation here in the Marriott Center. Jeffrey R. Holland was then the president of BYU. We also have very special feelings toward Provo, because as our daughter was working on her master's degree, she also gave birth to twin boys. I always knew that the women of the Church were very efficient, but our daughter really showed us how to use one's time wisely and productively. And those two boys even came seven weeks early.

My wife and I love you wonderful women of the Church! You are such a power for good in the world. You are truly a light to the nations, to communities, to families, and to the Church.

In the scriptures, reference is made to women who have blessed individuals, people, and generations with their intellectual and spiritual gifts. Names like Sarah, Rebekah, Rachel, or Martha, Elisabeth, and Mary, the mother of our Savior, will always be honored and remembered. But the

Elder Dieter F. Uchtdorf was sustained as a member of the Quorum of the Twelve Apostles of The Church of Jesus Christ of Latter-day Saints on October 2, 2004. Prior to his call, Elder Uchtdorf worked as a pilot for Lufthansa German Airlines. He also held several management positions for the airlines, including senior vice president of flight operations and chief pilot. Elder Uchtdorf is married to Harriet Reich Uchtdorf and they have two children and five grandchildren.

scriptures also mention women whose names are unknown to us but who bless our lives through their examples and teachings—like Jairus's 12-year-old daughter (see Mark 5:22–23, 35–43); the woman of Samaria whom Jesus met at the well of Sychar (see John 4); the ideal wife and mother mentioned in Proverbs 31; and, of course, Eve, the mother of all living.

Just think about it: After creating this beautiful world, God created Adam and, then, as His prime creation, He created woman—Eve! She was the sublime, the ultimate in all of His creations. She was the crowning creation.

Looking at the history of this earth and at the history of the restored Church of Jesus Christ, it becomes obvious that you sisters do hold a special place in our Father's plan for the eternal happiness and well-being of His children.

When I thumb through my own life's "who's who" in search of the most influential persons who had an impact for good at times of greatest need, I quickly realize that most of the defining moments in my personal development were positively shaped by faithful daughters of our Heavenly Father. First of all there is, of course, the great influence of my dear wife, Harriet, who is the sunshine of my life—always faithful and forthright and never hesitant to speak her mind. Once, during a press conference, she interrupted me and said, "Sometimes I am more like a thunderstorm than sunshine." I assure you, she is the sunshine in my life—a very lively sunshine—24 hours a day. How grateful I am for her! How much I love her!

Our daughter, Antje, and our daughter-in-law, Carolyn, are also great examples for me. They both live in Europe and raise their families there. Carolyn served a mission in southern Utah, and Antje graduated summa cum laude from BYU. They both returned to their home countries and use those great experiences of mission and education to build strong families and bless the Church there. I think you can sense that I am just a little proud of them.

Looking back to these very special and shaping moments of getting rooted in the gospel of Jesus Christ, three very special women appear in my life's book of remembrance: my mother, my grandmother, and my mother-in-law.

Toward the end of World War II, my family was living in Czecho-slovakia, where I was born. My father, a customs officer, was drafted into the army and sent to the western front of the war. As the war raged with more severity and the eastern front moved toward our town, my mother, alone with her four children and in an effort to protect them, made the decision to leave our home and all our earthly possessions behind and head west, toward the home of her parents in East Germany.

It was the winter of 1944—one of the coldest, harshest winters of World War II. My mother instructed us to take only warm clothes and food, but no other possessions. At this time, we were members of the Lutheran church, not even aware that there was a restored Church of Jesus Christ. Considering this, it is interesting that she took most of our family records and family pictures on our flight to the west.

As a four-year-old boy, I was so sad as we left behind our nice home with all my toys and a large balcony. How I loved this balcony and the view it provided, even though I once got my head stuck between two of its pillars; my ears—my pretty big ears—kept me from getting back out again. Fortunately, there was my mother to help and a big crowd to watch.

We were on one of the last refugee trains heading westward, and the journey, which would usually take one or two days, took us almost two weeks. Traveling in a freezing train, stopping over in refugee camps, and heading out toward the west again—exhaustion, hunger, and fear were the continuous ingredients of this perilous flight.

One night the train stopped again at a train station, and, as usual, my mother stepped out in search of some food for us children. Often, kind people came to those stations and brought milk and bread and other food for the refugee children. But this time when my mother returned with some precious food for us, the train was gone, with all of her four children in it.

During this time of the war, many family members were separated from each other, never to be united again. There she was, in a war zone, without her husband, alone on deserted railroad tracks, realizing that she had just lost all of her children! Later she shared with us how lonely and devastated she felt. The physical stress of the effort to flee to the west, and the emotional stress culminating in the apparent loss of all her children in a few minutes of time, was overwhelming to her. She started to pray— the only source of solace available to her at that desperate time. I know today that the Light of Christ moved her to pray with faith, as a good

Lutheran, and then to get up and look around to see if she could find the train somewhere else at the station. After a short period of terror and despair, she got on her feet and moved from one track to another and eventually found our train on a parallel track quite a distance away, where it had been moved during her absence.

With the protection of God, and under the inspired leadership of our mother, we reached her hometown and were reunited with her parents in Zwickau, East Germany.

Those dangerous days, as we fled in front of an oncoming army, and the following months, as the war came to an end, were among the most troublesome of our lives. Some of my memories of these days are of darkness, of night, of coldness. But with the help of God, we were moved into a place where a light was shining forth for all who came out of that darkness and coldness and who were willing to accept the Savior's invitation: "Come and see" (John 1:39).

It was in this town of Zwickau that my grandmother was invited by an elderly single woman to attend church with her. The setting was still desperate—the war was just over. Food was scarce, and so were all other goods, like coal to heat our homes or cook our meals. Houses were destroyed, and a family was fortunate if they were all still alive and had a roof over their heads.

My grandmother accepted the invitation of this dear single sister to attend sacrament meeting with her. This act of kindness might appear small and not too hard to do, but it changed our lives forever.

Looking back from today's circumstances of comfort, it is almost unbelievable what was happening then. We attended church in a cold, cramped, back room meeting place with electricity often failing, leaving us in the dark. But at the same time, this room was filled with the Spirit, and the divine light of the message of the restored gospel was in great abundance, and we were surrounded by the love, friendship, and helping hands of the dear members.

All of our family joined the Church. All were baptized except me, because I was only six at the time. Two years later I was baptized too, in a local indoor swimming pool by one of the Church leaders in our branch. Because of the circumstances during the postwar poverty, I had not learned to swim at this young age and was apprehensive to enter the water to be baptized. This was my first experience in a public indoor swimming pool. I will always remember the feeling of warmth, safety, and importance as I came out of the water after this sacred ordinance had been performed.

How grateful I am to these two women of the Church—my grandmother and my mother! They are true modern-day pioneers! They went before and ventured into new spiritual territory. They helped me to gain a testimony of the restored Church of Jesus Christ. They had faith, and they radiated love to a little boy, even in places and times of darkness, despair, and coldness.

The light of the gospel, bright as the sun, lighted up their life in these challenging times. And then in return, the warmth of their light and example helped me to feel secure and well grounded in the principles of the gospel.

I share these very personal experiences with you, hoping to impress upon you that wherever you live, whatever circumstances you live in, whatever your background or challenges might be, the gospel light has the power and purpose to bring blessings into your life and into the lives of those placed in your path. The gospel of Jesus Christ has been restored to bring blessings to our Heavenly Father's children. You are planted in your country, your community, your family to facilitate these blessings. I urge you to bloom where you are planted!

My dear sisters—grandmothers, mothers, aunts, and friends—please never underestimate the power of your influence for good, especially in the lives of our most precious children and youth!

President Heber J. Grant said, "Without the devotion and absolute testimony of the living God in the hearts of our mothers, this Church would die."[1] And the writer of Proverbs said, "Train up a child in the way he should go: and when he is old, he will not depart from it" (Proverbs 22:6).

President Gordon B. Hinckley counseled the women of the Church in January of 2004: "It is so tremendously important that the women of the Church stand strong and immovable for that which is correct and proper under the plan of the Lord. We call upon the women of the Church to stand together for righteousness. They must begin in their own homes. They can teach it in their classes. They can voice it in their communities."[2]

President Hinckley also says that big gates move on small hinges.[3] Your example in seemingly small things will make a big difference in the lives of our young people. The way you dress, the way you groom, the way you talk, the way you pray, the way you testify, the way you live every day will make the difference. This includes which TV shows you watch, which music you prefer, and how you use the Internet. If you love to go to the temple, these young people will also love to go. If you adapt your wardrobe to the temple garment and not the other way around, they will know what you consider important, and they will learn from you.

You are marvelous sisters and great examples. Our youth are blessed by you, and the Lord loves you for that.

A few years after my baptism, my family became refugees for a second time. The political regime in East Germany perceived my father as a dissident. His life was at risk, and we had to leave the country overnight, leaving behind everything we possessed. Again we had only the clothes we wore, some food for the trip, and family records, as well as family pictures. By the time I was 11, we had been refugees twice within only seven years. But this time we had already received the gospel of Jesus Christ. We had made covenants with the Lord through baptism, and we came to a branch in Frankfurt, West Germany, with other members who had the same principles and precious values.

Into this branch, just a few years later, came a young widow with her two daughters. The missionaries had found this beautiful family, which included my future wife, Harriet.

When I saw Harriet for the first time, with her dark brown eyes, I thought, "These missionaries are really doing a great job!" Even as a teenager I liked Harriet quite a lot. My bold advances, however, showed only marginal success. I tried, for instance, to influence the seating at the sacrament table so I could pass the sacrament to her. This did not impress her very much. On my way to Church activities during the week, I usually rode my nice bicycle and often stopped at their home to ask if Harriet would want to have a ride to church on my bicycle. Harriet never accepted; she always declined. Sometimes, however, her mother was there and would say, "Harriet will walk, but I will gladly ride with you on your bike to church." This wasn't really what I was hoping for at the time, but

I later realized it is an advantage to be on good terms with the mother of the girl of your dreams!

Sister Carmen Reich, my mother-in-law, was truly an elect lady. She embraced the gospel in a most difficult and dark time of her life, and she liberated herself from grief and sorrow. As a young woman and a widow, and the mother of two young girls, she emancipated herself from a world of old traditions into a world of great spirituality. She embraced the teachings of the gospel, with its intellectual and spiritual power, on a fast track. When the missionaries gave her the Book of Mormon and invited her to read the marked verses, she read the whole book within a few days. She knew things beyond the understanding of her peers because she knew them by the Spirit of God. She was the humblest of the humble, the wisest of the wise, because she was willing and pure enough to believe when God had spoken. She was baptized November 7, 1954, and was asked by the missionary who baptized her to write her testimony down in December, only a few weeks after her baptism. The missionary wanted to use her testimony in his teachings to help others feel the true spirit of conversion. Fortunately, Elder Jenkins kept the handwritten original for more than 40 years and then returned it to her as a very special and loving gift. What a wonderful act of love. Carmen Reich, my dear mother-in-law, passed away in 2000 at age 83.

Let me share with you parts of her written testimony. Please keep in mind that this is a sister who had heard about the gospel only a few weeks earlier. Before the missionaries came, she had never heard anything about the Book of Mormon, Joseph Smith, or Mormons in general. In 1954 there was no temple outside the United States, except in Canada. This is the English translation of her handwritten testimony:

"Special characteristics of The Church of Jesus Christ of Latter-day Saints which are not present in other religious communities include, above all, modern *revelation* given through the *Prophet Joseph Smith.*

"The *Book of Mormon,* in its clear and pure language, is next, with all the instructions and promises for the Church of Jesus Christ; truly a *second witness,* together with the Bible, *that Jesus Christ lives.*

"Bound together by faith in *a personal God,* that is, God the Father, God the Son, and the Holy Ghost, who facilitates prayer and also influences personally.

"Also, faith in the premortal life, the preexistence, the purpose of our earthly life, and our life after death is so valuable for us, and especially interesting and informative. It is clearly laid out, and our lives receive new meaning and direction.

"The Church has given us the *Word of Wisdom* as a guide to keep body and spirit in the most perfect shape possible to realize our desire and goal. So we keep our bodies healthy and improve them. All this from the knowledge that we will take them up again after death in the same form.

"Totally new to me, of course, is *temple work* with its many sacred ordinances, having *families together forever.* All this was given through revelation to the Prophet Joseph Smith." Marvelous.

There couldn't be two more different women than my mother and my mother-in-law. They looked different, they were different, but they both had the same strong faith that blessed them with the gifts of the Spirit. And they blessed not only my life but the lives of generations to come.

The lives of these women are a powerful witness of the fact that the gifts of the Spirit do not belong to men alone. Spiritual gifts, promises, and blessings of the Lord are given to those who qualify, without regard to gender (see D&C 46:9–26). In the Church of Jesus Christ, woman is not an adjunct to but an equal partner with man.[4]

The beliefs of the Church of Jesus Christ create a wonderful and unique feminine identity that encourages women to develop their abilities as true and literal daughters of God. Therefore, the Church's female membership has always played, and will always play, a central role in ensuring the success of Mormonism as a religion and as a society.

Through the Relief Society, Young Women, and Primary organizations, women obtain an ecclesiastical identity in the Church. The women of the Church are an important part in helping to "bring forth and establish the cause of Zion" (D&C 6:6). They care for the poor and the sick; serve proselyting, welfare, and humanitarian missions; and teach children and youth, realizing their contributions to the temporal and spiritual welfare of the Saints.

In accordance with the family-centered doctrine of the Church, a woman's role varies with her circumstances and the choices that she makes within the context of the restored gospel. She may fill many roles simultaneously, which will encourage her to acquire an education and training that will qualify her for two vocations—that of homemaking and that of earning a living outside the home, if and when the occasion requires.

We are living in a great season for all women in the Church. You are an essential part of our Heavenly Father's plan for eternal happiness; you are endowed with a divine birthright. You women are the real builders of nations wherever you live, because strong homes of love and peace will bring security to any nation.

President David O. McKay said the principal reason the Church was organized was "to make life sweet today, to give contentment to the heart today, to bring salvation today. . . . Some of us look forward to a time in the future—salvation and exaltation in the world to come—but today is part of eternity."[5]

What you sisters do today will determine how the restored gospel principles can influence the nations of the world tomorrow. It will determine how these heavenly rays of the gospel will light every land in the future.

By living up to this mission, in whatever life circumstance you find yourself—as a wife and mother, as a single mother, as a divorced woman, as a widowed or a single woman—the Lord our God has responsibilities and blessings in store for each of you individually, far beyond your imagination.

May I invite you to rise to the great potential within you. But don't reach beyond your capacity. Don't set goals beyond your capacity to achieve. Don't feel guilty or dwell on thoughts of failure. Don't compare yourself with others. Do the best you can, and the Lord will provide the rest. Have faith and confidence in Him, our Savior, and you will see miracles happen in your life and the lives of your loved ones. The virtue of your own personal life will be a light to those who sit in darkness, and it will be because you are a living witness of the fulness of the restored gospel. Wherever you have been planted on this beautiful but often troubled earth of ours, you can be the one to "succor the weak, lift up the hands which hang down, and strengthen the feeble knees" (D&C 81:5).

My dear sisters, let me assure you that the Lord loves you. He knows you. He listens to your prayers, and He answers those prayers, wherever on this world you may be. He wants you to succeed in this life and in eternity.

In the early days of the Restoration, the Lord spoke to Emma Smith through the Prophet Joseph Smith, giving her instructions and blessings. The Lord declared that this revelation was "my voice unto all." Remember that these same promised blessings apply to you. He said:

- "If thou art faithful . . . thou needest not fear."
- "A crown of righteousness thou shalt receive."
- "Where I am you [can] come" (see D&C 25).

Later the Prophet Joseph Smith added: "If you live up to your privileges, the angels cannot be restrained from being your associates."[6]

Of this truth, my dear sisters, I testify.

NOTES

1. Heber J. Grant, *Gospel Standards*, comp. G. Homer Durham (Salt Lake City: Deseret Book, 1941), 151.
2. Gordon B. Hinckley, "Standing Strong and Immovable," *Worldwide Leadership Training Meeting*, January 2004, 20.
3. See Gordon B. Hinckley, "A Prophet's Counsel and Prayer for Youth," *Ensign*, January 2001, 7.
4. See John A. Widtsoe, *Evidences and Reconciliations*, comp. G. Homer Durham, 3 vols. in 1 (Salt Lake City: Bookcraft, 1960), 305.
5. David O. McKay, *Pathways to Happiness*, comp. Llewelyn R. McKay (Salt Lake City: Bookcraft, 1957), 291–92.
6. Joseph Smith, *History of The Church of Jesus Christ of Latter-day Saints*, ed. B. H. Roberts, 2d ed. rev., 7 vols. (Salt Lake City: The Church of Jesus Christ of Latter-day Saints, 1932–51), 4:605.

ALL WE KNOW, ALL WE HAVE, ALL THAT AWAITS

Anne C. Pingree

One Saturday shortly after my husband and I began our missionary service in West Africa, we drove our way over the deep, potholed roads to Ikot Ekong, one of the first bush districts organized after the revelation on the priesthood was announced in 1978.

As we entered the simple concrete building nestled in the jungle among tall palm trees, we saw a beautiful, ebony-skinned Nigerian Relief Society sister who had obviously trekked some distance in order to clean the building before our conference. Bringing her short-handled broom made from the spines of dried palm fronds, she worked hard, bending over to sweep the rust-colored sand from the chapel's chipped concrete floor. I greeted her, thanking her in my strange American English. I then asked her a question about the meeting to come.

I will never forget her response. She answered in halting English, as she referred to her husband, "I will ask my master."

My master!

Those words hit me like a ton of bricks. As I stood speechless beside

Anne C. Pingree is currently serving as second counselor in the Relief Society general presidency. She earned a bachelor's degree from the University of Utah. In addition to her service as a homemaker, Sister Pingree has been a literacy volunteer for at-risk elementary school children and a tutor to Laotians for Literacy Volunteers of America. She served with her husband, George C. Pingree, during his assignment as mission president in the Nigeria Port Harcourt Mission. They have five children and seven grandchildren.

that magnificent sister, I was stunned by the realization of what those two words meant. And so was my husband. Later he said to me as we spoke of the experience, "Please teach these precious Nigerian sisters *who* they are."

Sisters, I rejoice to be a woman living when the gospel of Jesus Christ has been fully restored and we know who we are. When I ponder all we know, all we have, and all that awaits, my heart soars. We are, in fact, individually loved and valued by the Lord to such a degree that our prophet, President Gordon B. Hinckley, has said: "Let us, each one, resolve within . . . herself that we will add to the luster of this magnificent work of the Almighty, that it may shine across the earth as a beacon of strength and goodness for all the world to look upon."[1]

He has also said: "This is [the] season to be strong. It is a time to move forward without hesitation, knowing well the meaning, the breadth, and the importance of our mission [and responsibilities]."[2]

That call to shine across the earth, that reminder to be resolute in our faith, fills me with joy. It reminds me that the truths of the gospel apply to my life and family and circumstances. It tells me that my personal efforts to prioritize my actions and thoughts and time matter to the Lord.

Today I want to discuss several revealed truths that give us as women of these latter days such a cause to "press forward with a . . . perfect brightness of hope" (2 Nephi 31:20).

First, we are daughters of God, given the agency to prioritize our time and actions.

Second, we can better the world as we serve individually and in complementary roles with our brethren.

Third, our covenants bind us to the Lord; temple ordinances link us eternally to our families, in which we have sacred roles.

First, we are daughters of God, given the agency to prioritize our time and actions.

The restored gospel of Jesus Christ shines a great light upon our identity as women. Literally, we are "daughters of our Heavenly Father, who loves us."[3] Because this is true, each and every woman, regardless of her circumstances, can face her life with wonderful expectations of her own possibilities and purpose. My dear sisters in Nigeria were amazed and their eyes grew wide with disbelief as I taught them that they were beloved daughters of God, that He knew their names, their challenges, and the righteous desires of their hearts.

I cannot describe to you the joy I felt in being able to teach them the glorious doctrine that we are precious and of infinite worth to the Lord and that "he inviteth them all to come unto him and partake of his goodness; and he denieth none that come unto him, black and white, bond and free, male and female; . . . and all are alike unto God" (2 Nephi 26:33). That doctrine warms my soul just as it did the sisters of Africa.

Understanding that the Lord invites each of us as a beloved daughter to come unto Him profoundly influences *how* we think and *what* we do. Perhaps our greatest challenge today is not to become distracted from our most important responsibilities by the busyness of our lives. For the most part, we have sufficient testimony and enough life experience to have little trouble deciding between good and evil. Our challenge comes in choosing between *good* things and *needful* things. A scripture speaks of "lay[ing] aside the [good] things of this world, and seek[ing] for the things of a better" (D&C 25:10).

Sisters, a glorious gift of the Restoration to women is the knowledge that each daughter of God can prayerfully ponder her priorities, can carefully measure her choices with an eternal yardstick. In a most personal, profound sense, we can seek for the things of a better world.

Second, we can better the world as we serve individually and in complementary roles with our brethren.

Identifying a key priority, our prophet, President Gordon B. Hinckley, has made a clarion call to the Relief Society sisters of this day. He said: "We call upon the women of the Church to stand together for righteousness. They must begin in their own homes. They can teach it in their classes. They can voice it in their communities."[4] This inspired message reminds us that as we act upon Restoration truths, we can make the world a better place.

Let me share with you an example of a sister whose service blessed many in her land. Dr. Prisca is a Relief Society sister who heeds the prophet's call to stand for righteousness. She set a great example for her fellow countrymen by volunteering for three weeks to help vaccinate children during the Red Cross and Church-sponsored measles campaign in her island nation of Madagascar. When she attended a preliminary meeting for all the vaccinators, the other physicians focused on the payment they expected for their services. After listening to their discussion, she arose, less than five feet in height, and boldly declared that she was willing to work without any compensation. The moderator asked if she would sign a statement to that effect, which she did in the presence of more than 100 people. Her example of standing strong and immovable in doing what she knew was right blessed not only children in families but also many orphans in her homeland. She personally went into the city to bring street children to the clinic for their measles vaccinations.

What a blessing to the world committed Relief Society sisters like Dr. Prisca are because they "arise and shine forth . . . [as] a standard for the nations" (D&C 115:5) in which they live. They know who they are and what their responsibilities are, and they use their time, talents, and influence to better the world.

Significantly, as a result of truth revealed in the Restoration, we, as daughters of God, know our proper relationship with our brethren. Time after time as I taught the regal Relief Society sisters of West Africa that they are equal to their husbands in the sight of God, they would gaze at me in total amazement.

They could *not* believe that it was possible.

Thankfully, modern prophets have clarified our complementary roles as men and women. President Hinckley said of women: "They are our co-workers in building the kingdom of God. How great their role, how marvelous their contribution. How they add to the luster of life."[5] Sisters, this doctrine that we serve as partners with our brethren, in complementary roles to theirs, places us in the position to do great good in the Church and truly to add luster to the world. We are not only positioned to do so, but we are blessed because we *can* do so.

Belle Spafford, a general Relief Society president for nearly 30 years, reminded President David O. McKay that ever since the Restoration, women have built the kingdom of God along with men. She used this explanation: "The women stood side by side with the brethren when they were in Kirtland, in Missouri and in Nauvoo, and they walked across the plains with the brethren."[6] When I think of this joint labor, I recall that every step a man took, a woman walked. Every mountain a woman climbed, a man scaled, too.

Of course, our work as "fellow laborers" is not always the same as we build the kingdom of God. The example of how men and women worked in complement to build the first Nauvoo temple makes the point. The men constructed the building; the women housed, clothed, and fed those temple workers. The brethren hewed the timbers; the sisters sewed the temple veil. And so it went. All were needed to complete the house of the Lord.

Joseph Smith, whom we honor so appropriately this year, explained that the Church was never perfectly organized until the women were organized. Now, throughout the world in more than 160 nations, we are organized—priesthood and Relief Society—according to the Lord's order, and we walk and work side by side to accomplish our important responsibilities.

Sometimes we hear of sisters who don't feel listened to or supported by priesthood leaders. Some Relief Society leaders disagree with decisions and directions of their priesthood brethren. Whatever the case, dear sisters, may I suggest that we take to heart President Hinckley's statement that we are "co-workers" with the brethren "in building the kingdom of God." Let us believe in the greatness of our roles and our ability to make marvelous contributions.

Then let us add luster to our callings, to our joint service with our brethren, to our work in the world. The Lord is depending upon us to do so. Let us never be dissuaded from living according to who we are and what we must do. Rather, let us stand strong as women of these latter days who continue to take part in helping to "bring forth and establish the cause of Zion" (D&C 6:6).

Third, our covenants bind us to the Lord; temple ordinances link us eternally to our families, in which we have sacred roles.

The covenants we make in the temple bind us to the Lord. The saving ordinances we participate in link us to our families. The sisters who aided in the building and furnishing of the early Restoration temples knew this truth and understood the place of temples in the bringing forth of "the cause of Zion." As they officiated in temple ordinances and engaged in the saving work done in the house of the Lord, the sisters knew their service blessed both the living and their kindred dead.

Their temple covenants also gave them the peace and courage they needed to face their perilous times. In her journal, Sarah Rich, a Nauvoo sister, penned these poignant feelings: "If it had not been for the faith and knowledge that was bestowed upon us in [the Nauvoo] temple by the influence and help of the spirit of the Lord, our journey would have been like one taking a leap in the dark, to start out on such a journey in the winter as it was, and in our state of poverty, it would seem like walking into the jaws of death."[7] Driven brutally from their homes, forced across the frozen Mississippi, sent to an unknown destination, burying loved ones along the way, these sisters leaned heavily upon the spiritual bonds they felt with the Lord because of sacred ordinances performed and personal covenants made in the temple.

The performance of ordinances that link generation to generation brings spiritual stability and depth to family members on this side of the veil while offering our families on the other side the freeing blessings of the temple. As we do for our kindred dead what they cannot do for themselves, we draw our families together in a way that is meaningful across generations. It is, in fact, difficult to put into words the blessings of hearts turned to fathers and children.

After years of gathering old photos and searching for vital family records, the MacArthur family was blessed to have the opportunity to do temple work for family members whose names they bear. During the drive from their home in another city to the Portland Oregon Temple, Sister MacArthur said, "[All of us in the family] reviewed the names of the ancestors whose temple work we would soon perform. We shared what we knew about each person and made sure we understood all the family relationships. Each of us decided upon one individual for whom we could do all the necessary ordinances that day. Our younger son temporarily became family patriarch by serving as proxy for his third great-grandfather Hugh MacArthur, who had been born more than 200 years earlier. Serving as a proxy for a chosen ancestor helped us each see the ordinances of the temple through new eyes, and the significance of the promises and covenants took on new meaning." She said, "I will always recall the beautiful memory of my family in the sealing room and that comforting, joyful feeling in my heart. It was a time for *sealing* and *celebrating* seven generations of our eternal family!"[8]

Generation to generation, women's roles in the family—wife, mother, grandmother, niece, sister, aunt—are sacred and binding. When we are together, we women often talk about our roles in families, don't we? Maybe we discuss family so readily because we know that *all* we do in our homes, with our spouses, for our children, and in behalf of our extended family members matters deeply in both temporal and spiritual realms. What a gift that restored knowledge is to women! What a difference this knowledge can make in how we think and plan for the family.

Recently, I was in Guadalajara. Let me tell you about this amazing mother I met. In the midst of her demanding responsibilities as a mission president's wife in Mexico, Sister Anderson found an inspired way to prepare her own boys to be missionaries. Desiring that her 8-, 12-, and 14-year-old sons become more proficient in the Spanish language, she arranged for a tutor to come to the mission home regularly. She asked the tutor, a serious-minded, demanding, but loving teacher, to use the Spanish Book of Mormon as the tool by which the boys could develop their language fluency. Sister Anderson also asked the tutor to develop questions to ask her sons about the things they had read.

Through the months, the tutor listened to each boy read in Spanish from the Book of Mormon and then asked questions. Her heart was softened, and her testimony blossomed. She later shared that she saw light around the boys' heads each time they read from the Book of Mormon. The Spirit touched her, and she joined the Church. I met her as a new convert of just one day while I was on a training assignment in Mexico.

I like the response of an aunt who helped her recently returned missionary nephew as he struggled through a piercing personal tragedy. His mother—her sister—died unexpectedly only a few months after the missionary's return home. In his sorrow he lost some of the light of faith that had burned so brightly in his heart. His aunt, anxious for his welfare, gave him a photo of himself that she had taken on the day he returned from his mission. She urged him to remember *why* he had looked so radiant and happy and *what* he had taught on his mission about faith and hope.

Through subsequent months she encouraged and counseled with him. Often she reminded him that she longed to see that excited, hopeful expression again because it would mean that he was healing and living so that the Spirit of the Lord could rekindle brightness in his heart and countenance once more. The photograph, a very specific visual reminder, and his aunt's steady, prayerful, optimistic participation in his life served as a beacon to this young man, lifting and directing him.

I have often thought about Emma Smith as a remarkable wife to her prophet husband. Joseph Smith described his tall, dark-haired, dark-eyed wife as "undaunted, firm, and unwavering—unchangeable, affectionate."[9] Emma's mother-in-law, Lucy Mack Smith, wrote of her: "I have never seen a woman in my life who would endure every species of fatigue and hardship from month to month and from year to year with that unflinching courage, zeal and patience. . . . She has breasted the storms of persecution, and buffeted the rage of men and devils, which would have borne down almost any other woman."[10]

What strikes me about these tributes is that Emma, in so many ways an *ordinary* woman like you and me, did the *extraordinary* in the most trying of circumstances. In my experience, women bent on being Christlike and sincerely working for the betterment of their families are invariably extraordinary.

In an even broader sense, President Hinckley captures this idea. He said: "We are ordinary people who are engaged in an extraordinary undertaking. . . . Those who have gone before have accomplished wonders. It is our opportunity and our challenge to continue in this great undertaking, the future of which we can scarcely imagine."[11]

Sisters, I began my remarks today by sharing a story of African sisters new to the gospel who marveled at its revealed truths. I "stand all amazed" as well when I consider all we are, all we know, and all that awaits. These restored truths brightly beckon and bless us.

Like Mary, the first to see the Savior after His Resurrection, we look to Him and proclaim with joy and gratitude as she did, "Master" (John 20:16). What a gift it is to know that Jesus Christ knows and loves us personally, atoned for our individual sins, overcame the world, restored the gospel in this dispensation, and stands eternally as our Savior and Redeemer, our Lord and Master.

NOTES

1. Gordon B. Hinckley, "Condition of the Church," *Ensign*, November 2004, 6.
2. Gordon B. Hinckley, "This Is the Work of the Master," *Ensign*, May 1995, 71.

3. *Young Women Personal Progress: Standing As a Witness of God* (Salt Lake City: The Church of Jesus Christ of Latter-day Saints, 2001), 5.

4. Gordon B. Hinckley, "Standing Strong and Immovable," *Worldwide Leadership Training Meeting,* January 2004, 20.

5. Hinckley, "Standing Strong and Immovable," 21.

6. Interviews with Jill Mulvay Derr, *Belle S. Spafford Oral History,* 1975–76, 117.

7. Sarah Rich, in Carol Cornwall Madsen, *Journey to Zion: Voices from the Mormon Trail* (Salt Lake City: Deseret Book, 1997), 173.

8. Mary Ellen Romney MacArthur, "Our Seven-Generation Celebration," *Ensign,* July 1966, 30.

9. Joseph Smith, *History of The Church of Jesus Christ of Latter-day Saints,* ed. B. H. Roberts, 2d ed. rev., 7 vols. (Salt Lake City: The Church of Jesus Christ of Latter-day Saints, 1932–51), 5:107.

10. Lucy Mack Smith, *History of Joseph Smith, Revised and Enhanced,* ed. Scot Facer Proctor and Maurine Jensen Proctor (Salt Lake City: Bookcraft, 1996), 249.

11. Gordon B. Hinckley, "The State of the Church," *Ensign,* November 2003, 7.

"A Friend Loveth at All Times"

Mary Ellen Edmunds

I've chosen my title from Proverbs 17:17: "A friend loveth at all times, and a [sister] is born for adversity." I changed "brother" to "sister" just for today—maybe for tomorrow, too.

Do you remember your first friend? How old were you when you had your first friend? Where did you live? What kind of things did you do together with your first friend? I'm still close to the first friend I remember having. When I was three years old our family moved from California to Utah. We lived just across the street and down a few houses from the Palmers, and Zonie was my best friend. We'd sleep out on her lawn and we'd look at all the stars. (There were more back then.) And we would find one that we were sure no one else had ever, ever, ever seen. And then we would tell only our best friends about it. We kept it secret.

Having friends and being a friend has been important to me my whole life. We are honoring the Prophet Joseph Smith and the topic of friendship is based on what the Lord reminded him about his friends: that he

Mary Ellen Edmunds, popular author, speaker, and Relief Society teacher at the Missionary Training Center in Provo, earned a bachelor's degree in nursing from Brigham Young University and has served on the faculty there. In addition to her service on the Relief Society general board, she has been on four missions and was a director of training at the Provo Missionary Training Center. She has a fondness for the peoples of Taiwan, Hong Kong, Indonesia, and the Philippines, where she served on her missions.

had many friends who were standing by him with warm hearts and friendly hands.

This year we celebrate Joseph's 200th birthday, remembering that he's an example and a teacher of so many wonderful qualities, including the quality of being a true friend. I have thought so many times about what a difference it made for him to have friends in his own family, with his wonderful parents, with his brothers and sisters, especially Hyrum, who was to Joseph as Jonathan was to David. These brothers had a sacred bond of genuine friendship, unselfish and tender, a friendship of that pure quality of which there are but few instances on record. Hyrum watched tenderly over his younger brother Joseph. He was a peacemaker. He was faithful unto death as recorded in the Doctrine and Covenants: "In life they were not divided, and in death they were not separated!" (D&C 135:3).

Joseph expressed the following in August 1842: "Brother Hyrum, what a faithful heart you have got! Oh, may the Eternal Jehovah crown eternal blessings upon your head, as a reward for the care you have had for my soul! O how many are the sorrows we have shared together; and again we find ourselves shackled with the unrelenting hand of oppression. Hyrum, thy name shall be written in the Book of the Law of the Lord, for those who come after thee to look upon, that they may pattern after thy works."[1] We can become a friend to others as Hyrum and Joseph were to each other.

The Prophet Joseph Smith was an extraordinary friend to others. He taught: "Friendship is one of the grand fundamental principles of Mormonism. Friendship is like Brother Turley in his blacksmith shop welding iron to iron; it unites the human family with its happy influence."[2] In a letter to his dear wife Emma in the midst of their many trials, Joseph wrote, "Oh my affectionate Emma, I want you to remember that I am a true and faithful friend, to you and the children, forever."[3]

The Prophet Joseph knew from his own experience what a blessing and privilege it is to have a friend. He said, "Those who have not been enclosed within the walls of prison without cause or provocation, can have but little idea how sweet the voice of a friend is."[4]

One of the saddest things about the Prophet's life for me is how many of his closest friends and associates turned against him. I can't imagine how painful it must have been for him to see those who had been by his side through extraordinary experiences let go and turn away. President Wilford Woodruff recorded in his diary a statement Joseph Smith made in May 1843, wherein he said that only two of the original Twelve Apostles had not "lifted their heel against" him, namely Brigham Young and Heber C. Kimball.[5]

And yet the Prophet was so quick to forgive. I know you've read and heard the story of his friendship with William W. Phelps, who was baptized in 1832 and had a lot of wonderful spiritual experiences and opportunities for leadership. But he misused some Church funds and was disfellowshipped in March 1838. He became a bitter enemy of the Prophet and even testified against Joseph and others in Liberty Jail. He was finally excommunicated in March 1839.

The Prophet must have been deeply hurt by this former friend who turned against him with such animosity. But by the summer of 1840, Brother Phelps had experienced a mighty change of heart. In June he wrote a letter of true repentance to the Prophet, admitting he had done wrong and expressing how sorry he was. He wrote, "I want your fellowship; if you cannot grant that, grant me your peace and friendship, for we are brethren, and our communion used to be sweet, and whenever the Lord brings us together again, I will make all the satisfaction on every point that Saints or God can require."

On July 22, 1840, the Prophet wrote back quite a lengthy letter, including the following: "Dear Brother Phelps: . . . You may in some measure realize what my feelings, as well as Elder Rigdon's and Brother Hyrum's were, when we read your letter—truly our hearts were melted into tenderness and compassion when we ascertained your resolves. . . . It is true, that we have suffered much in consequence of your behavior. . . . One with whom we had oft taken sweet counsel together, and enjoyed many refreshing seasons from the Lord—'had it been an enemy, we could have borne it.' . . . Believing your confession to be real, and your repentance genuine, I shall be happy once again to give you the right hand of fellowship, and rejoice over the returning prodigal. . . .

> 'Come on, dear brother, since the war is past,
> For friends at first, are friends again at last.'"[6]

About one year later, Brother Phelps was rebaptized, and he moved to Utah in 1848. He wrote many hymns, including "The Spirit of God" (*Hymns*, no. 2), "Now Let Us Rejoice" (no. 3), "Redeemer of Israel" (no. 6), and "If You Could Hie to Kolob" (no. 284). There is one hymn, though, which has special meaning to the friendship of Joseph and William. It is "Praise to the Man" (no. 27).

One idea I have for each of us today is to search our hearts and see if there is anyone who needs to hear from us something like what Joseph said to Brother Phelps: "Come on, dear brother [or dear sister], . . . friends at first, are friends again at last."

Reconciliation. Forgiveness. Letting go. Is there anyone you can think of who needs to return to the circle of your friendship and love? Anyone you can forgive, perhaps as a gift to the Prophet Joseph Smith in this the year of his 200th birthday? Wouldn't that be a wonderful thing?

I love looking up the meaning of words in dictionaries. And I looked up *friend* and *friendship* and found lots of good stuff. Here's a sampling:

"To be ready, willing, or cheerful, or joyous—perhaps to frolick!" (Wouldn't that be fun as friends to frolic?)

"An in-depth relationship combining trust, support, communication, loyalty, understanding, empathy, and closeness."

"One who has sufficient interest to serve another."

On the value of friendship, President David O. McKay said, "Next to a sense of kinship with God comes the helpfulness, encouragement, and inspiration of friends. Friendship is a sacred possession. . . . 'To live, laugh, love one's friends, and be loved by them is to bask in the sunshine of life.'"[7]

A true friend is one with whom you can completely relax. Women especially serve as each other's therapists. We help each other make sense out of what is happening in our lives. Friends help us live longer and better and handle stress better. In one study, researchers found that people who have the most friends cut their risk of death by more than 60 percent! Another study found that the more friends women have, the less likely they are to develop physical impairments as they age, and the more likely they are to be leading a joyful life!

Some wise (anonymous) person has shared this thought: "A friend is one who hears the song in my heart and sings it to me when my memory fails."

In my life I have run across some examples of great friendships: the Savior with Mary, Martha, and Lazarus; Joseph and Hyrum; David and Jonathan; Ruth and Naomi; Heather and Ali; John Adams and Thomas Jefferson; Helen Keller and Annie Sullivan; Brian Piccolo and Gale Sayers; Bugs and Bidi; Batman and Robin; Kermit and Miss Piggy; Porgy and Bess. (You know I just got carried away. I had quite a few pages.)

Think of someone who is a friend to you right now. What are some of the things that make him or her such a good friend? Is it the joy and pleasure of just being friends? Do they make you want to live better and be better? Do they both laugh and cry with you? Are you safe with them? Is there trust?

Samuel Johnson said: "We cannot tell the precise moment when friendship is formed. As in filling a vessel drop by drop, there is at last a drop which makes it run over; so in a series of kindnesses there is at last one which makes the heart run over."[8]

How can we find and keep good friends? Look in your own family. You may find a best friend right in your own home!

This is true for me in my friendship with my younger sister Charlotte (who is currently serving in Sweden as a missionary with her husband). In spite of some spectacular disagreements in our childhood as we shared a room and everything all of our growing-up years, we have become the best of friends. I love her so much.

My friendship with my mother deepened when I went on my first mission. She fasted for me once a week and said to keep it just between the two of us. She sent letters and packages, and she'd send weird things—mousetraps and aprons from D. I. She helped me feel close even though we were 10,000 miles apart. I treasure my friendship with my family, some of whom are here today—my sisters and brothers, my sisters-in-law and brothers-in-law, my nieces, my nephews, and all the little "greats" who are starting to come along.

How can we be better friends? One thing I've thought of is to live the Golden Rule: to do to them what you wish they would do to you, even if they never do. To keep confidences, never betray a trust. To become better listeners. To read again the book by Dale Carnegie, *How to Win Friends and Influence People.* I looked through that again in getting ready for today and it's a great book. Cultivate a kind, friendly countenance. Can you think of a countenance that you just love? Maybe it's your mother or father or a grandparent or a teacher.

An Asian girl was introducing her friend to her bishop and said in her broken English, "He not mean, he just look mean." What kind of a countenance do we have? What do people see when they look at us?

Don't wait for someone to come and be your friend. It's been my experience that the best way to find a friend is to search and to be a friend. Open your heart and your doors and your windows. Or dig a hole to China. Did you ever do that when you were little?

The Lombardi brothers in our neighborhood were digging a tunnel all the way to China and I was just staying friends with them so I could get in the hole and go to China and see all those people and perhaps find a whole bunch of new friends!

I once read a wonderful little article about a woman who was visiting China. A 16-year-old boy in the park came up to her and wanted to practice his English, so they chatted for a while. Then she needed to leave, and as she turned he touched her sleeve and said, "Madam, I please tell you something more. You know when I was little boy, I dig hole to try to get to United States of America."

This woman couldn't believe what she was hearing. She said to him, "When I was a little girl, I tried to dig a hole to get to China!" Then she threw her arms around him and hugged him and said, "And now at last we meet!" What a wonderful thing.

Friendship isn't just about gathering people around you who are just like you, is it? There are some wonderful experiences in having friends with different talents, cultures, and traditions. I have friends I couldn't even really talk to because I didn't know their language and they didn't know mine, but we still became friends. Don't be too isolated or insulated.

Don't lose opportunities for being with others by spending too much time in front of the TV or in meaningless reading or computer games or online stuff. Follow what Church leaders have advised. They've encouraged us to get involved in life, rather than just contemplating it! Maybe we could do things like join an Institute class or a dance class. Get involved in service. I think of all the friendship and love that came to our family as our father passed away a few days after Christmas several years ago. I remember how many wonderful friends came to help me when I had a terrible flood a few years ago in my home. What a great friend my neighbor Shirley is when she calls up and says, "Let's walk!" And even when I think I don't have time, it does me so much good. I call her Mrs. Walker.

Jesus taught that by losing ourselves in the service of others, we find ourselves (see Matthew 10:39).

President Spencer W. Kimball put it this way: "The more we serve our fellowmen in appropriate ways, the more substance there is to our souls. We become more significant individuals. . . . Indeed, it is easier to 'find' ourselves because there is so much more of us to find!"[9]

Get tickets for plays, concerts, movies, and invite someone to go along. Join the ward choir, a book club, a neighborhood exercise group. Invite someone to bring their children and join you at the park. See if you can find someone who's lonely whom you could befriend.

Elder Jeffrey R. Holland said: "We could remember that Christ called his disciples friends, and that friends are those who stand by us in times of loneliness or potential despair. We could remember a friend we need to contact or, better yet, a friend we need to make. In doing so we could remember that God often provides his blessings through the compassionate and timely response of another. For someone nearby we may be the means of heaven's answer to a very urgent prayer."[10]

I love that sentence from Elder Holland. Let me repeat it: "For someone nearby we may be the means of heaven's answer to a very urgent prayer."

I think we could maybe write more letters, make more visits and phone calls than we do. Friendship is also not just about having friends who are our same age or the same season as we are. Many of us have dear friends who are lots older and lots younger. If you're my friend, you have a friend that's a lot older. I have a brand-new Medicare card.

I remember my sister Susan going to play Scrabble with Aunt Olive, 57 years older than Susan, and Aunt Olive always won. I asked Susan if she cheated. She said, "No, she was a schoolteacher."

Proverbs 18:24 says, "There is a friend that sticketh closer than a brother." Sometimes our paths cross so briefly with others, and yet we feel like we'll be friends forever. I've had some friends who have come into my life for 20 minutes and their influence has been so significant.

My patriarchal blessing has some strong counsel about choosing good friends, saying that there would be those I would meet who would try to convince me that the gospel of Jesus Christ was not the most important thing in my life.

Elder Robert D. Hales said, "Do you know how to recognize a true friend? A real friend loves us and protects us. . . . A true friend makes it easier for us to live the gospel by being around [her or] him."[11] While I've met a few people in my life who were not "of good report and praiseworthy," I've been blessed with wonderful friends.

When I was first working on this talk I began to include some examples, and they went on page after page after page. If I had a few hours I would tell you some wonderful stories, and they're all true.

It's hard to keep close to everyone, isn't it? Oh, how sad I feel at losing contact with some of my dear friends as the years have gone by.

I love this quote by Anne Morrow Lindbergh: "My life cannot implement in action the demands of all the people to whom my heart responds."[12] I feel that's so true in my life.

Some people collect coins, stamps, thimbles, frogs, boxes, and stuff, tumbleweeds. I seem to collect friends—all kinds of wonderful people all over the world to whom my heart responds. Oh, how I wish I had a way to keep close to every single one of them.

I had a time in my life when I needed a close friend. I really wanted a husband, and I hoped that would be the friend that would come dancing in. But it hasn't happened yet, and meanwhile I just talk to Heavenly Father a lot about the need for a friend. Through many years there were many wonderful people in my life—good friends—but I think you know what I mean if I say that I needed a close friend—someone with whom I could share my heart and my deepest feelings, my fears and my disappointments, my laughter and my tears, my memories, my dreams.

And not right away, but eventually, I received the gift of a friend who I had been searching for. It is such a blessing to have someone with whom I am so completely comfortable, with whom I can be real—honest and open and trusting. It is an extraordinary experience to have someone know you so well and love you anyway! Do you have someone like that in your life? Someone who knows you so well and they love you anyway? To be safe is quite a feeling. How do we thank Heavenly Father adequately for the gift of friendship?

Friendships remind me of a poem given to me by one of my wonderful friends, Marilyn B. Durrant. To each other we are MBD and MEE and we send each other stupid gifts and we can hardly wait to see the next thing that will come in the mail.

> *What made us friends in the long ago*
> *When first we met?*
> *Well, I think I know.*
> *The best in me and the best in you*
> *Hailed each other because they knew*
> *That always and always since life began*
> *Our being friends was part of God's plan!*[13]

I have learned a lot about friendship through my father's example with a friend of his whom he called his dear pal Lewie. They met in the '20s (that would be 19-, not 18-) when they were roommates in Chicago at Northwestern as they went to medical school. My dad wanted their friendship to be forever—an eternal, unending friendship. And so he kept in touch, and after almost 70 years, Lewie was baptized at the age of 90, with my father, age 92, by his side. I think they are now missionary companions over there!

Third Nephi 18:32 is a verse that reminds me of my dad and Lewis. Remember, almost 70 years after their friendship began, Lewie finally caught on. "Nevertheless, ye shall not cast him out of your synagogues, or your places of worship, for unto such shall ye continue to minister; for ye know not but what they will return and repent, and come unto me with full purpose of heart, and I shall heal them; and ye shall be the means of bringing salvation unto them."

Don't give up on others. Don't give up on yourself either. How about surprising someone with a burst of genuine friendship? Write a letter to someone who won't be expecting it. Visit someone who will be surprised to see you. Do something you've been meaning to do.

From the time we're little, we feel a strong need to belong, to know that someone loves us, that someone will "be there" for us, to know that we have a friend. I hope everyone here has at least one good, true friend. I hope there is no one here who feels friendless.

We've probably all had times when we've felt that while we had a lot of people around, we didn't feel especially close to any particular one. Maybe we've moved to a new place and we're just starting to get acquainted. And it seems like everybody else who is already there has their friends and their roots have sunk really deep. Maybe we feel there's not a place for us. What do we learn from these seasons, these experiences?

Well, today I want to say, don't ever forget that you have "friends in high places"! What a friend we have in Jesus, and in our Heavenly Father, and in the Holy Ghost, and in all of our loved ones who live over there. Some of them we don't remember, but they're interested in us and they love us and they surround us and help us. They will never forget you or turn away from you. I do love that song, "What a Friend We Have in Jesus."[14]

Elder Joseph B. Wirthlin taught: "The compassion of Christlike friends deeply touches and changes our lives. We should well remember that the Lord often sends 'blessings from above, thru words and deeds of those who love.' Love is the very essence of the gospel of Christ. In this Church, prayers for help are often answered by the Lord through the simple, daily service of caring brothers and sisters. In the goodness of genuine friends, I have seen the reflected mercy of the Lord Himself. I have always been humbled by the knowledge that the Savior regards us as His friends when we choose to follow Him and keep His commandments."[15]

Years ago I was talking to my little great-nephew Max. He was talking about spiders at Niagara Falls. I said, "Well, when you dream, do you dream about spiders?" He looked at me like, "You idiot!" "No," he said, "when we dream we dream about our friends and we love them. And we tell them that we love them and we take care of them." I will never forget the feeling I had as I learned from that little boy.

I want to go back to the title that I chose: "A friend loveth at all times, and a [sister] is born for adversity" (Proverbs 17:17). Maybe I was born to help you in some way. Maybe you were born to help me. Maybe you were born for someone in your life, in your family or not, whom you were meant to help and influence and be with, maybe just for 20 minutes or maybe for a long, long time. Maybe my dad was born to help Lewie. Maybe so.

The Savior said, "Ye are my friends, if ye do whatsoever I command you" (John 15:14). And He also said, "Verily I say unto you my friends, fear not, let your hearts be comforted; yea, rejoice evermore, and in everything give thanks" (D&C 98:1). The Savior will never leave us entirely alone—ever. He has promised, "I will not leave you comfortless: I will come to you" (John 14:18). "I will never leave thee, nor forsake thee" (Hebrews 13:5). I know this is true. I feel it. May God bless you with joy, contentment, hope, peace, and good friends.

NOTES

1. Joseph Smith, *History of The Church of Jesus Christ of Latter-day Saints*, ed. B. H. Roberts, 2d ed. rev., 7 vols. (Salt Lake City: The Church of Jesus Christ of Latter-day Saints, 1932–51), 5:107–8.
2. *History of the Church*, 5:517.
3. Joseph Smith, *The Personal Writings of Joseph Smith*, ed. Dean C. Jessee (Salt Lake City: Deseret Book, 1984), 367–68.
4. Joseph Smith, *Teachings of the Prophet Joseph Smith*, sel. Joseph Fielding Smith (Salt Lake City: Deseret Book, 1976), 134.
5. *History of the Church*, 5:412.
6. *History of the Church*, 4:142, 163–64.
7. David O. McKay, in Conference Report, April 1940, 116.
8. Samuel Johnson, in James Boswell, *Life of Johnson* (New York: Oxford University Press, 1970), 848.
9. Spencer W. Kimball, "The Abundant Life," *Ensign*, July 1978, 3.
10. Jeffrey R. Holland, "This Do in Remembrance of Me," *Ensign*, November 1995, 69.
11. Robert D. Hales, "The Aaronic Priesthood: Return with Honor," *Ensign*, May 1990, 40.
12. Anne Morrow Lindbergh, *Gift from the Sea* (New York: Random House, 1975), 118.
13. Attributed to George Webster Douglas.
14. Joseph M. Scriven, "What a Friend We Have in Jesus" (N.p.: W. Williamson, 1895).
15. Joseph B. Wirthlin, "Valued Companions," *Ensign*, November 1997, 32.

"I Am a Mother"

Jane Clayson Johnson

A few weeks ago, my husband and I attended a dinner meeting a few miles outside Washington, D.C. It was a wonderful gathering of about 75, mostly LDS couples, from their respective fields of law, business, education, and communications. After dinner, everyone was asked to take a minute or two and introduce themselves.

What struck me as we listened was how many of the men in the room confidently stated their professional accomplishments, which were impressive.

Then their wives stood up—beautiful, intelligent, spiritually minded women.

And this is how many of them described themselves:

"Oh, I'm *just* a mom."

"I don't have any *credentials*; I'm just raising our six children."

"My life's not very exciting; I'm just a stay-at-home mom."

"I can't offer much; I'm *just* a mother."

Jane Clayson Johnson is the former co-host, with Bryant Gumbel, of The Early Show *on CBS, as well as a network correspondent for* The CBS Evening News *and* 48 Hours. *At ABC News, she covered national and international stories for* World News Tonight *with Peter Jennings and* Good Morning America. *Jane has received many journalism awards, including an Emmy and the Edward R. Murrow Award from the Radio and Television News Directors' Association of America, as well as an honorary doctorate degree from Utah State University. Jane and her husband, Mark, live in Boston and are the parents of Ella and a new baby boy, William.*

We heard some version of that phrase, "I'm *just* a mother," repeated, almost apologetically, over and over again.

More than a half-century ago, the First Presidency proclaimed:

"Motherhood is near to divinity. It is the highest, holiest service to be assumed by mankind. It places her who honors its holy calling and service next to the angels."[1]

President J. Reuben Clark Jr. declared motherhood is "as divinely called, as eternally important in its place as the Priesthood itself."[2] And more recently, President Gordon B. Hinckley has said, "God planted within women something divine."[3] That is the precious gift of motherhood.

Sometimes, you can hear the clarion call to raise the image of motherhood *outside* the Church as well. Recently, I saw an interview with Maria Shriver, the wife of California Governor Arnold Schwarzenegger. She was explaining her new agenda as the state's first lady. She said one of her goals during her husband's administration is to *empower mothers!*

"How do we get women," she said, "to stop saying, 'I'm *just* a mother.' Or, 'I *used* to be such and such, but now I'm *just* a mother'?" She continued, "I want women to say, 'I am a mother!' and *stop* [because that is enough]."[4]

Sisters, our calling as mothers is surely the highest and holiest of assignments. It is, as President David O. McKay proclaimed, "the noblest office or calling in the world."[5] Elder Jeffrey R. Holland asks us to think of its importance from a historical perspective: "[Mothers,] yours is the grand tradition of Eve, the mother of all the human family. . . . Yours is the . . . tradition of Sarah and Rebekah and Rachel, without whom there could not have been those magnificent patriarchal promises to Abraham, Isaac, and Jacob. . . . Yours is the grand tradition of Lois and Eunice and the mothers of the 2,000 stripling warriors. Yours is the grand tradition of Mary, chosen and foreordained from before this world was, to conceive, carry, and bear the Son of God Himself. We thank all of you, . . . mothers, and tell you there is nothing more important in this world than participating *so directly* in the work and glory of God. . . . Yours is the work of salvation, and therefore you will be magnified, compensated, made more than you are and better than you have ever been as you try to make a honest effort, however feeble you may sometimes feel that to be."[6]

And then this from Elder Neal A. Maxwell: "When the real history of mankind is fully disclosed, will it feature the echoes of gunfire or the shaping sound of lullabies? The great armistices made by military men or the peacemaking of women in homes and in neighborhoods? Will what happened in cradles and kitchens prove to be more controlling than what happened in congresses?"[7]

There should be no doubt that the influence of righteous, diligent, daily mothering is powerful and more prevailing than any position or institution created by man. Having said that, "in our society we give plenty of lip service to motherhood. We pat moms on the head, bring them flowers on Mother's Day and honor them before crowds. But at the end of the day, we don't extend them the same respect we would a professor, a dentist, an accountant or a judge."[8] We don't validate mothers in the way we do women who "work."

But if *we,* as women, don't respect the sanctity of this divine calling, it's hard to imagine why anyone else would. I'm not *just* a mother. I AM A MOTHER! Surely, when a woman reverences motherhood, her children will arise up and call her blessed (see Proverbs 31:28).

I must admit, some afternoons I watch Oprah. And I'd like to quote "Sister Winfrey" here for a moment, because, for someone who is not a mother, she hits the nail right on the head, especially when you consider what she says in the context of our faith. "In our hands we hold the power to transform the perception of motherhood. We should no longer allow a mother to be defined as 'just a mom.' It is on her back that great nations are built. To play down mothering as small is to crack the very foundation on which greatness stands. The world can only value mothering to the extent that women everywhere *stand and declare that it must be so.* As we affirm other mothers and as we teach our sons, husbands and friends to hold them in the highest regard, we honor both the mothers whose shoulders we have stood on and the *daughters* who will one day, stand tall on ours."[9]

Sister Sheri Dew so beautifully adds a spiritual component to that thought.

"Satan has declared war on motherhood," she says. "He knows that those who rock the cradle can rock his earthly empire. And he knows that without righteous mothers loving and leading the next generation, the kingdom of God will fail. When we understand the magnitude of motherhood, it becomes clear why prophets have been so protective of a woman's most sacred role."[10]

My dear sisters, I have prayed and felt prompted to share with you the events of the last year and a half of my life. Last January, I decided to leave New York City and the world of network news to be a mother. As someone who spent fifteen years in gratitude for the incredible opportunities afforded me in broadcast journalism, I stand before you today remembering a very poignant moment. It was at Ground Zero in New York on the second-year anniversary of the September 11 terrorist attacks on our country. I was anchoring, with Dan Rather, CBS's anniversary coverage of that terrible day. I had just returned from Washington, D.C., two days before, interviewing First Lady Laura Bush in the blue room of the White House. In many ways, professionally, I was on top of the world. But I remember so vividly; there was such emptiness there.

Not that I wasn't grateful for these tremendous experiences. Not that I wasn't passionate about my work. Not that I didn't feel that this was a particular mission I was called to fulfill in my life. But, I felt that one of my deepest longings still had not been met. And that was to be a wife and a mother.

Shortly after that experience, the most wonderful man I have ever known asked me on the grounds of the Salt Lake Temple to marry him. We were married there seven short weeks later. What happened over the course of the next few months could not have been choreographed. In fact, I am convinced the timing of some of these events is more than an interesting coincidence. As Elder David A. Bednar has testified, the Lord's timing and His "tender mercies . . . are real. They do not occur randomly . . . [and that] helps us to both discern and acknowledge them."[11]

Mark proposed to me on a Thursday night about 8:00. The next day, Friday morning, not less than twelve hours later, I got a call from my long-time agent in New York City. He was very excited. With my contract up at CBS, he was calling to tell me he had brokered a deal for me—a lucrative, four-year network contract offer, working in New York, in prime-time television, on some very interesting projects. At that moment, it was so apparent to me that the Lord was laying out two very distinct choices, two very distinct paths. It could not have been more clear.

For weeks, Mark and I prayed about this. We fasted. We weighed the pros and cons of this wonderful, yet very demanding opportunity—what it would mean for our family, what it would mean for me to potentially walk away. Throughout this period, I had some of the strongest promptings, some of the most powerful spiritual moments of my life.

Finally, I decided to leave New York City and the world of network news. When I did that, I recognized I may not simply be putting my career *on hold*. I reflected often on these words from Elder Jeffrey R. Holland: "In those crucial moments of pivotal personal history, [we must] submit our-selves to God even when all our hopes and fears may tempt us otherwise. We must be willing to place *all* that we have—not just our possessions (they may be the easiest things of all to give up) but also our ambition and pride and stubbornness and vanity—on the altar of God, kneel there in silent submission, and willingly walk away."[12]

It takes a great deal of faith to do that, whatever the circumstance. But I can tell you, the rewards are exquisite. Not to say it was easy. The voices of the world told me I was crazy, that I was out of my mind. When I explained to my agent of ten years that I would not be taking that net-work offer, that I was moving to Boston, he told me I was making a ter-rible decision and that I would regret it for years to come. "What will you *be* without your job?" he asked. And knowing of my faith, he then said, "What are you going to do, move up there and teach Sunday School?" Well, as it turns out, that first Sunday in my new ward, they called me to teach Gospel Doctrine.

The fact that I was going to focus on a family just didn't compute with some people. I remember one network executive looking quite puzzled when she asked me what I was going to do once I got to Boston. I told her I was going to have a family. I was going to be a mother. "No, I understand that," she said, "but what are you going to *do*?" (As if that wasn't enough!)

"That *is* what I'm going to do!" And that is what I did. A little more than a year ago, I left New York and moved to Boston to be with Mark, who is a blessing I never thought would come to me. He has the purest heart and the deepest faith of any person I have ever known.

That first workday after my CBS contract expired, after I'd moved to Boston, I will admit I was a little nervous. After fifteen years and quite a different pace of life, how would I feel? It was on *that* day I found out Mark and I were expecting a child. Another coincidence? No, I don't think so. The Lord, in His love and tender mercy, sends signs and confirmations in the most wonderful ways.

In this story lies one of the important lessons of my life, which I feel impressed to share, often, especially with young women. There are *seasons* in life. Don't ever let anyone deny you the blessings and joy of one season because they believe you should stay in another season. And never— *never*—be afraid to aspire to be a mother.

I love these words from President James E. Faust: "Women today are being encouraged by some to have it all—generally, all simultaneously: money, travel, marriage, motherhood, and separate careers in the world. . . .

"Doing things sequentially—filling roles one at a time at different times—is not always possible, as we know, but it gives a woman the opportunity to do each thing well *in its time* and to fill a variety of roles in her life. A woman . . . may fit more than one career into the various seasons of her life. She need not try to sing all of the verses of her song at the same time."[13]

There are so many voices today, drawing us—especially women—in so many directions, pulling us away from what is really important. I believe that from the depths of my heart. "The Family: A Proclamation to the World" means something. A mother is "primarily responsible for the nurture of [her] children." That is a vital and "sacred responsibilit[y]."[14]

We must keep our priorities. From my perspective now, I know: There is more to life than a job. There is more to life than a successful career. As a woman, the most important job I will ever have is within the walls of my own home.

Our daughter Ella just turned eight months old. She is the joy of our lives. But I'll be honest—as moms everywhere can attest, it's not always easy. In fact, I have said it is easier to "go to work" than it is to stay home and be a mother. There are some days, now, when I am down on my hands and knees mopping up yet another mess, when I look up at the TV to see one of my old friends interviewing someone famous or globetrotting on a big story and I think, "*What have I done?*" But then I look at the little face of my sweet baby girl—and I would not trade it. Not for anything. You don't get this time back.

I know what I gave up. But I also know what I gave it up for. I traded in fancy lunches in fancy restaurants for the fine art of making my daughter delicious rice cereal. There's no one to do hair and makeup anymore. Some mornings I'm lucky to squeak in a shower. When I get up at 4:00 A.M. these days, it's not to be chauffeured off to a television studio. Now, in the wee hours of the morning you'll often find me tucked in the corner of the nursery, lulling a little baby back to sleep. No more pats on the back for booking exclusive interviews—they don't give awards for best diaper change of the day. And I don't get a paycheck you can cash at any bank. Now my rewards come in packages money can't buy.

I will *never* regret this.

When I was pregnant with Ella, I started a little stitchery project (which I'm trying very hard to finish!). It's a quote from the book of Alma, in the Book of Mormon. "They had been *taught by their mothers*, that if they did not doubt, God would deliver them. And they rehearsed . . . the words of their mothers, saying: *We do not doubt our mothers knew it*" (Alma 56:47–48; emphasis added).

In humility, I strive to be like the faithful mothers of Helaman's young army. This generation of children faces some of the most difficult challenges ever, moral and otherwise. As mothers, let us ask ourselves the question that was asked of Esther: "Who knoweth whether thou art come to the kingdom for such a time as this?" (Esther 4:14).

I love this next story from the life of our prophet's beloved wife, Sister Marjorie Hinckley. Her granddaughter Laura recounts it. Laura describes herself, as a mother, wondering what her children might think of her, how they might remember her when they look back in years to come.

"Will they say, 'My mother was a great pianist who brought a love for music into our home?'" No, probably not, she says. "Will they say, 'She was incredibly bright and a gifted teacher at home and in her profession?'" Likely not.

Will it be that she was "uniquely creative" or perhaps an exceptional seamstress? No, not those things either. Laura kept thinking how nice it would be to decide on one special thing, so that she could really focus on it, *now*, while rearing her children. But she couldn't come up with anything.

Then she remembered the framed collection of portraits and short biographies of seven generations of women in her family, written by her grandmother Hinckley. Each woman had special gifts and talents, but she began to notice a strong, golden thread repeated over and over as Grandma recorded the lives of those good women. Every one of them was full of *faith*.

Suddenly Laura had her answer. "If I could choose only one thing for my children," she said, "I would want them to develop faith in our Heavenly Father. I want my children to say that their mother was a faithful member of the Church who kept her [temple] covenants. And I want to show them by example how to be faithful themselves."[15]

If there is one thing my own mother has taught me it is the power of faith, whatever the difficulty, whatever the circumstance. What a tremendous gift, an eternal gift, for which I will always be grateful.

I want to close with this thought from President David O. McKay:

"She who can paint a masterpiece or write a book that will influence millions deserves the admiration and the plaudits of mankind; but she who rears successfully a family of healthy, beautiful sons and daughters, whose influence will be felt through generations to come, . . . long after paintings shall have faded, and books . . . shall have been destroyed, deserves the highest honor that man can give, and the choicest blessings of God. In her high duty and service to humanity, . . . she is *co-partner with the Creator himself.*"[16]

Sisters, *that* is a mother!

We are mothers, a "co-partner with the Creator himself."

May I leave you with this challenge?

The next time someone wonders what you do, or asks you to describe yourself, would you say, *I am a mother!*

NOTES

1. "The Message of the First Presidency to the Church," *Improvement Era*, November 1942, 761.
2. J. Reuben Clark Jr., "Our Wives and Our Mothers in the Eternal Plan," *Relief Society Magazine*, December 1946, 801.
3. Gordon B. Hinckley, *Teachings of Gordon B. Hinckley* (Salt Lake City: Deseret Book, 1997), 387.
4. *The Oprah Winfrey Show*, "First Lady Maria Shriver—Her New Life," April 29, 2004; emphasis added.

5. David O. McKay, *Gospel Ideals* (Salt Lake City: Improvement Era, 1953), 453.
6. Jeffrey R. Holland, "Because She Is a Mother," *Ensign*, May 1997, 36.
7. Neal A. Maxwell, "The Women of God," *Ensign*, May 1978, 10–11.
8. "The Best of Oprah's 'What I Know for Sure,'" supplement to O, *The Oprah Magazine* (May 2005): 65.
9. "The Best of Oprah's 'What I Know for Sure,'" 66; emphasis added.
10. Sheri L. Dew, "Are We Not All Mothers?" *Ensign*, November 2001, 96.
11. David A. Bednar, "The Tender Mercies of the Lord," *Ensign*, May 2005, 99.
12. Jeffrey R. Holland and Patricia T. Holland, *On Earth as It Is in Heaven* (Salt Lake City: Deseret Book, 1989), 127.
13. James E. Faust, "A Message to My Granddaughters: Becoming 'Great Women,'" *Ensign*, September 1986, 18–19; emphasis added.
14. First Presidency and Council of the Twelve Apostles, "The Family: A Proclamation to the World," *Ensign*, November 1995, 102.
15. Based on a story told in *Glimpses into the Life and Heart of Marjorie Pay Hinckley*, ed. Virginia H. Pearce (Salt Lake City: Deseret Book, 1999), 15–16.
16. McKay, *Gospel Ideals*, 453–54; emphasis added.

ESCAPING THE SUPERWOMAN SYNDROME

Susan Robison

A few weeks ago, a friend from New York and I happened to be on the same plane to Salt Lake City. He asked me what brought me to Utah at that time, and I explained I was meeting with my co-presenter for the BYU Women's Conference. He inquired about my topic, and I told him: "Escaping the Superwoman Syndrome." He looked at me, smiled, and said, "Something you've never been able to do." I'm hoping he isn't entirely accurate, but I have been there a few times in my life.

Let me see if I can give you an example of a woman suffering from the superwoman syndrome:

She is pursuing a successful, satisfying career while trying to maintain a successful, satisfying marriage and family life. Her children are well cared for and well adjusted—as is the family pet. She lives in a beautiful home, which is always clean and well maintained, and she drives the latest car. Added to that, she is a gourmet cook, preparing and eating well-balanced meals, and she exercises regularly, occasionally running marathons. She is well educated and well read, and that includes reading the newspaper

---

Susan Robison graduated from Columbia University with a Bachelor of Arts in English literature. She has served as a volunteer in her community and in various stake and ward leadership positions. Most recently, she served as stake Relief Society president of the New York New York Stake; she is currently serving as a temple worker in the Manhattan Temple. She and her husband, Ron, have three sons, one daughter, and eleven grandchildren.

every morning. She belongs to philanthropic organizations and is a recognized community leader. She not only volunteers at her child's school, she
is also the PTA president and fund-raising chairman. And, of course, she
is a soccer mom, and a ballet mom, and a music lesson mom, and a basketball mom. She spends quality time with her children, and if there is any
quality time left over, she spends it with her husband. She is also an active
member of The Church of Jesus Christ of Latter-day Saints, so along with
the important practice of daily scripture reading and personal and family
prayer, she serves in one or more Church callings, writes her name on all
the sign-up sheets passed around in Relief Society, sings in the choir, feeds
the missionaries, and works in the temple. She attends her regular Church
meetings—and any extra meetings just to be sure.

It's an effort just to think about that life, let alone try to live it.

However, is there anything wrong with any one of these activities?
No. They are all worthwhile endeavors and integral parts of our collective
lives. That's why the superwoman syndrome is so insidious. It is the siren
song that says: "You can have it all; you can do it all; you can be it all; and
you should because these things are all good." If you can't, you feel guilty.
If you don't, by your own assessment, something must be wrong with you.

I wanted to make sure I had an effective definition of "superwoman
syndrome," so I looked in the dictionary.[1] Words used to define *superwoman*—small *s*, all one word—include superhuman, several roles, apparent ease, fictional, and imaginary. Words used to define *syndrome* include
signs, symptoms, recognizable pattern, disease, disorder, and undesirable.

So here we have it—the superwoman syndrome: an imaginary or
fictional woman with superhuman powers who succeeds in combining
several roles and does it all with apparent ease; she exhibits a group of
signs and symptoms that together are characteristic or indicative of a
specific disease or other disorder and form a recognizable pattern of something undesirable.

As we continue to look at the superwoman syndrome, we are going
to consider how and why we continually flirt with this role; we are going
to look at the serious consequences this can pose to our physical, mental,
and spiritual health; and we are going to focus on four principles that can
help us better manage our lives and discourage us from the superwoman
syndrome in the future.

We don't plan to become part of the superwoman syndrome, but sometimes our life just falls into that category by default; it slips from our control when we are trying to do too much in too little time.

Certainly there are periods in our life when unexpected events occur, when too many things honestly and absolutely have to be done, and we find ourselves stretched beyond our capacities. This does not have to be most of the time. It should be the exception rather than the rule.

What is it that entices us either consciously or subconsciously to complicate an already busy life by pursuing more than we can handle? There must be a payoff or we wouldn't do it. I think there are a variety of motivations that contribute to our behavior, including trying to keep everything and everyone under control, constantly seeking attention, competing—trying to do everything better than other people, and thriving on crisis.

FOMO. But maybe we suffer from FOMO. F-O-M-O. This is a condition my daughter-in-law, Rachel, has discovered and named. She claims that her husband, my son Adam, suffers from FOMO—Fear of Missing Out. It goes something like this:

"Hey, Adam, let's go shoot some hoops."

"Sure!"

"Hey, Adam, why don't you and Rachel come with us to . . ."

"Right—we're there!"

"Hey, Adam, we're going on a great bike ride Saturday morning."

"Wouldn't miss it!"

"Hey, Adam, there's a party tonight."

"Well, we already committed to a dinner invitation, but we'll hit the party afterwards!"

Fear of Missing Out.

Part of FOMO is enjoying being with friends and participating in activities, but when we try to participate in every activity, we stretch ourselves too thin, we deplete our resources, and we invite more stress into other areas of our life.

Another part of FOMO is our not wanting to disappoint anyone. Women work very hard to make others happy; it's that women's disease—trying too hard to please. When the sole reason for our actions is to gain the approval of others, our lives become unbalanced, and we are disillusioned.

Doing Our Best. Another motivation that influences our behavior is striving to do our best. President Hinckley has counseled us to do our best, and to make sure it is our best.[2] I think some of us may have misinterpreted what he said. I certainly cannot speak for him, but my observation is this: trying to follow his counsel, we attempt to do more; we mistakenly think that "doing our best" means "doing the most," or "doing better than anyone else." He didn't say that. More is not necessarily better, and most is not always best. Best may be doing a few things well rather than many things in a mediocre manner.

In striving to do our best, we may compare ourselves to others. The trap door here is that we usually see others at their best, and we assume that their "best" is the full measure of who they are. It might work if we only watched one person, but we see and associate with many people, so there are many "bests," and we irrationally think we are supposed to be able to measure up to all of them. So we run faster and faster, and inevitably we fall short. We need to do *our* best, not someone else's.

Perfection. This leads us to a fundamental issue that pushes the Latter-day Saint woman into the superwoman syndrome: perfection—the notion that we have to be perfect and do everything perfectly. Thinking that we have to be perfect in this moment is a heavy burden. Understanding that perfection is a process and our task is to participate in that process is liberating. A few years ago, the monthly visiting teaching message addressed this idea of seeking perfection.[3] It pointed out that Christ's commandment to be perfect, even as He and His Father are perfect (see Matthew 5:48; 3 Nephi 12:48) may seem overwhelming and can lead to discouragement. The message also instructed us to remember the Lord's counsel, "Do not run faster or labor more than you have strength and means" (D&C 10:4). Elder Bruce R. McConkie said: "We have to become perfect to be saved in the celestial kingdom. But nobody becomes perfect in this life. . . . Becoming perfect in Christ is a process. We begin to keep the commandments today, and we keep more of them tomorrow, and we go from grace to grace, up the steps of the ladder, and we thus improve and perfect our souls."[4]

If our life continues to spin in the superwoman syndrome, we will suffer significant consequences.

Health. In researching this topic, I logged on to the Internet. I typed in
"superwoman syndrome"; there were 6,700 hits! This is no small issue . . .
it is a very big women's issue. The single fact that struck me the most was
how many of these sites were health-related. Seminars were sponsored by
hospitals, women's health professionals, physicians, psychologists, and
wellness centers. I had not realized or thought of the superwoman syndrome as a health-related issue, but it most definitely is. The sites I looked
at had similar messages. They pointed out the illusion of the superwoman
and, most important, they pointed out the serious health consequences
we as women can incur when we try to be a superwoman. These health
issues include sleep disorders, eating disorders, stress, chronic exhaustion,
low sex drive, anxiety, and depression. Do we understand that when we
push ourselves beyond our means, we are signing up for one or more of
these health-related problems?

Relationships. Whenever we live our life on the edge and exist in a
high state of anxiety, we damage relationships. When we try to do it all,
and the tension builds up, and we are pulled in multiple directions, our
tendency is to offer our best selves to friends, associates, and the outside
world. Whatever is left over, we take home to our family. We shortchange
those we love most. I look back, and I know there were times I succeeded
for friends or fulfilled responsibilities for an organization, but let down a
family member. This wasn't necessarily evident to someone else, but I
know the truth in my life just as you do in yours. When I tried to do too
much, when I tried to be too much, when I tried to have too much, I
failed someone.

Misleading examples. Each time we try to be something we are not, we
set a misleading example for other people. Marie Osmond recently spoke
at a fireside in our stake and shared an experience she had after one of her
pregnancies. She was told she had to get her body back into shape and be
camera ready six weeks after the birth of her child. She worked hard, but
did not achieve that goal. The reality was this was not her first pregnancy
and her body needed more time to recover and would not respond to this
artificial deadline. The pictures were taken anyway, and as can be done so
well and so easily with modern technology, they were altered and

enhanced. So, she said, "Here I was perpetuating the myth of perfection"[5]: the perfect career, the perfect mother, the perfect body. She acknowledged the problem and the misleading example this set for others. What example do we set for others, especially our daughters? How does our example influence the expectations our sons have of a companion? What do we teach them?

If we insist on pursuing the life of a superwoman, a time will come when we are so frustrated, so depressed, and so tired, we will realize that something is terribly wrong. We will recognize that we have lost our sense of self and our direction. We will recognize that we are listening to too many voices, to the wrong voices. We will recognize that we cannot be all things to all people. We will recognize that when we are overwhelmed, *we* have made choices that put us in that situation. We will recognize that even though there are many things we can do, we can't necessarily do them all by ourselves, and we need to learn to ask for help. We will recognize that it is time to evaluate our life and make some changes. As in the principle of repentance, recognition must take place before change can occur.

We now see the superwoman and the syndrome for what they really are—a myth and a malady. I would like to suggest a prescription for wellness: four principles that can help us manage our life and avoid the superwoman syndrome in the future.

1. Know Who You Are

I was recently walking in Times Square, and I looked up and saw a large billboard advertising a current Broadway musical. It said, "Discover who you are; remember where you come from." When was the last time you read your patriarchal blessing? Have you taken time—recently—to think about who you are? President Hinckley said: "You need time to meditate and ponder, to think. . . . We run from one thing to another. We wear ourselves out in thoughtless pursuit of goals which are highly ephemeral. We are entitled to spend some time with ourselves in introspection, in development."[6]

Another useful self-awareness tool is an honest assessment list where we write down our strengths and weaknesses, our fears, what makes us

happy, what we like and don't like, what we can and can't do, and what
we will and won't do.

2. SET PRIORITIES

When we know who we are, we are able to set our priorities and make
wise choices.

A number of years ago, when I served in the Young Women program,
we had a combined activity evening for the Young Women and Young
Men. We played a game called "Count Your Blessings."[7] Participants sat
in a circle. The blessings—50 to 100 of them—were written on various
colored cards—one blessing per card. The blessings covered all aspects of
life. The cards were scattered, face up, in the middle of the circle. The
players, in turn, selected the blessing they felt they could do without and
removed the card from the circle. This required each person to consider
what is really important in life, to prioritize their blessings, and to decide
which blessings they would be least willing to part with. (One young
woman had a very difficult time deciding to do without makeup!) This
type of an exercise, whether played as a game or done mentally, can help
us prioritize the many dimensions of our lives.

3. SAYING YES AND SAYING NO

These powerful words—yes and no—are the tools we use to control
our life. We must use them wisely, and we must take responsibility for how
we use them.

At the end of February, we held our stake women's conference. Our
theme was "Press Forward in the Face of Adversity." We featured a panel
of four women—Laura, Lucie, Lori, and Mirna—and a moderator,
Sharon. All sisters in the stake were invited to submit questions or
scenarios they would like to have discussed by the panel. The panel, the
moderator, and our stake Relief Society presidency met about two weeks
before the conference to go through the questions. Individual panel members volunteered to prepare to respond to specific questions. One question submitted was, "When is it okay to say no to someone in the
Church?" Laura volunteered to prepare for this question. We asked her to

make it clear in her response that we were not discussing official Church callings, recognizing that a calling is between the individual, her priest-hood leader, and the Lord. During the week that followed our meeting, I received an e-mail from Lucie. Let me share that with you.

"Sister Robison—Thanks for the evening. It was nice to get away and feast at your table. I did have one concern as I have pondered the questions. The first one has bothered me quite a bit: 'When is it okay to say no to someone in the Church?' I feel the responsibility to say yes quite often. I have felt the guilt many times before in my life, and yet very, very few times can I really come up with a good reason to say no, not to my priesthood holders, the Lord, and not to my fellow sisters. Hence, why I have agreed to do this panel, even though everything in me screams no, it's not comfortable, convenient, or what I want to do. My husband said—from a bishop's perspective—he is faced repeatedly with the 'no's' and that gave me perspective. I thought, yes. I feel like the women who say no are already comfortable saying no and will be validated by the response to the question: 'Sure, we need to say no.' The women who feel the responsibil-ity to say yes will continue to say yes and will not be very comforted by the idea: 'Sure, there are times to say no.' In all honesty, there are very few instances when no is necessary. My life has been woven together by yes's. Many have been hard and some I have even regretted, but they have made me who I am. The women who I love and respect the most in this world, the women who have made a difference in my world and the world period, are the women who weave the yes's into their lives. I feel if we all said more yes's we would have no need for the no's and the guilt—because the joy would be spread around more evenly. I just had to pass that idea along. Lucie"

Lucie's feelings are heartfelt and sincere. Her valuable observations give us a lot to think about. It is evident that she feels the great power and responsibility of saying yes and no.

We as women have a hard time saying no—to children, to husbands, to friends, to organizations, and so on. And yet we need to use both yes and no to direct our lives; one is not "good" and the other "bad"; both are necessary.

Knowing when to say yes and no is not always easy, and the difficulty often comes when we have to say no to something good.

A number of years ago, a good friend of mine was invited to be the president of a prominent women's organization. She was a wonderful leader and was eminently qualified to serve in that office. At about the same time—just a week or two before—her husband was called to a significant Church position, and she had committed to support him. She knew that the many demands of her husband's calling and the added responsibilities of her potential leadership role would be too heavy a load and could be detrimental to their family. So even though the invitation extended to her was an honor she would like to have accepted, she said no. Understanding our priorities helps us know when to say yes and no.

Yes and no are the center of the plan of agency. Heavenly Father selected Christ to carry out His plan, instead of Lucifer, to give man the right to choose and the obligation to be responsible for his choices. To exercise this right, we must say yes and no. What would be the point of moral agency if we were not intended to say both yes and no?

4. TURN TO THE LORD

When we are immersed in the superwoman syndrome, we rely more on ourselves and less on the Lord. It is ironic that when we need Him most, we turn to Him least. Our relationship with the Lord is entirely in our hands; it can be close and personal or it can be almost nonexistent. If we will allow the Lord to be an active participant in our lives, we will be directed in our choices and sustained in our efforts. He will comfort our hearts and calm our fears.

"A light shall break forth among them that sit in darkness, and it shall be the fulness of my gospel" (D&C 45:28).

The light of understanding, awareness, and resolve can shine into the darkness and sense of despair we feel when we find ourselves caught up in the superwoman syndrome. We may know with assurance that this dark place is not the Lord's plan for His daughters. The fulness of the gospel does not include the superwoman syndrome.

We have looked at the superwoman, and we have found her wanting. She is not real, and we fool ourselves if we think she is an ideal we should strive for or one we can attain.

We are the real women: real women with all our hopes, dreams, and imperfections. We are perfectly mortal. Every day we struggle with life's challenges; sometimes we fail, and many times we succeed. We do not do this alone. The Lord has blessed us with each other—with sisters all around us—to turn to for support, encouragement, and understanding. Isn't it remarkable how often it is another woman—a sister in the gospel— who embraces us and gives us that hug we need when we feel lost and abandoned? Most important, we are the real daughters of our Father in Heaven, and He loves us for who we really are. He will not ask us to "run faster or labor more than [we] have strength and means" (D&C 10:4). He wants us to have joy in life and peace in our souls.

I am grateful for all the wonderful women in my life—so many good friends, three special sisters, three outstanding daughters-in-law, my precious daughter, and my wonderful mother. We've shared our lives, and I've learned from you.

May the Lord bless each of you in your everyday efforts and in the choices you make. May you truly understand that you are His daughter.

NOTES

1. *Encarta World English Dictionary* (Redmond, Wash.: Microsoft Corporation, 1999).
2. Gordon B. Hinckley, "Standing Strong and Immovable," *Worldwide Leadership Training Meeting,* January 2004, 21.
3. "Seeking Perfection," *Ensign,* June 1989, 43.
4. Bruce R. McConkie, *1976 Devotional Speeches of the Year* (Provo: Brigham Young University Press, 1977), 399, 400.
5. Marie Osmond, unpublished fireside talk, New York New York Stake, February 20, 2005.
6. Gordon B. Hinckley, "Life's Obligations," *Ensign,* February 1999, 5.
7. Daniel H. and Luene Ludlow, "Count Your Blessings: A Family Activity," *New Era,* November 1983, 30–31.

"Old Variaunce" or "Newe Attonement": Marriage and the Imitation of Christ

John R. Rosenberg

Why are Adam and Eve standing on an elephant?

During the last third of the twelfth century, Christians in the Spanish village of Segovia built the Church of San Justo. Its murals depict the standard sacramental program that begins with the Fall and concludes with Christ's passion and resurrection. On the inside of the arched entrance to the altar, Adam and Eve pose just moments after the Fall, modestly covered with convenient (and scratchy) fig leaves. They stand on the back of a beast that looks like a hippopotamus, but is actually an elephant, as the letters *FAN* inscribed above the animal attest. Among all the possible choices from the medieval bestiary, why did the artist choose to have history's first married couple relate to a beast with which he obviously had no firsthand experience? The answer lies in the symbolism. The elephant is meek. He is a bearer of burdens. Without any danger to himself, he can bruise the serpent's head. He is, in other words, a figure of Christ.[1] Adam and Eve's marriage, activated by their understanding of the plan of salvation and the Atonement, finds perspective and hope in its happy acknowledgment that their union is Christ's burden.

Writers of both the Old and New Testaments emphasized the

John R. Rosenberg is a professor of Spanish literature and dean of the College of Humanities at Brigham Young University. He is married to Gaylamarie Green Rosenberg and is the father of two daughters, Karen Marie and Eliza.

association between earthly marriage and Christ's infinite offering.[2] John's Revelation is particularly detailed in this regard:

"Let us be glad and rejoice, and give honour to him: for the marriage of the Lamb is come, and his wife hath made herself ready. . . . And he saith unto me, Write, Blessed are they which are called unto the marriage supper of the Lamb" (Revelation 19:7, 9).

The New Testament builds on the Old Testament's view of marriage as a metaphor for Jehovah's covenant with Israel. Isaiah proclaims, "As the bridegroom rejoiceth over the bride, so shall thy God rejoice over thee" (Isaiah 62:5). Likewise, breaking that covenant by uniting with other gods, by approaching (*ad*) another (*ulter*) is "adultery," a loss of singleness of heart and mutual commitment: "And I saw . . . Israel committed adultery," Jeremiah laments. "Turn, O backsliding children, saith the Lord; for I am married unto you: and I will take you . . . and I will bring you to Zion" (Jeremiah 3:8, 14). Implicit in the use of the metaphor is the recognition that marriages can fail to meet their covenant purpose and may even become destructive and dangerous. However, it is not my purpose to discuss here these negative dimensions of marriage.

It cannot be coincidence that the Lord uses marriage as the primary metaphor to help us comprehend His covenant with us. There must be a special connection between His act of reconciliation, which makes possible at-one-ment with His children, and the lifelong process of a man and a woman becoming one. Could it be that part of His command to become Christlike involves learning to imitate His infinite Atonement in our eternal relationship?

While we may not be able to fully grasp how the Atonement operates as propitiation, that is, as payment of debt required by divine justice, we can understand the Lord's offering of mercy. That mercy becomes operative when we are blessed with the central epiphany of our spiritual life: although the Lord's understanding of my humanity, my failures, my pride, and my fear is thorough and perfect, so is His love and His optimism for my potential.

King David shares his recognition of this principle when in the eighth psalm he prayerfully asks, "When I consider thy heavens, the work of thy fingers, the moon and the stars, which thou hast ordained; what is man, that thou art mindful of him?" (Psalm 8:3–4). David stares at the stars and knows that he is nothing. Another king—Benjamin—calls us "beggars" to illustrate the same idea. Yet David in his smallness and sinfulness still declares, "Thou hast made [man] a little lower than the angels, and hast crowned him with glory and honour" (Psalm 8:5), and Benjamin tells us that because of Christ's sacrifice, "he hath spiritually begotten you; for ye say that your hearts are changed through faith on his name; therefore, ye . . . have become his sons and his daughters" (Mosiah 5:7). In other words, out of the Lord's perfect understanding of our imperfection we are lifted, taking with Him our first steps toward that ultimate lifting we call exaltation.

The hope we have for our future is grounded primarily in our faith in the Lord's intimate charity. The Book of Mormon expresses this intimacy with a lovely scriptural trio: Nephi prays, "O Lord, wilt thou encircle me around in the robe of thy righteousness" (2 Nephi 4:33); a few chapters earlier he affirmed, "I am encircled about eternally in the arms of his love" (2 Nephi 1:15); and, my favorite, Amulek promises that Christ's mercy "encircles [us] in the arms of safety" (Alma 34:16). We all want safety— physical safety, but also emotional safety. We especially want to feel safe with those to whom we are most intimately connected. Our experience of the Savior's ability to embrace us through our imperfections is one of the great healing experiences of mortality.

I have found a similar potential for healing in marriage. Next to the Savior, no one, not my parents, my sisters, my colleagues, my children, has a better view of my frailties than Gaylamarie. Likewise, our shared life reveals her to me with utter honesty. This knowledge bestows sacred power. We can use our knowledge to cleave us apart as a couple. This is the satanic option: knowledge of good and evil in each other is used to destroy. We remind our spouse of imperfections or differences we find unacceptable, pushing away rather than encircling, and in the process do perhaps irreparable damage to a divinely seeded self-image. Or, we may choose to imitate the Atonement. We love each other through our imperfections, cleaving with constancy to a few essential things.

One of the compelling attributes of the Atonement is constancy. As our advocate, the Lord is absolutely *loyal,* a word related to "legal" and "law." In other words, He is just; disloyalty is a violation of justice. He describes this advocacy to Isaiah, later repeated to the Nephites: "I have

graven thee upon the palms of my hands"(Isaiah 49:16; 1 Nephi 21:16).
Can there be a more enduring and endearing promise of constancy than
this? Just as we covenant to "always remember him" (D&C 20:77, 79), He
promises to remember us by keeping our image always before Him. We
imitate this trait of the Atonement as we live lives of unimpeachable loyalty to our spouse. In this regard I love the story about Joseph Smith's
loyalty to Emma. One of the Smiths' Nauvoo neighbors noted with disapproval that the Prophet's habit of "building kitchen fires, carrying out
ashes, carrying in wood and water, assisting in the care of the children"
was inconsistent with his stature as a "great man." The neighbor recorded:

"I reminded [the Prophet] of every phase of his greatness and called
to his mind the multitude of tasks he performed that were too menial for
such as he; to fetch and carry flour was too great a humiliation. . . . The
Prophet listened quietly to all I had to say, then made his answer in these
words: 'If there is to be humiliation in a man's house, who but the head of
that house should or could bear that humiliation.'"

Joseph's friend then arrived at the judgmental conclusion that his own
wife was more diligent in her household duties than was Emma:

"Thinking to give the Prophet some light on home management, I
said to him, 'Brother Joseph, my wife does much more hard work than
does your wife.' Brother Joseph replied by telling me that if a man cannot
learn in this life to appreciate a wife and do his duty by her, in properly
taking care of her, he need not expect to be given one in the hereafter. His
words shut my mouth as tight as a clam. I took them as a terrible reproof.
After that I tried to do better by the good wife I had."[3]

It is revealing that Joseph does not refute his neighbor's criticism.
Perhaps the neighbor woman did perform more physical labor than Emma.
The Prophet's point had nothing to do with the definition of a familial
role or how well that role was executed; it had everything to do with loyalty. In the Savior's Atonement and our imitation of it in marriage, we call
this loyalty "covenant."

The Savior is consistent in remembering His promises to us; one of
those promises is that as we repent He will cease to remember the ways
we offended Him. "I, even I, am he that blotteth out thy transgressions
for mine own sake, and will not remember thy sins" (Isaiah 43:25). While
we do not have the power to blot out our spouse's sins or offenses, we can

heal each other when we imitate the merciful dimension of the Savior's memory—His kind forgetfulness. Sometimes our human nature leads us to store memories of offense and hurt in anticipation of their usefulness in a future conflict. We stack them neatly in our mental pantry, organizing them into easily accessible themes. However, unlike our food storage, this provisioning of memories of offense does not nourish. How much easier it is for us to forgive when each accident of offense takes its place in the immediate context, without being joined by its embarrassing cousins from times past.

One of the most common stresses on the covenant of loyalty is the script that partners bring into marriage. Our parents, ancestors, local customs, and so on are dramaturges who compose the lines we will recite during our lifetime.[4] We are loyal to those lines: "Whate'er Thou Art, Act Well Thy Part." They often are fundamental to our self-image. We believe that our "part" is naturally and logically superior to ones played by others. These scripts tell us what to think and how to act with regard to home-making and interior design, child-rearing, money management, fashion, communication patterns, distribution of labor in and out of the home, and so on. Most of the things that cause daily irritation are trivial and are outside the table of contents of that essential script that we call scripture. I know of no place where it says, "Thou shalt not leave thy socks on the floor"; or "Thou shalt remove all the dishes after the cycle is completed so that thy spouse is not left to wonder which vessels are pure and which are filthy still." Scripture defines a single, transcendent role for each of us—disciple of Christ—and that role, humbly lived, blesses us with the ability to mercifully remember and kindly forget the *right* things.

If I were to select just one scriptural prompting on the drama of marriage, I would turn to the seventh chapter of Moroni. "And now I, Moroni, write a few of the words of my father Mormon, which he spake concerning faith, hope, and charity" (verse 1). Among other things, the chapter invites us to apply a single test for the appropriateness of marital responses: "Search diligently in the light of Christ that ye may know good from evil; and if ye will lay hold upon every good thing, and condemn it not, ye certainly will be a child of Christ" (verse 19). While letting go of evil and laying hold on good applies to all our decisions, the counsel is especially instructive for our marriages.

In the previous chapter, Moroni reaffirmed Christ's singular role as the "author and finisher of [our] faith" (Moroni 6:4). Christ is the "author" of a temple marriage, a fact easily understood as we recall the details of the ordinance of sealing. A marriage fills its measure to the degree that the Savior is employed as its "finisher"—like the finishing carpenter whose labors assure the beauty and durability of his creation. Our faith in His charity gives us the hope required to keep going. This same charity—the pure love of Christ—is the leaven in our marriages, and acquiring and nurturing it must be our principle concern. This charity is the constant light that eventually must replace courtship's fireworks. And it is this charity that soothes us as we contribute to the healing of a spouse. I have found that of all the gifts of Christ, this one is the most freely given. Mormon outlines the method:

"Wherefore, my beloved brethren, pray unto the Father with all the energy of heart, that ye may be filled with this love, which he hath bestowed upon all who are true followers of his Son, Jesus Christ" (Moroni 7:48).

This is a powerful witness of the reciprocal nature of charity. By experiencing the Lord's gift, or grace, for us, we are empowered to feel and then extend charity to our spouse: grace for grace. The product of that process is purification leading to our tentative steps toward becoming like Christ. Mormon's method works. When I am bothered by the fine print in the scripts Gaylamarie and I use, if I kneel and plead for charity, I find that Heavenly Father answers those prayers with urgency. Sometimes that answer teaches me that I am reading her script unfairly, or attaching undue importance to my own, or that I am reading the wrong script altogether. Regardless of the specifics, the exercise always, invariably, changes my heart.

One product of charity is patience. King Benjamin links the Atonement and patience when he describes the Savior's attitude toward us:

"Come to a knowledge of the goodness of God, and his matchless power, and his wisdom, and his patience, and his long-suffering towards the children of men; and also, the atonement" (Mosiah 4:6).

Likewise, as the Creator, the Savior patiently acknowledged that the process of forming the world would take place day by day, line upon line.

Part of our education in becoming like Christ is to learn to be creators, and our first experiment with creation in the proper order of things is marriage. This process is always slow and, because of the pace, painful. I recall a now humorous, but once disastrous, experience from early in my marriage.

Gaylamarie and I married later in life, and our union and subsequent blessing of two beloved daughters is my most tangible reminder of Christ's grace for me, that He records and seals our prayers with immutable promises (see D&C 98:2–3). Because we married late our courtship was *efficient*. When we faced each other across the altar we knew enough to give the right answer, but not much else. A week after our wedding we departed for Madrid, Spain, and were shortly joined on our honeymoon by thirty students registered for the study abroad program I was to direct for the next eight weeks. My professional obligations resulted in an unfortunate single-mindedness that was not particularly helpful during those early weeks of marriage. One day Gaylamarie came to me with a mournful countenance and muffled sniffle and said, "Sometimes I feel like you love Spain more than me."

Now, I had a witness that this marriage that had been created was "good"—as it might be described in Genesis. I knew what it felt like to have the Holy Spirit of Promise undeniably validate the ordinance we had shared. That conviction, however, did not automatically give me the skills to be wise, discreet, and sensitive in all my doings. So, to my bride's complaint that I loved Spain more than her, I feebly responded, "I have known Spain longer." In my defense, what I said is not what I meant. What I meant was that while our marriage was indeed "good," its process of creation would go on for many years. We were only in the first day, light still breaking away from darkness. My knowledge about and love for Spain had grown over the course of many years. I had faith that in due time our marriage too would enjoy its full measure. Now, had I said that, Gaylamarie would have interpreted my plea for patience as evidence of commitment.

Young Joseph experimented on James's promise that asking God leads to wisdom. In the verse immediately preceding, James links wisdom and patience: "Let patience have her perfect work, that ye may be perfect and entire" (James 1:4). Patience leads to wholeness: through patience we become "perfect," or complete, and "entire." The Lord's patience with us, and our "waiting patiently" on Him (D&C 98:2), lead to oneness with Him. God's patience is justified by His perfect understanding of our origin and our potential. Our "waiting patiently" is a sign of our covenant with Him. We formally enter that covenant through baptism, at which time we promise to "bear one another's burdens, that they may be light" (Mosiah 18:8), that is, to imitate Christ as represented by the elephant. Burdens come in many varieties: physical, economic, social, and emotional. Patience for those struggling with these burdens makes us "whole-some" with them. If this is true generally, its truth is even more urgent in marriage.

Our English word *atonement* evolved from ideas of "onement" or "to be at one" (*Oxford English Dictionary*). Its first known use is in Thomas More's 1513 *The History of King Richard the Third*, which describes the conflicts between the Dukes of Gloucester and Buckingham and Richard Lord Hastinges who have "more regarde to their olde variaunce than their newe attonement."[5] I find More's language suggestive: "olde variaunce"—differences in background, belief, and aspirations—was permitted to undo "newe attonement"—potentially productive alliances and singleness of heart and purpose.

The essence of marriage also involves modulating "olde variaunce" in order to achieve "attonement." This does not mean erasing differences, but rather recognizing and receiving those variations as gifts. These gifts enrich us by uncomfortably challenging us to read by new scripts, learning in ways not available to us if we were to remain singly with our "olde variaunce." For example, the script I am most at ease with is tightly composed and closely edited; Gaylamarie is a master improviser: the beat of my drum is classical, hers is jazz. She is open to emotional intimacy; I fail in most of my attempts to follow Paul's advice: "And to communicate forget not: for with such sacrifices God is well pleased" (Hebrews 13:16). Some of our differences may be driven by gender, others by background, still others by disposition. Separately, these "olde variaunces" make us interesting individuals; together they make us whole, perfect, entire.

In Plato's *Symposium*, Aristophanes tells a charming story about the creation of mankind. According to part of the tale, the first men and women were joined together in one being, round and symmetrical, with one head and two faces, four hands and feet, and so on. Their strength and beauty were such that they rebelled against the gods, causing Olympus's rulers to seek a way to humble them.

"At last, after a good deal of reflection, Zeus discovered a way. He said: 'Methinks I have a plan which will humble their pride and improve their manners.' He spoke and cut men in two, like [an] apple which is halved for pickling. After the division the two parts of man, each yearning for his other half, came together, and throwing their arms about each other, and intertwining in mutual embraces out of a desire to grow into one. So ancient is the desire of one another that is implanted in us, reuniting our original nature, trying to make one of two, and healing the state of man."[6]

Some early Christians found a similar model in Adam and Eve. Apart, their potential was limited; only by being "at-one" could they be complete. Elaine Pagels finds an example of this in an early "gospel":

"The . . . author of the *Gospel of Philip,* speaking in mythic language, said, for example, that death began when 'the woman separated . . . from the man'—that is, when Eve (the spirit) became separated from Adam (the psyche). Only when one's psyche, or ordinary consciousness, becomes integrated with one's spiritual nature—when Adam, reunited with Eve, 'becomes complete again'—can one achieve internal harmony and wholeness."[7]

Leaving aside the mystic discussion of "psyche" and "spirit" of this Gnostic gospel, its author nevertheless senses that Adam and Eve, separate and independent beings, must cleave unto each other and "be one flesh" (Genesis 2:24). "And Adam said, This is now bone of my bones, and flesh of my flesh" (Genesis 2:23). In Plato's story, *returning* to the state of wholeness or of being "at-one," intended for us by God, comes as we cling to each other in loyalty, constancy, and charity. M. Catherine Thomas puts this in a context more familiar for us when she writes, "The word rendered *at-one-ment* by the early translators of the Bible could perhaps have been more accurately rendered *re-at-one-ment* or *re-union.* That is, atonement seeks to restore us to a spiritual relationship with the Father and the Son in this life and to that organization and harmony we had together in the premortal world."[8] That restoration and harmony require the engagement of man, woman, and the Lord of them both.

"And the Lord God said, It is not good that the man should be alone"

(Genesis 2:18). Given that the Hebrew word *adam* can be rendered either as "Adam" or "man" (mankind), we might reasonably read this as a statement that it is not good for either man or woman to be alone—physically, emotionally, or spiritually. "So God created man *[adam]* in his own image . . . ; male and female created he them" (Genesis 1:27). That is, *adam* in the image of godhood is complete only with both male and female components. The fixed, immovable, and unchangeable charity of marriage is *an* "at-one-ment:" it is both the antonym and the antidote for "aloneness." The fixed, immovable, and unchangeable charity of the Savior's sacrifice is *the* Atonement (see D&C 88:133). By imitating its character, we give substance to our marriage; by receiving its power, we make it eternal.

NOTES

1. Luis A. Grau Lobo, *Pintura Románica en Castilla y León* (Junta de Castilla y León: Consejería de Educación y Cultura, 1996), 102.

2. M. H. Abrams, *Natural Supernaturalism: Tradition and Revolution in Romantic Literature* (New York: Norton, 1973), 37–46.

3. Hyrum Andrus and Helen May Andrus, *They Knew the Prophet* (Salt Lake City: Bookcraft, 1974), 145.

4. For discussion of theatrical metaphors, see Ernst Robert Curtius, *European Literature in the Latin Middle Ages*, trans. Willard R. Trask (Princeton, N.J.: Princeton University Press, 1983), 138–44.

5. Sir Thomas More, *The Complete Works of St. Thomas More, Volume 2: The History of King Richard III*, ed. Richard Sylvester (New Haven and London: Yale University Press, 1963), 16.

6. Plato, *Symposium*, trans. Benjamin Jowett (New York: Modern Library, 1996), 42–44.

7. Elaine Pagels, *Adam, Eve, and the Serpent* (New York: Vintage, 1989), 68.

8. M. Catherine Thomas, "The Restoration of the Doctrines of Marriage and the Atonement," in *Women and Christ: Living the Abundant Life*, eds. Dawn Hall Anderson et al. (Salt Lake City: Deseret Book, 1993), 89.

LIGHT OF THE EVERLASTING COVENANT OF MARRIAGE

———

Gaylamarie G. Rosenberg

In 1987, I spent the summer studying in Israel with students from BYU. It was amazing to visit the places where the Savior walked and where so many significant events took place. One day we spent several hours going through Hezekiah's Tunnel.

This tunnel was built about 701 B.C. to preserve Jerusalem against a possible attack from the Assyrians. It was more than 1,700 feet in length and built in a zigzag pattern. It was constructed through limestone rock, bringing the waters of the Gihon spring inside the walls of Jerusalem to the pool of Siloam.[1] Our director prepared us to walk through this tunnel by telling us to bring a flashlight, and wear sturdy shoes. He warned us that the path would be rocky and that we might be walking in several inches of water. The first half of the walk through the tunnel was a fun adventure. The second half was a surprise. Our director told us to turn off our flashlights and walk through the last half in the dark. I was stunned. Was he serious? How could I walk through the wet, rocky tunnel with no light?

My heart started beating like a drum. I was scared to death. I was sure that I would fall on the rocks and land headfirst in the water that was now

---

Gaylamarie G. Rosenberg earned a B.S. in education and an M.S. in family studies from Brigham Young University, where she has also taught classes for the Family Studies and Religious Education departments. She is married to John R. Rosenberg and is the mother of two daughters, Karen Marie and Eliza.

up to my knees. Most of all, I was nervous that I would panic with claustrophobia. However, I didn't want to be the only coward in our group, so I turned off my flashlight. It was pitch black and frightening. And I was the last person in line and didn't want to be left behind. As I tried to feel my way with my hands moving along the wet, slippery sides of the tunnel, I pled for comfort. I couldn't decide if I was frightened or just mad at our director for planning such a scary trip. All I knew is that I needed a little comfort.

Then, someone in another group about 30 feet behind me flashed his light for a split second, just long enough for me to see which way the tunnel was turning and what I was facing. This gave me assurance that I was okay. I continued in the dark, breathing deeply, I'm sure, and trying to listen to the people in front of me. Then I noticed that as I became fearful again, I would see another flash of light, once more filling me with confidence and assurance. This happened six or seven times. I made it to the end of the tunnel in the dark with those occasional flashes of light. Often the light came when I was the most fearful and uncertain.

Within our group there were cheers, laughter, and celebrations. Personally, I was relieved just surviving the experience. I was very thankful for the stranger behind me who gave me occasional light. Leaving the tunnel, I looked at a friend and said, "That was scary."

My whole life has been like that walk. I was deeply moved as I pondered the times in my life I felt I was walking in the dark and the Lord gave me light to see my way. Often I used my own knowledge and understanding and then, when I felt I was in the dark, I would plead for help and He would give me flashes of inspiration to renew my hope and rekindle my faith. When I stumbled in the dark, I knew that if I kept going, kept believing, He would always show me the next step to take, a corner to turn, or a new path to follow. His divine light would keep me steady and secure on a somewhat rocky path.

Jesus said during His triumphal entry into Jerusalem, "Yet a little while is the light with you. Walk while ye have the light, lest darkness come upon you: for he that walketh in darkness knoweth not whither he goeth. While ye have light, believe in the light, that ye may be the children of light" (John 12:35–36).

Then he added, "I am come a light into the world, that whosoever believeth on me should not abide in darkness" (John 12:46). Hence, our belief and dependence on His light will always carry us through the darker times.

In "The Family: A Proclamation to the World" we read, "Marriage between a man and a woman is ordained of God and that the family is central to the Creator's plan for the eternal destiny of His children."[2] The sacred institution of marriage across our nation and in the world seems challenged more today than ever. In many ways, attitudes and values regarding marriage are very much in the dark. There is a growing trend for cohabitation, premarital sex, abortions, same-sex relationships, and pornography. TV, radio, magazines, books, and the Internet provide easy access to society's view on marriage and family issues. Many of these attitudes and perspectives on marriage are not consistent with the teachings of our Heavenly Father. There has never been a more needful time to believe in His light. Our prophet, President Hinckley, has said: "The family is a creation of God. It is the basic creation. The way to strengthen the nation is to strengthen the homes of the people."[3]

President Heber J. Grant taught us: "The marriage vows taken in these hallowed places and the sacred covenants entered into for time and all eternity are [protection] against many of the temptations of life that tend to break homes and destroy happiness. . . . Eternal partnership under the everlasting covenant becomes the foundation upon which are built peace, happiness, virtue, love, and all of the other eternal verities of life, here and herafter."[4]

We can enjoy blessings from our marriage covenant on earth as well as in heaven, today, right now. Do we truly believe in a fulness of joy in our relationship? Do we trust the Lord that He will help us? We have powerful and beautiful promises that await our partaking—the promises of our sacred covenant of marriage. The words *sacred* and *covenant* both have interesting roots. The word *sacred* in Latin is *sacer,* which means "to set apart or separate" or, we could say, that which sets us apart or separates us from the world. The word *covenant* in Latin is *convenire,* which means "to come together." Hence, "sacred covenant" literally means "to set us apart from the world and come together under God's law."[5] President James E. Faust said in our recent general conference, "Holiness is the strength of the soul."[6] Coming together in holiness is likewise the strength of our marital relationships. We simply cannot afford to be complacent in our sacred covenants in a day when Satan is fighting a full-blown war against the sacredness of marriage.

In Doctrine and Covenants 45:9 we read: "And even so I have sent mine everlasting covenant into the world, to be a light to the world, and to be a standard for my people." In regard to our marriage relationships, do we look for the light to help us with our new and everlasting covenant of marriage?

Do we ever feel as if we are in the dark on how to enhance our marriage and enjoy the blessings of our eternal partnership? Let's begin where we are, wherever that may be, and seek the light, whether we have been married 5 months or 50 years. Elder Bruce R. McConkie said: "I start where I am, and I go forward from there. I start using such talent as I have, and I begin to apply the principles of eternal truth to my life. I consult and counsel with the Lord in the process, and no matter where I am, the gospel takes me forward and onward and upward, and blessings flow to me that will ennoble and sanctify and improve me in this life and eventually give me glory and honor and dignity in the life to come."[7]

I would like to discuss a few ways in which the light that abounds in this covenant can strengthen us. This light of divine, clear truth is often experienced in three ways: the light of love, the light of understanding, and the light of hope and optimism.

THE LIGHT OF LOVE

First, the light of love. We have all sung the song "Teach Me to Walk in the Light of His Love." How do we do that?

Orson Pratt said: "The children of Zion love in proportion to the Heavenly knowledge which they have received; for love keeps pace with knowledge, and as the one increases so does the other, and when knowledge is perfected, love will be perfected also."[8]

Our personal scripture study is not only imperative to our acquiring heavenly knowledge but the means through which we learn how to love more like our Heavenly Father. Light is always accompanied by love. In 1 John 4:16–17 we read: "And we have known and believed the love that God hath to us. God is love; and he that dwelleth in love dwelleth in God, and God in him. Herein is our love made perfect, . . . because as he is, so are we in this world." There is nothing sweeter than feeling the love of the Lord and likewise feeling His love work through us to strengthen another—especially a spouse. Love draws us toward more light. Darkness takes us away from loving. We simply don't love well when we are in the dark.

About 10 years ago, I had two surgeries to alleviate chronic pain in my jaw. My dear husband, John, took several weeks away from work to take care of me. He brought me home from the hospital with half my face completely numb and the other half throbbing. He made me milkshakes and fancy drinks. He slept on the floor next to our bed every night. He didn't want to disturb me—being the tornado sleeper that he is—but he wanted to be close in case I needed something. He surprised me with fun gifts, books from the library, and a mountain of videos. He spent all day literally at my service. This went on for two weeks; then we assumed that I was on the road to recovery and he could go back to work. To our dismay, when we returned to the doctor's office, we were informed that mistakes had been made and I would need to repeat the surgery. We started the process all over again. My heart was touched with John's devotion to take care of me for several more weeks. It was amazing to both of us how our perspective changed on many issues in our marriage. I could not focus on trivial things that bothered me when he was being so sweet in taking time to love and care for me. My perspective changed, my attitude changed, and my love for him increased dramatically. I was humbled as I felt his love and the Lord's love for us. It was one of those moments of coming out of the darkness and into the light for me. In Ecclesiastes 11:7 it says, "Truly the light is sweet, and a pleasant thing it is for the eyes to behold the sun."

In the 13th century, European monks invented the clock. Their purpose was to remind them to pray every few hours. It was an important tool for reminding them to turn their thoughts heavenward. Sadly, it clearly is not the main reason we have clocks today.[9] One of the adversary's greatest tools is distraction. Satan would fill our time and thoughts with so many distractions that we lose sight of what is most important. Are we simply too busy to take time to love and nurture one another? The little things in relationships are often the biggest: giving a hug, holding a hand, helping the other with a task, taking time to talk, saying thank you, expressing words of appreciation, and showing acceptance with our actions. Loving a spouse takes time. It's hard to feel the Lord's light if we are so distracted that we don't give our relationships the time and attention that they need or deserve.

We have the greatest power to nurture, love, and influence our spouse—more than any other person—because we are their spouse, because it is our stewardship. Next to our own personal righteousness, it is our role and greatest mission on earth to positively influence our eternal partner to accomplish all that Heavenly Father would have them do here on earth.

I know that as we increase in heavenly knowledge, humbly pray for love for our spouse—to see their potential and gifts the way Heavenly Father would see them, to love them the way that He would love them— a sweet light of love will permeate our hearts. We will see differently and love differently.

The Light of Understanding

Next, the light of understanding. This story of the Prophet Joseph Smith, which was related by Hyrum Andrus, gives us a wonderful example of why this light is needed in relationships: "I went one day to the Prophet with a sister. She had a charge to make against one of the brethren for scandal. When her complaint had been heard the Prophet asked her if she was quite sure that what the brother had said of her was utterly untrue. She was quite sure that it was. He then told her to think no more about it, for it could not harm her. If untrue it could not live, but the truth will survive. Still she felt that she should have some redress. Then he offered her his method of dealing with such cases for himself. When an enemy had told a scandalous story about him, which had often been done, before he rendered judgment he paused and let his mind run back to the time and place and setting of the story to see if he had not by some unguarded word or act laid the block on which the story was built. If he found that he had done so, he said that in his heart he then forgave his enemy, and felt thankful that he had received warning of a weakness that he had not known he possessed. Then he said to the sister that he would have her to do the same:

search her memory thoroughly and see if she had not herself unconsciously laid the foundation for the scandal that annoyed her. The sister thought deeply for a few moments and then confessed that she believed that she had. Then the Prophet told her that in her heart she could forgive that brother who had risked his own good name and her friendship to give her this clearer view of herself. The sister thanked [the Prophet] and went away in peace."[10]

The Prophet Joseph is a remarkable example in his humble approach in dealing with imperfect behavior in others and his concern to correct his own behavior.

In Matthew 7:3–5 we read: "And why beholdest thou the mote that is in thy brother's eye, but considerest not the beam that is in thine own eye? Or how wilt thou say to thy brother, Let me pull out the mote out of thine eye; and, behold, a beam is in thine own eye? Thou hypocrite, first cast out the beam out of thine own eye; and *then shalt thou see clearly* to cast out the mote out of thy brother's eye" (emphasis added). The Savior made it clear where our attention needs to be—on our own behavior—and then—only then—do we see clearly how to address others' behavior. In order to see a solution to a challenge in our marriage, we must take care of the beam in our own eye first. I am confident that the Lord will illuminate our understanding on these matters when we ask Him (speaking from personal experience, of course). Are we guilty of thinking that our marital frustrations are not important enough to resolve? Or of thinking that the Lord really doesn't care? Do we specifically ask Him for understanding? Do we think that we can't change and progress in our relationships? Sometimes we get caught in marital ruts. We may think, "Well, that's just the way I am, or that's just the way my spouse is." Heavenly Father would not have us see their, or our, divine potential like that. Change, improvement, and growth are foundational to our eternal progression. Surely, He cares about our sacred relationships. He will help us to distinguish between what is essential and what is not.

There is a Latin saying that translates as: "In essentials let there be unity: in non-essentials, liberty; and in all things, charity."[11] When improving ourselves and taking care of our own beams becomes a quest instead of an irritation, the light of understanding becomes clear and bright.

The Light of Hope and Optimism

Lastly, I'd like to talk about the brilliant light of hope and optimism.

My brother-in-law Kent is the most optimistic person I know. His cheery tone and optimism are contagious. I have been deeply influenced by his hope as well as my sister's equal hope and courage. Over the last 15 years, my sister Karen has endured the deaths of her baby son, father, brother, two nephews, and mother-in-law; lymphoma cancer; congestive heart failure; lung, throat, and spine disorders; mechanical heart pumps; a heart transplant; and a neuromuscular disease. Have their married years been easy? No. They have gone through the refiner's fire. Kent and Karen have had many reasons to be discouraged—trials that could have robbed them of marital joy but have not.

Kent has given me permission to read a journal entry he made on January 20, 2003. He wrote: "Last night and this morning, I have had very tender feelings. I thought about how much I love Karen—how blessed we are to have such a strong, powerful love that has kept us together for 25 years, and especially during the 13 years of Karen's poor health. . . . God has blessed our marriage with an even stronger, sweeter, and more tender love and commitment than ever before. With so many marriages falling apart, I count this as the greatest blessing of my life, and a great blessing to our children. We are one of the poorest couples in the world financially, but we are one of the richest in blessings that money cannot buy." On Saturday, December 28 (13 days after her heart transplant and 3 days after major surgery), "Karen and I celebrated our 25th anniversary in the intensive care unit of UCLA Medical Center. On this night, Karen's nurse, Tina, came up to us and told us that she was very impressed with the glow in our faces. She said we looked so happy we were together and radiated mutual respect and admiration for each other. She was so intrigued with how much we loved each other. She asked us, 'How have you kept your love and relationship so strong after all these years?' Karen and I explained to this sweet young nurse that we had to work at our marriage to make it strong. We talked about our commitment to each other and how we were determined to make it work. We then explained to her about our deep religious beliefs."

I know that Kent and Karen's faith in the Savior has strengthened their hope and optimism. I am sure that it has influenced Kent over the years to greet each morning with a smile and a happy tone. I cannot count how many times I have been in their home and have seen him raise his arms in the air and say, "It's going to be a great day." Then he'll look at Karen and say, "Everything is going to work out, dear. Don't worry; we will be fine; I sure love you, honey." Karen has often said, "It takes more energy to be negative than positive. I'd rather use what energy I have to be happy." I know of their deep belief and reliance on the grace of the Savior. Their confidence in Him is unwavering. Their choice to rely on His light for hope is inspiring.

For some, simple yet profound joy may be found in looking more for the positive—all that is going well in a marriage. It's amazing how bad our spouses look when we look for the bad. Likewise, it's amazing how good our spouses look when we look for the good in them. So, *what are we looking for?* Let us look to see the good. Light and sight always go together. In Alma 37:46–47, we read: "Look [that] they might live. . . . Take care of these sacred things, . . . look to God and live." We simply must be aware of what we are seeing, especially regarding our sacred relationship with a spouse.

Elder Jeffrey R. Holland said: "Believe that . . . faith has everything to do with your romance, because it does. . . . Jesus Christ, the Light of the World, is the only lamp by which you can successfully see the path of love and happiness. How should I love thee? As He does, for that way 'never faileth.'"[12] We must believe that the closer we become to the Lord, the closer we can become to each other in marriage. The blessings of our marriage covenants promise us it is so.

In Doctrine and Covenants 132 we read: "If a man marry a wife by my word, which is my law, and by the new and everlasting covenant, and it is sealed unto them by the Holy Spirit of promise, . . . ye shall come forth in the first resurrection . . . and shall inherit thrones, kingdoms, principalities, and powers, dominions, all heights and depths—then shall it be written in the Lamb's Book of Life. . . . Then shall they be gods, because they have no end; therefore shall they be from everlasting to everlasting, because they continue; then shall they be above all, because all things are subject unto them" (D&C 132:19–20).

Marriage is an essential part of godhood. We are given a sacred privilege to be procreators in bringing children into this world; we learn how to have dominion over others—our children—how to raise them in truth and righteousness, and how to put gospel principles into practice with one another. Surely we must recognize the sacredness of our stewardship. Let us not flinch in our determination to keep our covenants by taking the Lord's hand and following His light. We have blessings of eternal life with God, to live as He lives, to have eternal increase, to have one another for all eternity, to have the fullness of His joy; this we are promised. As we seek to keep our sacred covenants, we will find hidden reservoirs of strength,[13] confidence cemented in our divine nature, and love more sweet than we could have imagined.

In Jerusalem, the light of the Lord is abundant in many locations, such as the Garden of Gethsemane, the Garden Tomb, the Temple Mount, and even in Hezekiah's Tunnel. Each path I walked in Israel has left sweet memories and a reminder of the glory of His light. I testify that the Lord is mindful of our marriages, that He cares, that He loves our spouses, that He loves us. He wants us to partake of the fulness of His joy through our eternal partnership under the everlasting covenant. I testify that His light will lead us as we experience the light of love, light of understanding, and light of hope and optimism.

NOTES

1. LDS Bible Dictionary, s.v. "Hezekiah's Tunnel," 702.
2. First Presidency and Council of the Twelve Apostles, "The Family: A Proclamation to the World," *Ensign*, November 1995, 102.
3. Gordon B. Hinckley, "Living Worthy of the Girl You Will Someday Marry," *Ensign*, May 1998, 51.
4. *Teachings of Presidents of the Church: Heber J. Grant* (Salt Lake City: The Church of Jesus Christ of Latter-day Saints, 2002), 54.
5. *Oxford English Dictionary*, s.v. "sacred" and "covenant."
6. James E. Faust, "Standing in Holy Places," *Ensign*, May 2005, 62.
7. Bruce R. McConkie, "Agency or Inspiration," *New Era*, January 1975, 42.
8. Orson Pratt, *The Seer* (Orem, Utah: Grandin Books, 1990), 156.
9. Stewart Brand, *A Clock from the Long Now* (New York: Basic Books, 1999), 42.
10. Hyrum and Helen Andrus, *They Knew the Prophet* (Salt Lake City: Bookcraft, 1974), 144.
11. Quoted by B. H. Roberts, in Conference Report, October 1912, 30.
12. Jeffrey R. Holland, "How Do I Love Thee?" *New Era*, October 2003, 4.
13. Bruce C. Hafen, "Covenant Marriage," *Ensign*, November 1996, 26.

BUILT UPON A FOUNDATION OF FRIENDSHIP

――◆――

Richard B. Miller

Few things in life are more exciting than a couple falling in love. They want to spend countless hours together as they bask in each other's company while planning their wedding and their eternal future. It is a magical time in their lives, as their love for each other grows. They can hardly believe that this is really happening to them, and they get caught up in the amazing excitement of falling in love. This love is consecrated in the house of the Lord, where the couple makes eternal covenants. Happily, they rush off on a honeymoon to begin their lives together.

Shortly after the honeymoon, though, reality hits. While still madly in love, they must return to unfinished school assignments, final exams, internships, and jobs. They find their lives becoming busier. At some point they graduate, move to another part of the country, begin careers, and settle into a new house. In addition, parenthood is introduced into their lives, which makes their earlier perceptions of being busy seem naïve. These former newlyweds find themselves trying to keep up with T-ball practice, piano lessons, carpooling, Cub Scouts, activity day, Relief Society enrichment night, soccer games, carpooling, parent-teacher conferences, Church callings, dance recitals, dental appointments, visiting teaching, ward dinners, carpooling, and compassionate service.

Richard B. Miller is a professor in the School of Family Life and an associate dean in the College of Family, Home, and Social Sciences at Brigham Young University. He and his wife, Mary, are the parents of four children.

The endless hours that they spent together during their courtship have been reduced to exhaustion-filled minutes. In a recent study that I conducted, I asked more than six hundred married people between the ages of 40 and 50 a question: "If you could change one thing in your relationship with your spouse, what would it be?" *By far,* the most common response to this open-ended question was that they wished that they could spend more time together. This response was twice as common as other issues that are more commonly discussed, such as money, physical intimacy, or child-rearing practices.

Many are able to overcome the time demands and stresses of life and maintain the love that they felt when they were first married. In my study of midlife couples, sixty percent said that their love is stronger now than when they were first married. Unfortunately, though, some couples develop patterns of anger, hostility, and chronic conflict that eventually lead to divorce.

There is a third group of couples, one that we don't talk about as much, who stay married but gradually lose their love towards each other. Over the years, their love dies, the battery becomes dead, the flame goes out, and the spark is gone. They no longer feel anger, frustration, or hurt; they are past that. They simply don't feel much of anything at all. In many cases, these couples stay married because of the commitments that they have made when they married or because of their desire not to disrupt their children's lives by getting divorced. Or they may simply be afraid of getting divorced and living separately. So they live their lives emotionally separate from each other, simply carrying on the work of keeping the family running. The great love that they once felt for each other is gone.

President Kimball has described these couples. He said, "Many couples permit their marriages to become stale and their love to grow cold like old bread or worn-out jokes or cold gravy."[1]

And on another occasion he said, "There are many people who do not find divorce attorneys and who do not end their marriages, but who have permitted their marriage to grow stale and weak and cheap. There are spouses who . . . are in the low state of mere joint occupancy of the home."[2]

Why and how do these couples fall out of love? Of course they lead busy lives that make it a challenge to find the time to nurture the love that they felt when they first married. However, couples who are able to maintain their love and grow closer together over the years are usually just as busy. Couples don't drift apart because they are busy; rather, their love dies because they have violated vital principles of creating and maintaining love, which eventually leads to an erosion of love.

In order to understand how loves dies, it is important to understand the nature of marital love. Elder Joe J. Christensen has offered a compelling description of marital love. It is noteworthy that scientific research on love has echoed these same principles. He said:

"Love is a difficult word to understand in the English language. For example, I could say to someone that 'I love you.' I used exactly those same words this morning speaking to my wife, Barbara, and I meant something very different. We need to know who is speaking to whom in what context. The Greeks don't have the same problem because they have three different words for *love*. The first is *eros,* or romantic love. The English word *erotic* comes from that Greek root. . . .

"The second is *philia,* or brotherly love. The U.S. 'City of Brotherly Love,' Philadelphia, gets its name from that Greek root. The third is *agape,* or Godlike love, the kind of love that enables our Father in Heaven and the Lord to love us even though we are not perfect. I understand that each time in the Greek text of the New Testament when the Lord commands us to love our enemies, it is *agape* that is used."[3]

Marital love, then, consists of three components: romantic love, friendship, and Godlike love. I am convinced that the key factor in maintaining a strong love that remains vibrant over the years is to foster friendship in the marital relationship. A marriage that is built upon a foundation of friendship is most likely to withstand the daily hectic schedules and occasional storms that inevitably hit every marriage.

Of course, Godlike love is also very important. But my experience is that couples who have drifted apart and are leading parallel lives usually still care about each other. Most of them still feel some level of Godlike love for each other. That usually isn't the part of their love that has died.

Romantic love is also important. Couples need to nurture their romantic love by being affectionate with each other and sharing tender expressions of love that are reserved for married couples. However, I'm convinced that friendship is the foundation upon which romantic love flourishes over the years. This is especially true for women. Like a flower, romantic love soon withers and dies without the foundation of a strong root structure of friendship. Friendship is the steady, stable foundation that keeps a marital relationship firmly rooted so that expressions of romantic love can continue to bloom over the years.

Elder Marlin K. Jensen has said: "Friendship is . . . a vital and wonderful part of courtship and marriage. A relationship between a man and a woman that begins with friendship and then ripens into romance and eventually marriage will usually become an enduring, eternal friendship. Nothing is more inspiring in today's world of easily dissolved marriages than to observe a husband and wife quietly appreciating and enjoying each other's friendship year in and year out as they experience together the blessings and trials of mortality."[4]

Family scientists have found in their research that a strong friendship is a key component to happy marriages. For example, one study asked 100 happily married older couples what they believed were the most important reasons why they were still happily married after being married for an average of 45 years. Out of a list of 37 possible answers, the most common response was that their partner was their best friend. They also frequently reported that they liked their partner as a person, that they were proud of their spouse's achievements, and that they laughed together frequently, all of which are attributes of friendship. The authors of this study concluded that "the sense of friendship, the enjoyment of being with each other and sharing in various activities, are a most important component of the glue that provides older as well as younger people with a satisfying marital relationship."[5]

Similarly, Dr. John Gottman, the foremost marital researcher in the world, has concluded that "happy marriages are based on a deep friendship. By this I mean a mutual respect for and enjoyment of each other's company. These couples tend to know each other intimately— they are well versed in each other's likes, dislikes, personality quirks, hopes, and dreams. They have an abiding regard for each other and express this fondness not just in the big ways but in the little ways day in and day out."[6]

Good friends *want* to spend time together. Even though they are busy, they are willing to take the effort to arrange their schedules to be together.

They value their relationship and try to make the other person happy. Good friends are unselfish and loyal. Good friends earn each other's trust; they are dependable and keep confidences. Good friends enjoy talking with each other and are interested in what the other person feels and says. They say, "I'm sorry," and forgive each other.

Most couples begin their marriage on a foundation of a strong friendship. In today's world, almost every young adult says that they want to marry their best friend, and most of them do. After countless hours spent together during their courtship, talking and laughing, and sharing their deepest hopes and fondest dreams, they have forged a close friendship. What happens over the years that erodes the friendship and, subsequently, the romantic love that is so dependent on that foundation? I would like to briefly discuss two issues that I believe erode friendship in marriage. The erosion process may take years, and it may even be unnoticeable for a long time, but, like tooth decay, it quietly and gradually creates damage until there is a serious problem. These two issues are equality and equity.

A strong, lasting marital friendship is based on equality. Even though the husband is the patriarch of the home, with the responsibility of providing spiritual leadership, our prophets have made it very clear that husbands and wives are equal partners. Notice the reference in "The Family: A Proclamation to the World" that husbands and wives are equal partners.[7] In addition, President Hinckley has said, "Marriage, in its truest sense, is a partnership of equals, with neither exercising dominion over the other, but, rather, with each encouraging and assisting the other in whatever responsibilities and aspirations he or she might have."[8]

On another occasion, he said: "Under the gospel plan marriage is a companionship, with equality between partners. We walk side by side with respect, appreciation, and love one for another. There can be nothing of inferiority or superiority between the husband and wife in the plan of the Lord."[9]

A friendship in marriage that is based on equality values the opinions of both partners. Both partners feel that their voice is respected in the relationship. They both know that their "vote" matters, that the other person won't act until they reach consensus on a decision. Elder L. Tom Perry described this righteous process in some detail:

"Remember, brethren, that in your role as leader in the family, your wife is your companion. As President Gordon B. Hinckley has taught: 'In this Church the man neither walks ahead of his wife nor behind his wife but at her side. They are coequals.' . . . Therefore, there is not a president or a vice president in a family. The couple works together eternally for the good of the family. They are united together in word, in deed, and in action as they lead, guide, and direct their family unit. They are on equal footing. They plan and organize the affairs of the family jointly and unanimously as they move forward."[10]

The equality of husbands and wives in marriage is a doctrine of God. The violation of that doctrine erodes away at the friendship within the marriage. No one likes to be controlled. No one likes to feel that they don't have a voice in the marriage. Feelings of inequality lead to resentment, and *resentment is the poison of friendship.* Failed attempts to change the structure of the marriage to one of equality lead to more resentment. After repeatedly trying to gain a real voice in the marriage, the spouse often quits trying and starts to pull away from the relationship. They usually still try to be a good spouse and perform the tasks that they have in the marriage and the family, but they gradually feel differently and eventually find that the friendship with their partner is gone.

Equity is also a vital factor in a strong marriage. Equity refers to feelings of fairness in the relationship. In a healthy marital friendship, both partners feel that the relationship is fair, with both partners making strong contributions to the relationship. There are times, though, when one spouse perceives that the relationship is unbalanced. They feel like they are "doing all of the giving" while their partner is "doing all of the taking." At first these perceptions lead to mild annoyance, but chronic feelings of inequity create resentment, the poison of friendship. Over time, the resentment grows until the friendship has been eroded and their feelings of love are gone.

Equity is commonly an issue with the division of labor in the marriage, especially among women. Our Church leaders have made it very clear that husbands and wives *both* have the responsibility of taking care of the home. The proclamation on the family clearly teaches that husbands and wives are "obligated to help one another as equal partners." Elder Boyd K. Packer has stated:

"It was not meant that the woman alone accommodate[s] herself to the priesthood duties of her husband or her sons. . . . Holders of the priesthood, in turn, must accommodate themselves to the needs and responsibilities of the wife and mother. . . . There is no task, however menial, connected with the care of babies, the nurturing of children, or with the maintenance of the home that is not [a husband's] equal obligation."[11]

In addition, Elder Joe J. Christensen, when talking to the priesthood brethren, said: "Be a true partner in home and family responsibilities. Don't be like the husband who sits around home expecting to be waited on, feeling that earning the living is his chore and that his wife alone is responsible for the house and taking care of the children. The task of caring for home and family is more than one person's responsibility. Remember that you are in this partnership together. Barbara and I have discovered that we can make our bed every morning in less than a minute and it's done for the day. She says that she lets me do it to help me feel good about myself all day, and I guess there may be something to that."[12]

Thus, husbands and wives, when they are reunited at home in the evening, should work together and pitch in to do whatever needs to be done with children and around the house. It isn't the man's job or the woman's job; they are partners and they work together in performing household and family tasks. I have long believed that there are few things that nurture the friendship of a woman towards her husband more than hearing him run the vacuum, bathe a young child, or assist an older child with homework—especially if he does it without having been asked. Such sounds of full participation in the responsibilities of family life build friendships much more effectively than the sounds of a ball game on TV or a video game—or snoring.

In truth, inequality is related to inequity. This is because a lack of equality often prevents the correction of imbalance in the relationship. In every marriage, spouses at times may feel that the relationship is unbalanced, with one contributing more than the other. Responsibilities and the demands of family life are constantly shifting, and it is common for the division of labor to be temporarily inequitable. However, in an equal marriage, the partners are able to discuss the issue as equal partners. With the issue on the table, they are able to negotiate a revised division of labor, where both partners believe that the relationship is fair. However, when one partner holds power over the other, that person is usually unwilling to listen to the concerns of the spouse, preferring to maintain the status quo. In such cases, the problem remains unresolved and feelings of resentment—the poison of friendship—grow. Thus, equality is usually a prerequisite of equity.

Hopefully, we can follow these principles of equality and equity, as well as other important principles, so that we can maintain strong friendships in our marital relationships and keep our love alive and vibrant. However, there are some people whose marriages have already grown "stale," "cold," and "worn out," to use President Kimball's words. What should they do?

I believe that the solution is found in the gospel of Jesus Christ. When we feel hurt, frustration, and eventual resentment in our relationships, the scriptures clearly teach us that we are to go to the person and resolve it.

The Savior taught, "Moreover if thy brother shall trespass against thee, go and tell him his fault between thee and him alone: if he shall hear thee, thou hast gained thy brother" (Matthew 18:15).

In many cases, the offending party has no idea that they have been offensive. Several years ago, I worked with a couple who came to me because the wife didn't feel love for her husband anymore. Her resentment towards him had grown over the years to the point that it had poisoned all of her feelings of love towards him. She had a long list of complaints and grievances. One was particularly interesting; she was upset many years before when she was delivering one of their children. While she was in the process of pushing, her husband asked her to hurry up because a football game on TV was about ready to start. She was understandably upset, but the interesting thing was that this was the first time—many years later—that she had ever talked with him about it. Her husband hardly remembered the incident and had no idea that it was a big deal to her.

So the Savior teaches us that we should go to our spouse if there are unresolved hurts and resentments and resolve them. That gives our spouse the opportunity to repent, to say "I'm sorry," and to change behavior. It also expedites the process of forgiveness, where we turn our hurts and resentment over to the Lord. The great miracle of the Savior's Atonement will heal our hearts and allow us to love again.

Marital love is like the coals of a campfire. Sometimes it looks like the fire is out, but if you sift through the ashes, you will find a coal, often buried deep and almost unnoticed. But, as you gently remove the ashes around it, you can still see the embers glowing. By carefully blowing on it, the embers expand and become hotter. With patience and care, the little piece of coal that was hidden and taken for dead can be reignited and burst into a wonderful fire. So it is with love.

Several years ago, I met with a couple who were in their 70s. She told me that she no longer loved her husband, that she hadn't felt loving feelings towards him for many, many years. Although they still worked well together in being parents and grandparents, and they had served together in the Church—including a mission—their personal relationship had been nonexistent for a long, long time. She said that she was committed to the relationship and that she had no interest in being divorced, but she definitely didn't love her husband.

As we visited over the next several weeks, she talked about some of the hurts that had occurred in their relationship over the years. The marriage had been characterized by great inequity, with him making many demands on her, with little expectation that he should contribute to the family, other than providing a living. He had also been unkind in many ways. Not wanting to make trouble, she had never really voiced her concerns and dissatisfactions with her husband. Consequently, she had built up a wall of resentment that created a great divide between them, and her feelings towards him gradually changed from hurt to resentment to apathy. As she talked about her past hurts, her husband responded marvelously. He told her repeatedly how sorry he was and how much he wanted to treat her better. As he repented, the miracle of forgiveness came over *both* of them, and her feelings started to change. She started *wanting* to do things with him again, and their level of interaction increased. They worked on rebuilding their friendship. They talked, went for walks, and laughed. On the last time that we met, she told me, "I'm finding myself falling in love all over again. For the first time in 40 years, I can say that I truly love him."

My hope and prayer is that we can build our relationship upon a foundation of friendship, that we can live consistent with the principles that maintain our friendship and allow it to grow. With such a foundation, our love will remain strong for eternity.

NOTES

1. Spencer W. Kimball, "Oneness in Marriage," *Ensign*, March 1977, 5.
2. Spencer W. Kimball, *Marriage* (Salt Lake City: Deseret Book, 1978), 44, 46.
3. Joe J. Christensen, "Ten Ideas to Increase Your Spirituality," *Ensign*, March 1999, 60.
4. Marlin K. Jensen, "Friendship: A Gospel Principle," *Ensign*, May 1999, 64.
5. Robert H. Lauer, Jeanette C. Lauer, and Sarah T. Kerr, "The long-term marriage: Perception of stability and satisfaction," *International Journal of Aging and Human Development* 31 (1990): 193.
6. John Gottman, *The Seven Principles for Making Marriage Work* (New York: Three Rivers Press, 1999), 19–20.
7. First Presidency and Council of the Twelve Apostles, "The Family: A Proclamation to the World," *Ensign*, November 1995, 102.
8. Gordon B. Hinckley, "I Believe," *Ensign*, August 1992, 6.
9. Gordon B. Hinckley, *Teachings of Gordon B. Hinckley* (Salt Lake City: Deseret Book, 1997), 322.
10. L. Tom Perry, "Fatherhood, an Eternal Calling," *Ensign*, May 2004, 71.
11. Boyd K. Packer, "A Tribute to Women," *Ensign*, July 1989, 75.
12. Joe J. Christensen, "Marriage and the Great Plan of Happiness," *Ensign*, May 1995, 64.

MARRIAGE WITH A LESS-ACTIVE CHURCH MEMBER

Jacqueline S. Thursby

I have been invited to give you a message out of my earthly experience. I am both humbled and elated at the opportunity to share some of what I have learned, and at the same time preparing this presentation has been a journey of renewal for me. The day in 1968 when my husband announced that he was going to withdraw from activity in the Church, I resolved that I would be the very best wife of a less-active that I could possibly be. I have a firm testimony of the gospel and a very active conscience, so there was little else I could consider doing. I am not sure if I have fulfilled that resolve perfectly, but I can honestly say that I have given and will continue to give it my best effort. With the aid of Jesus Christ's teachings, the Atonement, and the constant guidance of the Holy Spirit, this mortal assignment (that of being married to and loved by my beloved apostate) has been more full of joy than I expected. With my conversion, I reconstructed my life in terms of the Church guidelines. Where our lives had been good, I wanted them better. Where my scripture reading and prayers had been daily, I wanted my scripture study to be more probing and my prayers to be more constant. That is the way it has been

Jacqueline S. Thursby is an associate professor in the English department at Brigham Young University. A folklorist and member of the Secondary English Education team, she has authored four books, written several articles, and presented her research nationally and internationally. She and her husband, Denny, live in Provo, Utah, and are the parents of four children.

219

since. My husband has been supportive because he knows that I believe what I profess to believe.

He is a good man, and well worth whatever investment in prayer, fasting, and patience I may be asked to give. We were converts and parents of three young children. We were baptized on the same day, and then, a little more than a year later, we traveled from our home in St. Louis to the Salt Lake Temple to be sealed as a couple and as a family. That sealing is in effect for all time and eternity. Like many others, and with Heavenly Father's aid and support, I have had to learn how to make the marriage and sealing work with a good but spiritually reluctant companion. Our home is a refuge, a holy place that is usually in order. We share our evening meals, and when the children were still at home, or when they visit, mealtime is a gentle ritual. The talk is positive, the food simple and wholesome, and respect is simply the expected behavior. That is the way our parents' homes were and now our children's. That setting provides a foundation for bonding with Christ and one another.

My message to you is one of hope, of caring, of deep respect, of compassion, of faith, of honor, and of dignity. You, my sisters, are to possess all of those attributes now and throughout all eternity. You have been chosen, called, and set apart to serve a complex mission in our Father's kingdom. You are saviors on Mount Zion, a chosen group of sisters engaged in what I call, in very human terms, "a rescue mission." A few years ago I wrote a book about nurturing relationships with less-active family and friends. In a few minutes, I'd like to share the preface of that text to you. It isn't very long, just a page and a half, but it explains what I believe to be the basic position that most of us find ourselves in with one human relationship or another. In my case, the position describes many of my family interactions. Though many of my deceased family members have had the temple work done for them, my living relatives are not interested in conversion to The Church of Jesus Christ of Latter-day Saints. I pray for them, stay in touch with them, and respect their agency. We love one another and rush to support each family member when there is a need or occasion to celebrate. I hope you do that too. And now, the preface with a few significant scriptures interjected:

"Long ago, by the human measurement of time, there were great councils in heaven. We were all there, and I think most of us were excited for the time to come for decision making about our future. Heaven was a spirit world, and we wanted our spirits to be clothed with mortality, with flesh and bones, so that we could live on earth and take the next steps toward our destiny. We would be able to make our own decisions in mortality. There would be laws, and there would be authority, but whether we obeyed the laws and authority was clearly to be our choice. Our teacher, exemplar, and Savior was Jesus, the Christ. He promised to show us the way to live together on earth and the way to prepare to return with honor to the spirit world when our bodies could no longer house our spirits.

"It was his Father's plan.

"Many did not like the plan. They were afraid that if humans could choose, they would choose wrongly and fail on earth. Those who rejected the Father's plan of agency followed Lucifer. Lucifer's plan was absolute control. He and his followers were permanently cast out of heaven. They will never have bodies of flesh and bone, and it is they who tempt humans to be disobedient. It is they who tempt those who struggle with faith.

"Some spirits who voted for the Father's plan were stronger than others. Faith would be a requirement for success in the mortal probation, and many probably believed and were anxious to learn and obey every law. But there were probably varied reactions to the plan among the obedient spirits. Perhaps some had less faith, and they needed concrete facts and visual affirmations of truth; such spirits would need assistance on earth in order to return to their Heavenly Father at the end of their mortality.

"I believe that those of us who received the gift of faith . . . were given assignments to minister to those who have less faith."

First Corinthians 12:4–12 reminds us: "Now there are diversities of gifts, but the same Spirit. And there are differences of administrations, but the same Lord. And there are diversities of operations, but it is the same God which worketh all in all. But the manifestation of the Spirit is given to every man to profit withal. For to one is given by the Spirit the word of wisdom; to another the word of knowledge by the same Spirit; to another faith by the same Spirit; to another the gifts of healing by the same Spirit; to another the working of miracles; to another prophecy; to another discerning of spirits; to another divers kind of tongues; to another the interpretation of tongues: But all these worketh that one and the selfsame Spirit, dividing to every man severally as he will. For as the body is one, and hath many members, and all the members of that one body, being many, are one body: so also is Christ."

"Thus, loving—really loving—the less-active or inactive Church members or members of other faiths in our homes, families, and neighborhoods is not simply a noble act of endurance; it is a matter of being obedient and keeping covenants."

As Mosiah 18:8–9 states: "And it came to pass that he said unto them: Behold, here are the waters of Mormon (for thus were they called) and now, as ye are desirous to come into the fold of God, and to be called his people, and are willing to bear one another's burdens, that they may be light; yea, and are willing to mourn with those that mourn; yea, and comfort those that stand in need of comfort, and to stand as witnesses of God at all times and in all things, . . . even until death, that ye may be redeemed of God, and be numbered with those of the first resurrection, that ye may have eternal life."

In conclusion, the preface states:

"It is a matter of commitment, integrity, and eternal worth. There is nothing more important than to lead our loved ones to Christ. We who have spouses, children, extended family, and friends who have not gained testimonies of the truthfulness of the gospel have a sacred responsibility to love them into receiving a witness from the Holy Ghost. We are sent to gently coax the light of Christ in each one of them until it becomes a steady flame of testimony. We must treasure and feed our own gifts of faith. We must be gentle, patient, and forgiving. We must learn to listen and be watchful. This is a responsibility that can be borne with honor and dignity, and it is a matter of eternal destiny."[1]

And so, how do we do this? Your bishop has probably counseled you to return to your home, or to the temple, and fast and pray often. He may have said, "Hang in there," as my favorite stake president used to say to me regularly. Or you may have been told, repeatedly, "Endure to the end, with righteousness, patience, and faith." Okay. But how do you make yourself feel better in the midst of varying levels of depression, unfulfilled promises, indifference, and whatever else the adversary can construct to prevent you from having joy? Well, the bishop and stake president are right. You must fast and pray, and then you tie a knot at the end of the rope and hang on (and by the way, it is okay to cry). Remember Alma

37:36? "Yea, and cry unto God for all thy support; yea, let all thy doings be unto the Lord, and whithersoever thou goest let it be in the Lord; yea, let all thy thoughts be directed unto the Lord; yea, let the affections of thy heart be placed upon the Lord forever."

My best counsel to you, dear sisters, would be to hang on with a positive attitude of faith and trust. The Lord has a safety net under you, and for every sting the adversary constructs and flings at you, Jesus Christ has an antidote. Through the Atonement, and through the counsel of the scriptures, priesthood and patriarchal blessings, prayer, and the still, small voice of the Holy Spirit, we can receive guidance for every situation. For every insult, there is an appropriate response, and that is often silence. For every act of indifference, one can respond quietly with one's own engagement; for every missed meeting or social, one can respond with a beautifully planned evening at home (even with children). More often than not, honest, respectful communication is the answer for bringing peace to most differences.

I would like to share a few tips for you to try to keep in mind concerning your value and capabilities. You know that you were created in the image of God. God and Christ are creative, self-determining, all-powerful beings who live according to law. You too are creative and self-determining, and you have the power to take charge of your life and shape it as you will. Yet with your agency, you have the responsibility to obey His righteous desires for you to become like Him. What are your capabilities? Do you really understand and respect the meaning of agency? Can you tap into the powers of the universe through Jesus Christ and free yourself from the preoccupation of your companion's choices concerning the Church? Yes, you can.

These seven suggestions could be applied to any life. I have gleaned them from a variety of mostly unidentifiable sources and blended them with my own life experience to share some of what I have learned after nearly forty years of practice. There is a little "Jackie" here as well as a little gospel.

1. Stay in the present. Stop mentally wandering into the past or the future. I am not suggesting that you stop planning for the future, but stop worrying. Actually, we have been reminded of this in several conference talks in the last few years. You cannot change the past, and you cannot

adequately predict the future. There is an ancient Zen meditation that I
share with my students at stressful times of the semester. For just a minute
or two, simply be where you are. Feel your feet in your shoes, your clothes
on your body, the very skin on your hands. Stop thinking momentarily, let
go of both the past and the future, and focus on simply being in the now.
Be still, and you will feel the presence of God within you. You might not
want to try this at a stoplight for fear of going to sleep, but try it now or
in another safe place. It centers, calms, and refreshes, and reminds you
that you are never alone.

2. Push away victim mentality and learn to laugh. So, your husband
won't join the Church, or he won't commit to becoming active and honoring his priesthood. If he is good to you and your children, you are still
much better off than many who have no life companion. If he does not
treat you as well as you would like, look for the good in your situation.
Have you remembered to express gratitude to him for what he does that
pleases you? Victim mentality is a blaming position that drains you of your
power to find and be yourself. Bad things do happen to good people. You
know that! It is all a part of your training, and you succeed by responding
prayerfully, bravely, and positively to whatever you are called upon to
experience. Your spouse most likely enjoys you most when you are positive and even demonstrating a sense of humor. Go to the library; get a
book of jokes or some comedy videos. Lighten up. Christ is patient, and
so should you be.

3. Speaking of victim mentality, do you really think it is your parents'
or husband's fault that you aren't closer to some mythical perfection? Did
they forget to teach you a few things about the mysterious workings of,
well, (you fill in the blank)? Forgive them. There is no compromise on
this. We are commanded to forgive, and forgiveness is a process that we
learn to master over time. Neither your parents, your spouse, your teachers, nor your professors could give you everything you need to know.
Neither can you give that to anyone else. As long as you are unable to forgive, or to even begin working on forgiving, you are holding on to a black
cloud that, no matter how familiar and comfortable, needs to be cut loose.
It is sort of like being overweight. It is so comfortable, but so dangerous.
Many of us manage to hurt ourselves pretty thoroughly through ignorance
of one kind or another, and that is why prayer and scripture study keep

circling back as key components of joy and peace of mind. Only the Lord knows all of our needs, and we have to forgive everybody else for not quite understanding.

4. Try to remember that less is more. When I look at the bookcases in my home, and at my book-lined office, I have to stop and wonder. Then I rationalize about having so many books. Rationalization, that is, constructing plausible reasons for sometimes less than perfect choices and behavior, is one of humankind's most useful mental exercises. Having a ton of books relates to my job as a professor: I read, I tell, and I read some more, and I push the button for Amazon.com used books because I am under contract to stay current. Even so, there is a library! Simplify. Having running credit card debt is a killer of the peaceful marriage relationship. My husband used to say (before I was employed, and even now occasionally), "Is that a want or a need?" Usually it was not a need. Children need shoes that fit; each room needs so many lamps; each meal needs to be balanced; each person needs food, clothes, and shelter. However, we can only sleep in one bed at a time, wear one outfit at a time, and read one book at a time, and excellence can sometimes be purchased at very reasonable prices. Be careful, and don't overload your marriage with material encumbrances. Remember that the counsel of our leaders is to avoid debt.

5. Find something you both really like to do and get into it! Our joint interests have varied over the decades. We have been married for forty-five years, and our common interests have moved from tending our babies together to golf, bike riding, and antiquing. It would be so delicious to me if we could study the scriptures and history of the Church together, but that does not interest him so I do that early in the morning before he awakens. He likes TV sports, which do not interest me, so now and then we spend evenings in separate rooms. We both like to garden, but my job is year-round, so I have little time for that. Lately the common ground has been carefully selected videos from the library. We watch world classics, mysteries, dramas, and comedy films. We have vicariously and inexpensively traveled to most of the world through the DVD and VCR. I have made recipes that range from Italian Easter Pie to an almond paste Danish Christmas Tree as we have read about and watched beautiful faraway places through the technology.

6. You must learn what agency is and respect it. You were some of the

spirits in the front lines cheering for moral agency in the preexistence. For most of us, understanding what agency really means is a life-long learning process. It is not bribery or a rewards system. One of the most important points of respecting another's agency is to avoid manipulation of any sort. There have been popular books published about using manipulative methods to charm or delude husbands so that wives might be treated with some surreal respect. In my opinion, those methods are simply dishonest. Be yourself, and respect yourself enough to be honest. Your husband deserves to be treated with truth and dignity. Allow him the freedom to make his choices; the consequences will follow. In time, he will come to realize what his best choices are.

7. Empower yourself with the spiritual strength of Jesus Christ. You don't have to understand how it works, but memorize the little scripture that was in one of our visiting teaching messages last year: "I can do all things through Christ which strengtheneth me" (Philippians 4:13). I first learned about the empowering quality of that little scripture from my mother's Norman Vincent Peale books on positive thinking, and I learned just how quickly it worked. There was quite a bit of opposition to my joining the Church when I was in my twenties. Like Nephi of old, "I was led by the Spirit, not knowing beforehand the things which I should do" (1 Nephi 4:6), but trusting Christ to strengthen me, I followed His summons. Because I continue to trust Him, He has led me like a shepherd through many rocky paths of surprise and disappointment, and I know His power is there to guide and comfort you as well.

Try working on these tips over time. You might try the one-a-day method. There are seven, and the concepts overlap, but you might try a daily focus on one at a time and see if they help. It is imperative that we reach our highest capacity of spiritual understanding as we move through mortality. Personal understanding of spiritual pathways is the only way to live in harmony and peace with those who view the gospel differently. This is a process, and one of my colleagues, Professor Nancy Christiansen, recently gave a College of Humanities devotional called "Whence Then Cometh Wisdom and Where Is the Place of Understanding? (Job 28:20)." In that talk, she suggested that many of the steps to secular learning in university studies are the same as steps to spiritual understanding. Similar to beginning a secular study of a topic unfamiliar to us, we must have, as she said, "a willingness to face a challenge"; we must understand that we will "stumble, make mistakes, and look less than adequate"; we realize that through testing, we receive "correction and feedback"; we must have "diligence and determination" and be willing to practice, practice, practice. We "must engage all of [our] faculties: memory, analysis, synthesis, imagination, and judgment in order to transform [our] behaviors." "Finally," Christiansen notes, "this process requires the sacrifice of time, effort, money, and activities of lesser value." Our purpose on earth is to become like God, and "if we wish to live in a paradise where peace, plenty, love, freedom, power, and joy abound, then it is only reasonable that we submit ourselves to Christ's tutoring."[2] The worth of a soul is priceless in the eyes of our Maker, so what could be more significant in His work than to labor to assist His noble sons and daughters to return to Him with honor?

Proverbs 4:7 states: "Wisdom is the principal thing; therefore get wisdom: and with all thy getting get understanding." You have been chosen, called up, and assigned to do the work you are doing in your homes. You are blessed beyond measure with the capacities to make of your homes and the relationships within them places where the Spirit of the Lord can and will be felt. The Lord has a place reserved for you in the celestial kingdom, and He will rejoice with you when the period of repentance is completed for each loved one and you witness their joy at receiving and acknowledging Christ, the Redeemer. Seek and obtain and practice wisdom as the Lord reveals to you the ways to create those kinds of homes and relationships. Love and grace are at the center, and they must be nourished and kept glowing through you.

My mother passed away a little over a month ago, and another colleague, Professor Suzanne Lundquist, wrote a poem for me in honor of that rite of passage. There will be a time on the other side of the veil when my mother, my husband, and other members of my family will recognize and accept the gospel. In the poem, Lundquist wrote about a "ransom season," a mending where repentance will be "ministered alongside a honeyed bowl of grace."[3] Because of faith, sisters, you can enjoy that "honeyed bowl of grace" daily in your lives. It is an inward peace granted to those who wait. In the meanwhile, there is no loss in your stature or empowerment to serve your companion well. Love him, support him, and be that little bit of honey stirred gracefully into his life on this side of the veil.

NOTES

1. Jacqueline S. Thursby, *Begin Where You Are: Nurturing Relationships with Less-Active Family and Friends* (Salt Lake City: Deseret Book, 2004), xiii–xiv.
2. Nancy L. Christiansen, "Whence Then Cometh Wisdom and Where Is the Place of Understanding? Job 28:20," College of Humanities devotional, Brigham Young University, January 20, 2005, 2–4.
3. Suzanne Lundquist, "For Jackie (on the death of your mother)," unpublished poem, Provo, Utah, March 26, 2005.

THE ADVERSARY EXPOSED IN THE LIGHT OF THE RESTORATION

Truman G. Madsen

Once I had the rare privilege of driving with President Gordon B. Hinckley on the east side of the Sea of Galilee. We spoke of Jesus' ministry. We looked up to traditional Gadara. "What does this experience tell us?" I asked. "Jesus permits evil spirits to enter into the bodies of the Gadarene swine. Then the swine rush down the mountain and are drowned. What does it all mean?" He replied thoughtfully, "The worth of a human body" (see Matthew 8:28–34).[1]

In this one sentence the President was echoing the Prophet Joseph:

"We came to this earth that we might have a body and present it pure before God in the Celestial Kingdom. The great principle of happiness consists in having a body. The Devil has no body, and herein is his punishment. He is pleased when he can obtain the tabernacle of man and when cast out by the Savior he asked to go into the herd of swine showing that he would prefer a swine's body to having none."[2]

We have also been taught that the business of the adversary and his host is to destroy. Destroy they sometimes do. Even if they can only retard or, as it were, clip our wings they achieve their end, to make all men miserable like themselves (2 Nephi 2:18, 27). The devil is the saddest sadist in the universe.[3]

Truman G. Madsen is a professor emeritus of philosophy at Brigham Young University. He is currently serving as a stake patriarch and Gospel Doctrine teacher. He and his wife, Ann, are the parents of four children.

One morning I ran into Mary Ellen Edmunds. That's always an experience. She is cheerful and buoyant and blessed with many funny bones. I asked, "Do you think we can bind the adversary by humor?" "Well," she said, "I don't like to rile him up. But sometimes I say to him, 'Is that really the best you can do?'" Indeed there are times one can see clear through the campaign of the devil. But sometimes he is so subtle and works so invisibly he is like a band of termites. At all times he is venomous.

I tend to picture him in the lower regions walking back and forth saying, "I ain't got no body." In that jocular spirit, years ago I wrote a fable with apologies to C. S. Lewis.[4] It's about an imp who is assigned to buffet a teenager. With demonic curiosity he reverses his role. He tempts to do good instead of evil. The adversary himself casts him out. Then he is taken to the lower regions and put on trial for low treason. The devil loses control, slams his pointer down, and says, "How could you do it?" The imp replies with a distant smile, "Just for the heaven of it."

We can make two opposite mistakes. One is to underestimate the devil's influence and power. The other is to overestimate it, or to assume there is no way out. He delights in either error, for they play into his hands. We are counseled to avoid both.[5]

So now seriously.

THE ENCOUNTER WITH MOSES

On record is an interview with Moses. He is blessed with face-to-face communion with God. (This manifestation is clearest in the Pearl of Great Price.) Repeatedly the account refers to Moses as "in the similitude of mine Only Begotten" (see Moses 1:1–16).

Immediately after that awesome experience, the adversary appears to Moses and says, "I am the Only Begotten, worship me" (Moses 1:19). Moses asks, "Where is thy glory . . . ? And I can judge between thee and God" (Moses 1:15). The adversary rants and raves. And Moses cries out, "In the name of the Only Begotten, depart." And Satan departs (see Moses 1:19–22).

Satan, we are taught, appears as an angel of light (see 2 Nephi 9:9; D&C 128:20). But compared to the Savior, his light is darkness.

What does the name *Lucifer* mean? It means the morning star. A star—that sounds like an honorary title. But what happens when the sun comes up, the S-o-n or the s-u-n. The star is eclipsed. You can't even see it. The devil will be eclipsed by the Savior; he will eventually be exiled to outer darkness. He will be gone. "How art thou fallen from heaven, O Lucifer, son of the morning!" (Isaiah 14:12). In the meantime he and his host are permitted to taunt us in this world.

LEARNING TO DISCERN

We have a home court advantage in judging between the Lord and the blandishments of Satan. Modern revelation teaches that we are all born into this world possessed of the light of Christ. And "that which was from the beginning is plainly manifest unto [us]" (D&C 93:31).

Then, says the revelation, "that wicked one cometh and taketh away light and truth" (D&C 93:38–40). So one of his strategies is subtraction, not addition. (Lewis observes that the devil does his worst work not by putting ideas in our head but by keeping certain ideas out.[6])

In Jerusalem once we took students into a cave and closed it off. When we were in total darkness we lighted an olive lamp. Its tiny flame lighted all the faces and the walls. Just as Jesus promised: "It giveth light unto all that are in the house" (Matthew 5:15). Then we lit another lamp and placed it close to the first. The flames bent toward each other, then blended. Just as Jesus promised: "Light cleaveth unto light" (D&C 88:40).

Your spirit is native to light and truth. By its very nature it seeks and responds and embraces truth. Intelligence cleaves to intelligence, not to ignorance. Virtue loves virtue, not the opposite (see D&C 88:40).

So how does the adversary rob us of what we start with? He perverts, misleads, stupefies, and confuses.

First, by disobedience. When we refuse to receive and honor counsel from above, our inner power diminishes. Modern revelation says, "They receive not the light. And every man whose spirit receiveth not the light is under condemnation" (D&C 93:31–32). "[When] we revolt at anything which comes from God the devil takes power."[7]

Second, "because of the tradition of their fathers" (D&C 93:39). There are lots of false traditions out there, including traditions about the devil, amidst elements of truth. They surround us. But the Lord commands Latter-day Saints to bring up their children in light and truth. Sometimes the only place we can do that is in the home.

OF LIMITS, BOUNDS, AND CONDITIONS

We know of certain bounds the adversary cannot pass.

First, he cannot coerce. He cannot force.[8] The statement "The devil made me do it" is always a fiction. He can't make you do anything. Said the Prophet Joseph, "[He] cannot seduce us by his enticements unless we in our hearts consent and yield."[9] (It is crucial to know that neither will the Lord Jesus Christ resort to force. The Atonement of Jesus Christ is a pattern of persuasion, not of coercion [see D&C 88:33–35].)

Second, apparently he cannot know our thoughts. Revelation says "that there is none else save God that knowest thy thoughts and the intents of thy heart" (D&C 6:16). At first this is a frightening idea. He really knows my thoughts, my heart, my secret and deepest concerns? On second thought it is gloriously reassuring. Someone truly understands you and cares for you; it is God and not Satan. Satan knows who you were and are, and his memory has not been covered with amnesia. But he cannot read your thoughts. If you pray secretly in the hour of temptation he cannot know what you are doing, whatever his shrewd guesses. Joseph taught that when you receive the Spirit through prayer, the spirits of evil will withdraw.[10]

Third, he is overcome by the power of the name of Jesus Christ when it is spoken in genuine faith and humility. "Not with railing accusation, that ye be not overcome, neither with boasting" (D&C 50:33). We bear his name, and "no combination of wickedness shall have power to rise up and prevail over thy people upon whom thy name shall be put in this house [the temple]" (D&C 109:26). To this name he must yield. Thank God for that.

Fourth, he cannot stay here or in the spirit world forever. He cannot be destroyed. But he will be exiled.

HIS TARGETS

Where does he point his "fiery darts" (1 Nephi 15:24; compare D&C 3:8; 27:17)? Wherever he can deceive and take off our relish for spiritual things he goes after us. For example:

He goes for the frontal lobe. That is where moral discrimination and nuances of spiritual sensitivity are lodged. Hence he sponsors the epidemic of the use and abuse of hard drugs and mind-dulling drink. This is the real drug war. According to the party line, drugs expand consciousness. Yes, they do, as the bomb expanded Hiroshima. In contrast, the Word of Wisdom promises us increasing knowledge and treasures of knowledge and wisdom.

He goes after "the still small voice." There are a thousand ways he has devised to numb and drown out Spirit impressions and the voice of conscience. The sheer omnipresence in our culture of noise and deafening music is one symptom of his hold and the almost universal appeal of this multimedia barrage.

He attacks the home and especially you, mothers and motherhood. He degrades, ridicules, and worse. There are two kinds of blasphemy. One uses the name of God in vain. Another maligns the most sacred power in the universe, surrounding it with gutter language. Teach your children to avoid it. Exalt the glory of the home. Re-enthrone in your own home the proclamation on the family.

Overall the adversary targets, as Neal Maxwell has written, the "crown jewels"[11]: Christ himself, of course. But then Joseph Smith, the Book of Mormon, and the temple, all of which center on the Savior. Constantly he reviles. When we edited the *Encyclopedia of Mormonism* we included an article on anti-Mormon literature. We learned that during the same period temple building has increased fourfold, so also has virulent anti-Mormon literature. It is clear the devil hates the temple. That is a high compliment to the temple.

LEARNING TO OVERCOME

Brigham Young taught: "When you are tempted, buffeted, and step out of the way inadvertently: when you are overtaken in a fault, or commit an overt act unthinkingly; when you are full of evil passion, and wish to yield to it, then stop and let the spirit, which God has put into your tabernacles, take the lead. If you do that, I will promise that you will overcome all evil, and obtain eternal lives. But many, very many, let the spirit yield to the body, and are overcome and destroyed."[12]

Notice he says "let it" not "make it." Your divinely sired spirit can do what it is predisposed to do.

The Apostle James wrote, "Resist the devil, and he will flee from you" (James 4:7). President McKay, after reviewing the adversary's assaults on Jesus, taught, "Your weakest point will be the point at which the devil tries to tempt you. . . . Resist him and he becomes weaker and you become stronger, until you can say, no matter what your surroundings may be, 'Get thee behind me, Satan: for it is written, Thou shalt worship the Lord thy God, and him only shalt thou serve.'"[13]

My grandfather tells of a donation requested, and a man decided to give a ham. He had a smokehouse full of hams. When he went in there, he picked out a nice large ham, and a spirit came over him: "Now, that is a big ham; you don't need to give that person such a large ham; give him a little one." He said, "Shut up, Mr. Devil, or I will give him two hams," so he had no more trouble—none whatever.

All of us face times in the Church when we are called or assigned at apparently the worst time and situation. Of such a moment, President Heber J. Grant said: "I had made the promise to myself that I would accept the mission and make no excuses, and as Brother Snow was talking the thought came to me: 'It is not an excuse to tell your condition financially,' and I remarked to myself, 'Shut up, Mr. Devil, if I should tell my condition financially there isn't a man in this room that would let me go to Japan. That is the best excuse I could possibly make.'"[14] He accepted the call and was blessed financially and otherwise.

Sometimes the devil's game is to foster extremes. Some religions, for example, teach that the only way to live a righteous life is to mortify, mutilate, and get rid of the body. The truth? The body is the temple of God. The other extreme concludes the body is everything. It acknowledges no soul, no spirit—also a falsehood.

The adversary is an accuser. He works hard to make us feel guilty or inferior or stupid or worthless when we are not. And he hits us hardest when we are down. He encourages the constant replay of our mistakes. He tries to convince us we have not sinned when we have and to tell us we have sinned when we have not. Either way the attempt is to lead us away from Christ.

On the other hand, he is the arch-advocate of pride and arrogance.

Pride may be the ultimate cause of his own decline and fall.[15] He sought to become a law unto himself. He goads us to do the same. He sought for what was unlawful, and then rebelled. He portrays God as the great spoilsport and claims he alone can provide freedom, even while he himself is the slave of corruption.

The answer to all this is to trust the Lord.

OF LIGHT AND LOVELINESS

Ann and I attended the open house of the Manhattan Temple. We found ourselves sitting at a table with Mike Wallace. He did not know until then that President Hinckley had lost his wife. He showed obvious sympathy.

I said to him, "At the end of your *60 Minutes* interview, President Hinckley was talking about eternal marriage. You said, 'I don't think so.' He replied, 'Then you haven't thought about it enough.' So, Mike, have you thought about it?"

"You're not going to like my answer," he said. "I've been married four times." He did not speak disparagingly of his wives. But he said, in effect, his career is hardly compatible with a good marriage. Then he reached over and took Ann's hand. "Why are Mormon women so beautiful?" (I thought he said, "lovely." Both are true.) I blurted out, "It is the best-kept beauty secret in the world. It is the Spirit of God that contributes to beauty of person, form, and feature." (This is a phrase from Parley P. Pratt.[16])

Ann looked him in the eye and wisely said it in one word: "fidelity." I think he understood. She meant fidelity to God and His Christ; likewise fidelity to one's partner and family and to one's mission in life.

How, we asked Wallace, had he felt when he walked into the Manhattan Temple? He marveled that from the bustle and tension and competition of downtown New York he took only a few steps, and instantly there was peace and serenity. The contrast was vivid for him. He, with many others, felt the sweet peace of the house of God.

Sisters, you who are living temples, I suggest that your best fortress against the adversary is simply to be who you are; to know that in the pantheon of heaven there is no higher order of personality and being than woman and sweetheart and mother. You have received promises in sacred places. They are real. You are, as Moses was told, "in the similitude of the Only Begotten." That is the beauty of holiness.

The devil and the works of the devil are ugly. He keeps no promises; his reward is always the same—defeat and death of your highest aspirations. But he is thwarted and bound by your righteousness.

I close with a passage I have memorized and sometimes review at night in the midst of trial: "Fear not, little children, for you are mine, and I have overcome the world, and you are of them that my Father hath given me; and none of them that my Father hath given me shall be lost. And the Father and I are one. I am in the Father and the Father in me; and inasmuch as ye have received me, ye are in me and I in you. Wherefore, I am in your midst, and I am the good shepherd, and the stone of Israel. He that buildeth upon this rock shall never fall" (D&C 50:41–44).

I testify that He is the good shepherd and the rock of our salvation. As you draw close even into oneness with Him, you will defeat the adversary.

NOTES

1. The Prophet taught, "They who have tabernacles, have power over those who have not" (Joseph Smith, *Teachings of the Prophet Joseph Smith*, sel. Joseph Fielding Smith [Salt Lake City, Deseret Book Company, 1976], 181, 190).
2. Joseph Smith, *Words of Joseph Smith*, ed. Andrew F. Ehat and Lyndon Cook (Provo: BYU Religious Studies Center, 1980), 60.
3. A classic apostolic address on the devil is Marion G. Romney, "Satan, the Great Deceiver," *Ensign*, February 2005, 52–57.
4. See C. S. Lewis, *The Screwtape Letters*, rev. ed. (New York: Macmillan, 1961). Lewis cleverly invents a series of diabolical instructions from the devil to his imps.
5. On one hand, Joseph said: "The devil is an orator, &c: he is powerful: he took our Savior onto a pinnacle of the temple, & kept him in the wilderness for forty days." On the other, "it matters not to me if all hell boils over I regard it only as I would the crackling of thorns under a pot" (Smith, *Words of Joseph Smith*, 12, 327–31).
6. C. S. Lewis, *The Screwtape Letters* (New York: Macmillan Publishing, 1982), 20.

7. Smith, *Teachings of the Prophet Joseph Smith*, 60.

8. "The devil cannot compel mankind to evil, all was voluntary. Those who resist the spirit of God, are liable to be led into temptation, and then the association of heaven is withdrawn from those who refuse to be made partakers of such great glory—God would not exert any compulsory means and the Devil could not; and such ideas as were entertained by many were absurd" (Smith, *Words of Joseph Smith*, 72).

9. Smith, *Words of Joseph Smith*, 65.

10. Smith, *Words of Joseph Smith*, 44: "If he is a spirit from God he will stand still and not offer you his hand. If from the Devil he will either shrink back from you or offer his hand."

11. Neal A. Maxwell, *We Talk of Christ, We Rejoice in Christ* (Salt Lake City: Deseret Book, 1984), 31.

12. Brigham Young, in *Journal of Discourses*, 26 vols. (London: Latter-day Saints' Book Depot, 1854–86), 2:256.

13. David O. McKay, in Conference Report, October 1959, 88; see Luke 4:8.

14. Heber J. Grant, in *Improvement Era* 44 (January 1941): 56.

15. The Prophet Joseph said, "All the religious world is boasting of its righteousness—it is the doctrine of the devil to retard the human mind and retard our progress by filling us with self-righteousness" (Smith, *Words of Joseph Smith*, 123).

16. "The gift of the Holy Spirit . . . develops beauty of person, form and features. It tends to health, vigor, animation and social feeling. It develops and invigorates all the faculties of the physical and intellectual man. It strengthens, invigorates, and gives tone to the nerves. In short, it is, as it were, marrow to the bone, joy to the heart, light to the eyes, music to the ears, and life to the whole being" (Parley P. Pratt, *Key to the Science of Theology* [Salt Lake City: Deseret Book, 1965], 101).

HIDE AND SEEK

———◆———

Wendy L. Watson

Sisters, do you remember the childhood game called Hide and Seek? I loved playing it outdoors with my friends at the end of a long, hot summer day, starting right around dusk, or playing it inside at my grandmother's house with all its nooks and crannies.

Well, I believe that as latter-day women of God, we need to engage in a different kind of Hide and Seek: a kind of Hide and Seek that is crucial to the building of really strong lives, marriages, and families. The Hide and Seek I invite you to think about today is our need to hide from the adversary and to seek the Spirit. To seek the Spirit is to do everything we can to live within the illumination of His light. To hide from the adversary means to do everything we can to live far away from Lucifer's darkness.

Because of Satan's intense attacks, we need to put on the full armor of God *and* we also need to do as Gideon did in order to get people to safety: We need to go through "the back pass, through the back wall, on the back side of the city"! (Mosiah 22:6). We need to hide from the adversary and seek the Spirit. Satan wants just the opposite. He tempts us to seek him and his diabolic ways—and, to hide from God. The adversary wants us to

---

Wendy L. Watson holds a Ph.D. in family therapy and gerontology. She is a professor of marriage and family therapy at Brigham Young University and is an author of several books and talks on tape. Sister Watson chaired the BYU Women's Conference in 1999 and 2000. She is a Relief Society teacher in her Cottonwood Heights ward.

hang out in his hangouts, to spend more and more time with his products and productions.

The adversary has a long history of luring people to seek him and to hide from God. No one and nothing is sacred to him; nothing and no one is off limits. Satan started with our first parents in the Garden of Eden. Almost immediately he was right there in their faces—beguiling Eve and then telling her and Adam to quickly hide from God. The irony is that their act of hiding actually revealed their transgression—not to the Lord, as He already knew, but to themselves. Adam and Eve learned that you can neither run nor hide from God nor ultimately from yourself.

Unfortunately, many of us have not learned that lesson. We try to hide from God, from ourselves, and from each other. But once again, our hiding is so very revealing. A child hides his eyes with one hand while his other hand is in the cookie jar—believing that if he can't see his mother, she can't see him! A teenager hides away in her room just wanting to be left alone because she doesn't feel like she fits in—with anyone! A young man and woman hide under blankets thinking to cover their immoral thoughts, feelings, and actions.

A woman hides her longing for a heart-to-heart connection with her husband by secluding herself away within the illusions of love offered by one more chat room or one more romance novel. Another hides her grief about her life by eating another bag of cookies.

A husband hides his addiction to pornography—from his wife and, perhaps more importantly, from himself—by stashing his latest download from the Internet in the most obscure area of their unfinished basement, mistakenly believing that no one will ever find it. Another hides his feelings of never measuring up to his wife's expectations by lying more and more—about everything!

Many of us try to hide our anxieties and actions, our attitudes and addictions. But somehow, sooner or later, they all sneak out! And the very fact that we're hiding reveals that something is wrong.

Now sisters, in this world so filled with Satan's relentless onslaughts, where can we hide from him? Where can we be safe?

Our covenants provide such a place. While blankets can't protect us from Satan's attacks, priesthood ordinances can. We can wrap ourselves in the power that is in the priesthood and be secure. Very secure. We can't hide under the covers, but we can seek refuge within our covenants. Every time we do anything to increase the exactness with which we keep our covenants, we go underground, so to speak, from the adversary.

Our covenants will keep us safe—as we keep our covenants!

Temples are another oasis from the ominous railings of the adversary. No unclean thing is to enter into the house of the Lord. And that counts the adversary out for sure! He is not, nor will he ever be, welcomed inside those hallowed walls. The adversary was cast out long ago from God's presence. And that decision stands. Therefore, when we worthily serve in the Lord's holy house, we can not only come closer to the Savior and to our Heavenly Father than ever before, we can also be further away from our greatest antagonist—and his madding crowd. We can be safer than ever before! And the further good news is that every time we leave the temple we leave armed with more power and more protecting assistance.

As we stand in holy places and keep our covenants, we can withstand unholy attacks!

Now think for a moment about another consoling truth that is almost too good to be true. Our Heavenly Father has given us Someone to be with us—always! We really never need to be alone. We can arm ourselves each and every hour of each and every day with the Holy Ghost. Does it ever cease to thrill you that we can have as our very closest companion the third member of the Godhead? There is no better bodyguard, no greater security for your spirit. There's only one hitch—well, two actually: We need to seek Him. And we need to live worthy of His association.

The Spirit can be your own personal detector and protector. He is the very best security system on earth!

I'm sure you've noticed how the adversary sometimes uses unbelievably sophisticated ways to disguise himself and his traps. But the Holy Ghost can identify every whiff of evil. So, what can we do to have the Spirit of the Lord with us? Let me offer four suggestions:

1. Increase the intensity and frequency with which we pray for the companionship of the Holy Ghost. Many women have found that by praying at crucial times for His companionship, profound changes occurred. What were the crucial times?

After praying in the morning for the Spirit to be with them throughout the day, as these women encountered any tempting, trying, or difficult situation they prayed in that very moment for the Spirit to be with them. They visualized the Holy Ghost being right there by them and then followed through on what they felt drawn to do, say, or feel. They experienced the guidance of the Spirit in ways they never had before.

2. Increase the earnestness and frequency of our pleadings to learn how He personally speaks to us. If you're not sure how it feels or sounds when He's talking to you, ask for Him to teach you how to recognize His promptings. He may not speak to you through a burning in your bosom. He may speak through the line of a hymn that comes to your mind, disquieting feelings that persist, flashes of ideas you've never considered before, or scriptural passages that seem written exclusively for you.

3. Decrease the time between receiving an instruction and acting on it. The Holy Ghost is eager to help us. Showing Him that we're grateful for His guidance by actually following through on His promptings will increase our ability to receive even more.

4. Toss out, turn off, quit purchasing, and stop participating in anything that would prevent His companionship. By the way, we can quickly tell which thoughts, feelings, behaviors, videos, Internet activities, TV offerings, books, magazines, clothes, and music need to be discarded—because the Spirit will flee in the presence of anything that offends Him. We can simply ask ourselves: Can the Spirit be with me when I watch, wear, do, hear, read, think, or feel the following? If the answer is "No," we know what to do. We need to create an environment in our homes, minds, and hearts where He will want to be. Where He *can* be!

So, forget about cleaning up for company. Clean up for the companionship of the Spirit!

Now, think for a moment about the Holy Ghost and Satan. Neither have bodies. Both are spirit beings. Elder Bruce R. McConkie taught that the Holy Ghost's work of sanctifying the souls of men "can only be performed by a spirit being."[1] And since we know that there must be "opposition in all things" (2 Nephi 2:11), while the Spirit is helping to sanctify us, guess what the adversary's doing.

Everything about these two spirit beings is diametrically opposed—including their desires for you and the intent of their influences. Satan is the ultimate contaminator. His goal is to entice you to be as impure as possible—as often as possible—in your thoughts, feelings, and actions. We could call him "the great putrifier"! The Spirit, on the other hand, is the great Purifier. And the more pure He helps us become, the more heightened our sensitivity is to Satan's sinister influences.

With the Spirit of the Lord right by our side, we can both run and hide so much more swiftly and securely from Satan—because we can tell more and more quickly when there is something we need to run and hide from.

One woman knew she needed to hide from the adversary when she was a member of a committee that was studying the effects of pornography. She said, "I shut my eyes every time anything pornographic was shown." She was not about to get hooked, and then chained, by that old line which has destroyed so many: "What is pornography? I'll know it when I see it." This wise woman made sure that her mind and spirit were protected, by simply closing her eyes. How simple! And how very effective!

Now, think of another difference between the Spirit and Satan. While the adversary is the great concealer, the Holy Ghost is the great revealer. The Spirit can show us things about ourselves and others, about life and love, that we could never discover on our own, no matter how hard we tried. His work involves light and truth and love. The more He can reveal to us, the more His purposes are fulfilled. His joy comes as we discover new joys. He wants to reveal truths to us so we can become more and more free to be like our Heavenly Father and His Only Begotten Son, our Savior.

On the other hand, Satan wants to keep us from understanding truths. His work involves darkness, counterfeits, illusions, lies, and lust. The more he can conceal from us, the happier he is. His joy comes from our misery. He wants to conceal truths from us so we are held more and more captive by him, and become more like him.

One truth the adversary seems particularly invested in concealing is the truth about sexual intimacy. His efforts to conceal these eternal truths are extraordinary. He has developed an entire arsenal of impure goods and services to seduce men and women, youth, and even children into defiling themselves and others. What a bastion of corruption. And he's not finished yet. Clearly, Satan is afraid of the power that is available to those who keep themselves morally clean before, and within, marriage. Personal purity is power—power that Satan will never have.

Satan is desperate to dupe people into participating mentally, emotionally, and physically in his distortions of sexual intimacy so that their spirits become impure. It appears that Lucifer tempts almost everyone to be immoral. And so many succumb to something—fornication, adultery—in all their forms, including Internet affairs, sexual abuse, self-abuse, homosexuality, pornography.

And, as women, we support the adversary's agenda if we or our daughters yield to certain so-called fashion trends by wearing second-skin clothing, short skirts, cleavage-displaying tops, and belly- and hip-exposing slacks or skirts. As Elder Dallin H. Oaks recently stated: "Please understand that if you dress immodestly, you are magnifying this problem [of pornography] by becoming pornography."[2]

While Satan wants us to inappropriately expose our bodies, he wants us to conceal our sins—for that is another way we give him power over us. When we attempt to hide our sins in any way, it almost guarantees that we will repeat that sin, again and again. Conversely, the Holy Ghost wants us to reveal our sins. For that is the first step we need to take to gain access to the power that is in the Atonement for us. Secrets about sins are spiritual suicide. And they offend the Spirit.

There are other things that offend the Spirit, things like contention—contention born of resentment. I've been struck lately with just how resentful many of us are:

One woman resents that her neighbor—who is not even close to being as spiritual and charitable as she is—was called to be the Relief Society president! She resents that her best friend can eat anything she wants and never gain a pound, that her perpetrator was not punished severely enough, that her brother never follows through on his commitments (ever!), and that her sister has been slacking off helping with their aging parents.

Another woman resents that her children don't listen to her advice, that one daughter isn't married (or dating!), that her house hasn't sold, that a client has never paid his bill, that her mother died before she arrived at her bedside, that her friends are always in the limelight! And that her husband wouldn't let her have her hair in an up-do for their wedding photos—twenty-five years ago!

One woman is resentful that the buff, professionally aspiring, greatly inspired, impeccably honest stud-muffin she married quickly turned into a fat, lazy, lying spiritual pygmy!

And another woman is resentful that she doesn't have a husband to be resentful about!

Sisters, if thirty years of counseling individuals, couples, and families has taught me anything, it is that **resentment is toxic!** It prevents us from feeling love. It can stop us from experiencing light and truth. And perhaps most serious of all, resentment keeps us from seeking and fully enjoying the companionship of the Holy Ghost. Resentment also prevents us from hiding from the adversary. And it supports Satan's agenda to destroy marriages and families. How so?

Resentment's powerful negative emotions swell within us and attract other negative emotions. All that negativity plays havoc with our relationships and makes us much more vulnerable to the adversary's attacks. Sisters, when resentment begins to rule us, darkness gathers.

I can think of a very good woman with great desires who is under the influence of resentment. Let's call her Donna. Her countenance is dark. Her understanding of gospel concepts is impaired. Her judgment of many situations is off. She often feels lonely and misunderstood. Now, this is not a woman who is involved in blatantly sinful practices. In fact, her checklist of gospel practices is rather complete and, I'm sure, tallied daily. Yet, her countenance does not reflect the joy of gospel truths, the love of the Savior, the light of the enabling and redemptive power of the Atonement. Many things in Donna's life have been unexpected, disappointing, and down right painful. And resentment rules her.

Perhaps resentment rules some of us right here today. Now please don't feel resentful that I'm suggesting that some of us might be struggling with resentment! But resentment seems to fuel many fiery problems in our individual lives, marriages, and families.

If we are under the influence of resentment, we need the Spirit's help more than ever! And yet, resentment limits the presence of the Holy Ghost in our lives. So, what can we do?

We can begin with prayer. The moment we express our desire to be

freed from resentment—or even our desire to have a desire to be freed—
I believe we turn a key that increases our access to the Spirit. When we
let our Heavenly Father know—really know—that we want to lay down
our resentments, the Spirit comes to our aid. If we pray, He *will* come.

The Spirit can bring important things to our memories, such as our
strengths we've been overlooking. He can help us remember situations
that initially generated our resentment, not for the purpose of marinating
our hearts in others' mistakes, or brooding about others' blunders, but so
that we can finally remove these weapons of war from our hearts, one by
one, and bury each one of these weapons of war in order to have peace,
just as the converted Lamanites did. As we look at each experience by the
revealing light of the Holy Ghost—instead of through the dark shadows
of the adversary—I believe past experiences can look very different.

Imagine what could happen to our resentment if we considered the
following two questions:

1. What if I could view my premortal videotapes, and as I reviewed
them I discovered that I courageously signed up for some difficult life
experiences—the very experiences for which I have felt so much resentment! What would change?

2. What if I discovered that part of my mortal mission is to be a kind
of pioneer in my family—to blaze a new trail, to be someone who behaves
so differently from previous generations that I turn the tide on the adversary's influence on our family? What would I want to stop doing? Start
doing?

Now let's put the premortal videotapes away. But let me just add that
I believe if we could view even five minutes of our premortal life many of
our resentments and much of our suffering would simply fall away!

Let's consider four more questions that might help us to be freed from
resentment.

1. What if, as I look at the resentment-generating experiences of my
life, I were to discover that in some instances I actually, although very
unintentionally, gave others permission to treat me poorly? What would
happen to my feelings of resentment then?

2. What if I saw a videotape (not a premortal one) of one of my per-
petrators, showing him or her pacing the floor at 2 A.M., weeping in

anguish and saying, "I am so sorry for the pain I caused (fill in your name)"? What difference would that make?

3. What would happen to my resentment if I acknowledged that some of my resentments are actually related to my disappointment in myself, because I didn't speak up or take action for such a long time?

4. What would I want to stop doing immediately if I had eyes to see the tremendous price that my family members have paid for my devotion to the "care and keeping" of resentment? Our family members will give us clues about the effects of our resentment on them. One woman discovered that her unpredictable anger—which was generated by resentment—had not gone unnoticed by her 4-year-old daughter. This little girl developed a morning routine of asking her older brother before going downstairs to breakfast, "Is Mom in a good mood today?"

Another woman learned that her son moved out of their home because he didn't want to live anywhere that the Spirit didn't and couldn't reside. What was preventing the presence of the Holy Ghost in their home? His mother's relentless resentment toward his recently repentant father!

Sisters, resentment keeps us from fully experiencing the Spirit and makes us much more vulnerable to the buffetings of Satan. In fact, I believe that resentment is one of the most powerful tools of the adversary and it can be just as corrosive to our souls, over time, as things we would regard as much more serious sin.

We may feel rather safe at this point in our lives against the adversary's seduction toward immorality. We may even think that Satan can't get us to be immoral; however, he can get us to be resentful—if we're not careful. Resentment is inspired by Lucifer, encouraged by him, and perpetuated by him, all for the purpose of damaging our souls and our relationships. Therefore, we need to seek out resentment in our lives and get rid of it. And to do so, we need the Spirit's super-sleuthing skills. He will reveal to us where resentment may be hiding!

The secret hiding place of resentment may be

- in the word jabs and barbs that slip out in our conversations.
- in our sarcastic comments.
- in the disparaging remarks we make about others.

• in the negative assumptions we make about why others behave the way they do.

Resentment may be underneath

• our inability to be happy for others' successes.
• our inability to make decisions.
• our inability to make the changes we so desperately seek.

And resentment may even—and oh so tragically—be behind our inability to really believe that there is power in the Atonement for us.

In conclusion, sisters, now is the time to hide and seek! It's time to hide from the adversary—within our covenants and within the Lord's holy temples—with greater commitment than ever before! For when we do so we make it so much more difficult for Satan to find us. We need to seek the Spirit—with more vigor than ever before. He will help us detect every one of Satan's ploys to deceive us and to rob us of our power, the power that comes from personal purity. The Holy Ghost will help us to hide from that which seeks to destroy us and to seek for those harmful things which have been hiding in our lives. For example, the Spirit will help us to seek out, and get rid of, one of the adversary's most life-putrifying, and relationship-destroying, tools: resentment.

Sisters, as we hide and seek in this manner, we will be able to build really strong lives, marriages, and families. And we'll be able to do exactly what the Lord is counting on us to do at this most crucial time for us, as laborers in His vineyard.

NOTES

1. Bruce R. McConkie, *New Witness for the Articles of Faith* (Salt Lake City: Deseret Book, 1985), 265.
2. Dallin H. Oaks, "Pornography," *Ensign*, May 2005, 90.

THE THREADS OF FAITH

Carolyn Colton

Does a blanket signify anything special to you? Perhaps a memory of being tucked in tight by your parents? Something you wrapped up in when you felt bad and needed comfort? The blanket you clutched as a toddler to give you courage? A collection of scraps combined together to make something better? A community offering of affection and well-wishing?

Universally, quilts and blankets are used for safety, warmth, and expressions of love. A blanket that keeps a person wrapped in it dry and warm is made of many strong threads woven tightly together, without any holes.

An unshakable faith is like a tightly woven blanket. It shelters us from the storms of life, from anger, rejection, fear, loneliness, and all the ills of the world. It gives us the courage and stamina to keep seeking for God's light when a path is misted in darkness. Father Lehi had such a faith when he exclaimed, "I am encircled about eternally in the arms of his love" (2 Nephi 1:15).

Throughout all time, prophets of God have pled with us to seek for and partake of the most desirable of all things: to drink from the fountain

---

Carolyn Colton is a longtime resident of Bethesda, Maryland, where she works as an assistant general counsel for Marriott International, Inc., and a Primary teacher in the Rockville Ward, Washington D.C. Stake. She is a graduate of Brigham Young University and the J. Reuben Clark Law School. Her spare time is filled with friends and family, reading, and making quilts.

of living waters, to come unto the arms of our Savior, and to be one with Him, encircled by and filled with the love of God.

How can we gain this faith?

I wish I could give you a checklist with a promise that, if you tick off each point, you will have this kind of unshakable faith, but I can't. The problem is that no one else is exactly like you; no one else is exactly like me. Our perspectives and beliefs have been shaped by our family, our culture, our genetics, our experiences, our knowledge, and our past choices. Not one of our checklists looks like another's. Something that might build my faith might not build yours. What might shake my faith might not shake yours. But, with the help of our Savior and the promptings of the Holy Ghost, we can each know what we must personally do to weave an unshakable faith that will withstand every challenge and allow our souls to be filled with the gospel's promised light and joy.

HAVE MANY STRONG THREADS

There are some universal principles that, if understood, can help us as we seek to strengthen our faith. The first such principle is that, just as a tightly woven blanket is made of hundreds of threads, your faith is made up of many parts. Each thread of faith can be strengthened or unraveled, reworked or broken, repaired or removed, and new threads can be added.

Try this exercise. List all the parts and subparts of your faith. For example, a few threads of my faith are that God lives, I am His spiritual child, and God knows me personally. After you list all the threads of your faith, evaluate how strongly you believe in each one. Think how long each has been part of your faith. Has your understanding of any thread of faith ever needed to be reworked—perhaps after you realized it was based on an incorrect assumption or understanding? When you finish this exercise, look at the whole. Does your blanket of faith look like a loosely woven cheesecloth? A doll's blanket? Or is it a large and tightly woven blanket of felted wool?

LOOK, LOOK, AND LOOK AGAIN

The next principle is to look, look, and look again.

Jean Louis Agassiz was a professor of natural science who taught at

Harvard in the 1860s—that's around the time the pioneers were settling Utah. Professor Agassiz believed students should study nature itself rather than acquire facts through lectures or books. To effectively master such a study, a student needed to develop the critical intellectual tools of observation and comparison. An unforgettable lesson he used to develop this skill was jokingly named by his students "The Incident of the Fish." As I share with you a paraphrase of the words of one student's memory of his encounter with "The Incident of the Fish," I want you to think of how the fish might be like a thread of faith.

"Agassiz brought me a small fish, placing it before me with the rather stern requirement that I should study it but should on no account talk to any one concerning it nor read anything relating to fishes, until I had his permission so to do.

"'What shall I do?' I asked.

"He replied, 'Find out what you can, and by and by I will ask you what you have seen.'

"I was disappointed. I concluded gazing at a fish did not relate to the study of insects—which was my desire. In ten minutes I saw all that could be seen in that fish. Half an hour passed, an hour, another hour—the fish began to look loathsome. I turned it over and around; looked it in the face—from behind, beneath, above, sideways, at a three-quarters' view—just as ghastly. I was in despair. So I decided it was time for lunch. For an hour I was free!

"On my return, I slowly pulled forth my mute companion, that awful fish, and with a feeling of desperation, I looked at it again. At last a happy thought struck me—I would draw the fish. With surprise, I began to discover new features in the creature. Just then the Professor returned.

"'That is right,' said he, 'a pencil is one of the best of eyes. So what have you seen?'

"He listened attentively to my brief rehearsal of the parts of the fish. When I finished, he waited, expecting more, and then, with an air of disappointment said, 'You have not looked very carefully; why, you haven't even seen one of the most obvious features of the animal, and it is plainly before your eyes! Look again! Look again!' And he left me to my misery.

"I was mortified. Still more of that fish! But now I set myself to my task with a will, and I discovered one new thing after another, until I saw how correct the Professor's criticism had been. The afternoon passed quickly, and at the end of the day, the Professor asked, 'Do you see it yet?'

"'No,' I replied, 'I am certain I do not, but I see how little I saw before.'

"'Well,' he said, 'put away your fish and go home; perhaps you will be ready with a better answer in the morning.'

"This was disconcerting. Not only must I puzzle over my observations of my fish all night without it in front of me, but the next day I was going to have to give an exact account of my discoveries without verifying them, and I had a bad memory! So I walked home by the Charles River, pondering over my problem.

"After a sleepless night, I arrived at the lab the next morning. The Professor seemed to be as anxious as I that I should see for myself what he saw.

"'Do you perhaps mean,' I asked, 'that the fish has symmetrical sides with paired organs?'

"'Of course! Of course!' he said. He was thoroughly pleased.

"Then I ventured to ask, 'So what should I do next?'

"'Oh, look at your fish!' he said. And so for three more long days he placed that fish before my eyes, forbidding me to look at anything else or to use any artificial aid. 'Look, look, look,' was his repeated injunction. Only later did I come to realize that this was not only one of the best lessons of my life but a turning point as well."[1]

This story teaches: First, at any given time you are limited by your perceptions. Second, it is necessary to analyze what you saw and then articulate your conclusions to help you figure out what you really saw. Third, by constantly refining and analyzing what you perceive, you can move closer and closer to a complete understanding of the truth. And fourth, you must come to your own understanding and not rely upon secondhand observations.

The Lord directs us to seek wisdom, and if we will ask Him, we will "receive revelation upon revelation, knowledge upon knowledge," and we will "know the mysteries and peaceable things" that bring joy and eternal life (D&C 42:61).

Look, look, and look again is also what Nephi heard when he sought to understand the meaning of his father's vision. Nephi first desired to know the things his father saw in a vision. He believed the Lord could make such things known to him. As he pondered, the Spirit of the Lord began to teach him. In Nephi's description of this wonderful experience, I counted that the Spirit of the Lord directed Nephi to either "Look!" or "Behold!" 48 times (see 1 Nephi 11).

Periodically Nephi was asked to analyze and articulate what he saw. Because of this exercise, Nephi became able to see and comprehend the entirety of Christ's mission and conclude that the beautiful tree and the fountain of living waters that his father saw were representations of "the love of God, which sheddeth itself abroad in the hearts of the children of men; wherefore, it is the most desirable above all things" (1 Nephi 11:22). Nephi sought, pondered, asked, and the Spirit taught him truth.

Once a thread of faith is gained, it can be strengthened by following the Lord's repeated admonition to learn of Him, listen to His words, and live according to the truths we have been given (see D&C 19:23). With prayer and study, we can determine whether each thread of our faith is based upon truth or whether we have woven into our beliefs uninspired philosophies of men or incorrect assumptions. And as we rework our faith, we understand each thread better and better and better, and the Spirit confirms to us that it is true. I am realizing more and more that as we rework each thread of our faith, we will inevitably find that at the core or foundation of each thread is the love of God and the Atonement of Christ.

Luckily, we are not limited, as Professor Agassiz's students were, by the prohibition against the use of tools as we look, look, and look again. We have the scriptures, and we have prophets, and we have the Holy Ghost to help us see the truth. In fact, we are directed, "As all have not faith, seek ye diligently and teach one another words of wisdom; yea, seek ye out of the best books words of wisdom; seek learning, even by study and also by faith" (D&C 88:118). We also have the tool of prayer and the promise that if we ask Heavenly Father in faith, believing that we will receive, and keep the commandments diligently, the Lord will pour out His Spirit upon us and bless us with knowledge and understanding (see 1 Nephi 15:11; D&C 19:38).

Remember that knowledge and faith do not distill upon us automatically with no effort on our part. The Prophet Joseph underscored the effort we must put forth when he said:

"The things of God are of deep import: and time and experience, and careful and ponderous and solemn thoughts can only find them out. Thy mind, O man! If thou wilt lead a soul unto salvation, must stretch as high as the utmost heavens, and search into and contemplate the darkest abyss and the broad expanse of eternity—thou must commune with God."[2]

In other words: look, look, and look again!

BEWARE OF THE GREAT UNRAVELER

The third principle is the realization that each thread of our faith, no matter how strong, is constantly being attacked by the great unraveler. Remember that the Lord beckons us to open our eyes and ears so He can fill our souls with light and joy, and Satan fights to blind us and fill our souls with darkness, fear, and anger.

A Chinese military theoretician, Sun-Tzu, wrote the *Art of War* around 400 B.C. His ideas about combat have been followed by successful military commanders ever since. He believed the way to win was to shatter cohesion, produce paralysis, and bring about the collapse of an opponent by generating confusion, disorder, panic, and chaos. That is why such strategies as surprise, deception, speed, and shaping the opponent's perception of what really is happening are so successful. In fact, a key focus he taught was to unravel the opponent before the battle even starts.

A commander must get inside the mind and the decision process of his opponent in order to make sure the opponent is dealing with outdated or irrelevant information and will thus become confused and disoriented and unable to function. The commander should look for gaps in the defense and not hit the strong points but go around them like water going downhill—bypassing obstacles, always moving, probing, and then, when an opening is found, pouring through it, pushing deeper and deeper, punching through the weaknesses, following the path of least resistance.[3]

Don't Sun-Tzu's theories sound an awful lot like the list of Satan's tools given to us by Nephi? Nephi's catalog of the devil's strategies includes:

• Stirring us up to anger to rage in our hearts against that which is good

• Pacifying us into thinking we don't need to nourish our faith because we are okay, "all is well in Zion"

• Flattering us into believing that there is no hell nor is there a devil

• Enticing us to follow the precepts of men and deny the power of God and the gift of the Holy Ghost

• Letting our pride blind us to the truth and causing us to tremble with anger against the truth of God in fear that, if it is indeed true, then, perish the thought, we will be proven wrong, and

• Tempting us to lose patience and forget the principle that God teaches us line upon line so we conclude that, because we have received the word of God once, we have no need for additional revelation on that thread of our faith (see 2 Nephi 28:20–31).

Another strategy Satan seems to use is to magnify our doubts in one principle. Then he perpetrates the deception that this thread of our faith is the keystone. Then he tempts us to put all of our energy into justifying our doubts. The natural consequence of this strategy is that we are left without energy or motivation to nurture the other threads of our faith. The other threads will then weaken with neglect and break, and bit by bit our faith is all unraveled.

We shouldn't ignore our feelings or doubts. Nor should we fail to acknowledge the fact that one part of our faith is unraveling or is broken. And we *need* to put energy into figuring out the reasons for such trauma. But rather than *embracing* a doubt, we should put energy into *doubting* the doubt. Examine the source and soundness of the information that led to the doubt. Hopefully, we will then realize that our understanding of a principle or a source of doubt is too limited to justify giving the doubt the power to unravel the entire blanket of our faith. It is critical that while we sort out a faith-shaking doubt, we spend an equal if not greater amount of time and energy embracing, reinforcing, and nurturing those threads of our faith that *are* strong.

It is clear that, while the Savior helps give us the threads of truth to weave a protective blanket of faith, Satan gives us a flaxen cord that grows into an awful chain with which he binds us and happily drags our souls down to his "gulf of misery and endless wo" (Helaman 5:12; Alma 12:11; 2 Nephi 26:22).

Henri Nouwen, a Catholic priest, in his book *The Return of the Prodigal Son*, describes the kind of unraveling confusion Satan can cause. Listen to how he describes the continual attack on his belief that he is a beloved child of God.

"The same voice that speaks to all the children of God and sets them free to live in the midst of a dark world while remembering the light . . . is the never-interrupted voice of love speaking from eternity and giving life and love whenever it is heard. When I hear that voice, I know that I am home with God and have nothing to fear.

"As the Beloved of my heavenly Father, . . . I can confront, console, admonish and encourage without fear of rejection or need for affirmation. As the Beloved, I can suffer persecution without desire for revenge and receive praise without using it as a proof of my goodness. . . . Yet over and over again I have left home. I have fled the hands of blessing and run off to faraway places looking for love . . . and the true voice of love is a very soft and gentle voice speaking to me in the most hidden places of my being. It is not a boisterous voice, forcing itself on me and demanding attention. . . . It is a voice that can only be heard by those who allow themselves to be touched. . . .

"But there are many other voices, voices that are loud, full of promises and very seductive. These voices say, 'Go out and prove that you are worth love by being successful, popular and powerful. . . . ' They are always there and always reach into those inner places where I question my own goodness and doubt my self worth. They suggest that I am not going to be loved without having earned it through determined efforts and hard work. They want me to prove to myself and others that I am worth being loved, and they keep pushing me to do everything possible to gain acceptance. Almost from the moment I had ears to hear, I heard those voices, and they have stayed with me ever since. They have come to me through my parents, my friends, my teachers and my colleagues, but most of all they have come and still come through the mass media that surround me. And they say,

"'Show me that you are a good boy.'

"'You had better be better than your friend!'

"'How are your grades?'

"'What are your connections?'

"'Are you sure you want to be friends with those people?'

"'These trophies certainly show how good a player you were!'

"'Don't show your weakness, or you'll be used!'

"'When you stop being productive, people lose interest in you!'

"As long as I remain in touch with the voice that calls me the beloved, those questions and counsel are quite harmless. Their warnings and advice are well intentioned. . . . But when I forget the voice of the first unconditional love, then these innocent suggestions can easily start dominating my life and pull me into a distant country. It is not very hard for me to know when this is happening; anger, resentment, jealousy, desire for revenge, lust, greed, antagonisms, and rivalries are obvious signs that I have left home. . . . Before I am even fully aware of it, I find myself wondering why someone hurt me, rejected me, or didn't pay attention to me. Without realizing it, I find myself brooding about someone else's successes, my own loneliness and the way the world abuses me. Despite my conscious intentions, I often catch myself daydreaming about becoming rich, powerful and very famous. All of these mental games reveal to me the fragility of my faith that I am the Beloved One on whom God's favor rests."[4]

Nouwen gives us a barometer to *signal* us when our faith is being shaken. He tells us our faith is somehow being shaken when we have feelings of anger, resentment, antagonism, and other feelings that aren't compatible with the feelings of love, joy, and peace that you feel when filled with the Spirit.

How do we combat the assaults on our faith? The answer is also found in Nephi's interpretation of his father's vision, when he identifies the meaning of the rod of iron:

"Whoso would hearken unto the word of God, and would hold fast unto it, they would never perish; neither could the temptations and the fiery darts of the adversary overpower them unto blindness, to lead them away to destruction.

" . . . Give heed to the word of God and remember to keep his commandments always in all things" (1 Nephi 15:24–25).

LIVE ACCORDING TO THE LIGHT YOU HAVE

The last principle I would like to highlight in our individual quest for an unshakable faith is to live patiently according to the light you are given and more light will be given to you.

Alma admonishes us to "worship God, in whatsoever place ye may be in, in spirit and in truth" (Alma 34:38). I think Alma was referring not only to the physical places we can worship, he also was referring to whatever place you have reached in your spiritual journey. In other words, you don't have to have the faith of Joseph Smith or of Enoch to have effective faith or to worship God. You need to pray to Heavenly Father with whatever faith you do have and ask for more truth. If we do this, our seeking will be answered with truth and our knowledge and understanding will be added upon.

The Prophet Joseph taught: "We consider that God has created man with a mind capable of instruction, and a faculty which may be enlarged in proportion to the heed and diligence given to the light communicated from heaven to the intellect; and that the nearer man approaches perfection, the clearer are his views, and the greater his enjoyments, till he has overcome the evils of his life and lost every desire for sin; and like the ancients, arrives at that point of faith, where he is wrapped in the power and glory of his Maker, and is caught up to dwell with Him. But we consider that this is a station to which no man ever arrived in a moment."[5]

I pray that these four principles I've discussed ring true to you. First, have many strong threads. Second, look, look, and look again. Third, beware of the great unraveler. And fourth, live and worship according to the light you are given.

May we heed the admonition of the prophet Nephi, son of Helaman, to "remember, remember that it is upon the rock of our Redeemer, who is Christ, the Son of God, that ye must build your foundation; that when the devil shall send forth his mighty winds, yea, his shafts in the whirlwind, yea, when all his hail and his mighty storm shall beat upon you, it shall have no power over you to drag you down to the gulf of misery and endless wo, because of the rock upon which ye are built, which is a sure foundation, a foundation whereon if men build they cannot fall" (Helaman 5:12).

Then together we can sing in faith Nephi's psalm: "O Lord, wilt thou encircle me around in the robe of thy righteousness!" (2 Nephi 4:33). And we will know for ourselves that it is the most precious of all things.

NOTES

1. Paraphrased from Samuel H. Scudder, "In the Laboratory with Agassiz," in *Every Saturday* 16 (April 4, 1974): 369–70.

2. Joseph Smith, *Teachings of the Prophet Joseph Smith,* sel. Joseph Fielding Smith (Salt Lake City: Deseret Book, 1976), 137.

3. See Robert Coram, *Boyd: The Fighter Pilot Who Changed the Art of War* (Boston: Little, Brown, and Company, 2002), 333–37.

4. Henry J. M. Nouwen, *The Return of the Prodigal Son: A Story of Homecoming* (New York: Image, 1994), 37–42.

5. Smith, *Teachings of the Prophet Joseph Smith,* 51.

INDEX

coercion and, 237; hiding from,
238–47; as unraveler of faith, 253–56
Scriptures, 83–93
Sealing, 50–52, 73–74
Seasons, in women's lives, 175
Self-awareness, 184–85
Self-improvement, 205
Selflessness, 126
Service: women and, 152–54; Spencer
W. Kimball on, 165
Seth, 126
Shriver, Maria, on motherhood, 171
Simplify, 225
Skinner, Andrew C., 43–52
Sloan, Tim, 105
Smith, Emma, 157
Smith, Hyrum, Joseph Smith on, 160
Smith, Joseph: and First Vision, 1–2,
13–14, 38; restoration of gospel and,
3–4; on growth of Church, 4–5;
name of, to be had for good and evil,
5; organization of Relief Society and,
6; reactions to, 14; testimony of,
14–15; knowledge of, 15–16; on faith
and knowledge, 23; prepared for First
Vision, 34–37; history of, 39–40;
memorizing First Vision account of,
41; prophecies on, 43–44; on
learning, 45, 257; on priesthood keys,
45–46; on obtaining priesthood, 51;
loves "A Poor Wayfaring Man of
Grief," 54–55; charity of, 55–61;
taught through scriptures, 89;
receives revelation on trials, 97;
influence of home and family on,
121–22, 131; on Emma Smith, 157;
friendship and, 159–62; loyalty to
wife of, 192; as example of dealing
with imperfect behavior, 204–5; on
Satan and bodies, 229; on coercion,
232, 237; Satan's attack on, 233; on
power of those with bodies, 236; on
discernment, 237; on pride, 237
Smith, Joseph F.: on priesthood in spirit
world, 46–47; on missionary work in
spirit world, 47
Smith, Joseph Fielding: on priesthood in
premortal existence, 46; on Elijah

and sealing keys, 50, 51; on obtaining
priesthood, 51
Smith, Lucy Mack: as example of faith,
122; on Emma Smith, 157
Snow, Eliza R., 6
Spafford, Belle, 153
Spain, 195
Spiders, 168
Spirit. *See* Holy Ghost
Spirit world, priesthood in, 46–47
Spiritual Lightening, 135
Standards, 63–72
Stewardship, 111
Subtraction, 231–32
Sunday dress, 70–71
Sun-Tzu, 253
Superwoman syndrome, 179–88
Swinton, Heidi S., 54–61
Symbols, 10

Tanner, Susan W., 121–29
Taylor, John, on Joseph Smith, 5, 44
Temperance, 138
Temple: Accra Ghana, 7–8; as means to
fullness of priesthood, 51–52;
everyday work of, 74–81; modeling
homes after, 127; ordinances,
154–57; Satan's attack on, 233;
Manhattan, 235; as hiding place, 240
Temple Square, 134–35
Temptation: Gordon B. Hinckley on
resisting, 66; Brigham Young on
overcoming, 233
Test, mortality as, 95–96
Testimony: of First Vision, 2–3, 31–33;
of Joseph Smith, 14–15; gaining,
14–18; David O. McKay on, and
faith, 17–18; of Gordon B. Hinckley,
64; of Carmen Reich, 146–47
Thomas, M. Catherine, 135; on
atonement, 197
Thoughts, Satan cannot know our, 232
Threads, 248–56
Thursby, Jacqueline S., 219–28
Time, 203–4
Times of restitution, 35–36
Timing, 173
Today, 148
Traditions, as temptation tool, 231–32
Train, 141–43